Out of the Holding Tank

A Balanced Program of Language Arts for

Homeschooling Middle School Students

Dena M. Luchsinger

Crecer Publications
Wasilla, Alaska

Crecer Publications
1161 N. Iroquois Drive
Wasilla, Alaska 99654

Includes bibliographical references and index.
ISBN 978-0-9848313-3-3 (paper)

Printed in the United States of America
First edition published 2012

To Kristen and Lauren,

From "Lions, Tigers, and Jaguars, Oh My!" to "Double Take,"
and
from The Audition Mystery to Chaderick,

I've loved playing words with you.

Table of Contents

CHAPTER ONE

UNDERSTANDING LANGUAGE ARTS:

DIFFERENT APPROACHES AND THE PHILOSOPHIES BEHIND THEM

"Mom?" Kristen called from the other room. I heard a note of panic in her twelve-year-old voice. "Mom, they're not moving!"

I wiped my hands on a kitchen towel and joined her. She'd been cleaning her aquarium, which had become positively disgusting with green algae. Since the aquarium and fish were hers, I'd told she would have to be responsible for it herself. Sure enough, the fish weren't moving; they were floating on top of the water. Not a good sign.

"Oh, honey," I said. "Did you use detergent when you cleaned the tank?"

"No!" she insisted. "I only used hot water!"

So chemicals hadn't killed the fish. "Well, it could have been shock. Were you careful to use the same temperature water when you filled the aquarium again?"

"Um," Kristen said, looking a bit sick.

Then I noticed what she was looking at. "Is that steam?" I asked.

It was. Not wanting to harm her fish, Kristen had conscientiously used only hot water to scrub the aquarium walls, but upon finishing, she'd refilled the tank with the same, scalding water she'd used to clean it. Then she had very gently returned her goldfish to the aquarium . . .

"Well," I said, realizing what had happened and going into comforting mother mode, "at least they didn't suffer long."

Middle School Students: Big Kids or Young Adults?

Middle school is a time of many minor catastrophes. Middle school students want to make grown-up choices and prove that they're not kids anymore, but they sometimes lack the savvy, experience, and persistence to pull it off. It's a time of contradiction and confusion: middle school students never quite know where they stand or who they want to be, whether they want to be responsible and mature or free to explore and play just a few years longer. Caught in this internal tug-of-war, middle school students can be moody: playful one day, and serious, thoughtful, or ambitious the next, and even when they want nothing more than to prove their maturity, they need a lot of support and direction. Though they crave the freedom to make their own decisions, they secretly yearn for the support they know will help them succeed. More than ever, they need encouragement when they're on the right track, and comfort when they accidentally cook their own fish. In short, middle school is a tough, awkward, crazy, but fun and often wonderful time.

The Middle School Language Arts Conundrum

Whereas homeschooling parents generally have few problems getting elementary-aged students to comply with almost any program of language arts, in middle school students can suddenly struggle, flounder, and even balk. Consider each of the following scenarios:

- Grant loved reading the Percy Jackson books and talked animatedly about their plots, but his interest in reading suffered when his mother insisted he read the much slower paced book that she'd loved when she was his age next.

- Shelly loved most of her subjects, but her mother insisted that she diagram sentences now that she was in middle school. She could do the work, but she found the work tedious and cumbersome, and it took her a long time to diagram long sentences neatly.

- Charlie did the writing assignments he was given, but until his mother showed him what he ought to have written, he never knew what she meant when she told him to develop his ideas more.

- Rose got to pick every other book in her reading program, and while she really enjoyed liked the ones she chose, she kept "losing" the more quality books her mom picked.

- Aaron hated the writing program his dad picked out for him, and he thought the assignments were stupid. One day, he decided that his dad couldn't make him write any more stupid stories—and as it turned out, he was right.

- Brianna did okay with language arts. She liked reading books from her favorite series, and she got good grades on worksheets and the short compositions her mom made her write. The only problem was, her reading and writing skills never seemed to actually improve.

Each scenario reflects a lack of understanding. In some scenarios, programs lack clear goals, which results in students doing work they see as pointless, while parents see evidence of work but no progress. In others, assignments strike students as inefficient and irrelevant, and they resent the imposition of other peoples' tastes on them for reading and writing. Students feel frustrated, bored, and even a little oppressed, and though they may comply, they do not love the work they have to do. In every case, one has to ask, "What, exactly, is the point?" And therein lies the problem.

To a certain extent, confusion about goals is unique to the middle school level. In elementary school, children must learn to read and write; in high school, students analyze and compose. But in middle school, goals are fuzzy. Is middle school language arts best seen as glorified elementary-school work, dumbed-down high school, or a little of each? Fuzziness about goals leads many people, including curriculum designers, to turn middle school language arts into a sort of holding tank for middle school students.

The Middle School Holding Tank

When Kristen cleaned her aquarium, she put her goldfish in a temporary holding tank, which in our case was a simple glass bowl. But serious aquarium owners often keep more sophisticated holding tanks to keep their expensive fish collections healthy. Their concern is twofold: new fish may become stressed if kept too long in confined spaces, but they may also carry contagious diseases that could contaminate an established collection of valuable and presumably beloved fish. In the holding tank, the new fish get used to a new diet and receive treatment for any parasites or bacterial infections they may have. They also adjust to their new environment, as owners replace about 10% of the water on a regular basis until the fish acclimate themselves enough to enter the established aquarium.

In many ways, most middle school language arts programs resemble the holding tank. Middle school is, after all, the designated place for students to prepare for high school: a place to debug any persistent issues left over from elementary-level learning and get a jump start on the real work they'll do in high school. All of this is accomplished through assignments: to read certain books, to write to creative writing prompts, to practice editing compositions and inferring meaning from books. In theory, after three years of this kind of debugging and prepping, students should be well prepared and ready to roll by the time they become high school freshmen.

Unfortunately, the holding tank approach to middle school language arts that prevails in public schools doesn't quite work the way it should. Fish survive in holding tanks, but they don't thrive. Certainly, it's good to cure oneself of ailments such as parasites and infections, but convalescence is a very different thing from building strength or experiencing growth. And while gradually adjusting to a new environment seems like a good idea, what happens in language arts often involves overly difficult tasks and expectations. Assignments feel oppressive, confusing, or unfair—and like Kristen's fish, many middle school students just seize up and stop learning.

Some teachers suggest approaching middle school language arts differently: "If I look at my classroom as a holding tank," middle school English teacher Nancie Atwell (1998) writes, "learning stops" (p. 66). In her seminal work, *In the Middle*, Atwell observes that kids forced to read what someone else wants them to read slow down and rarely get into reading (p. 37). She points out that assigning creative writing tends to result in either lackluster efforts from the students who don't really care, or unnatural, almost saccharine attempts at impressing or pleasing a teacher from the ones that do (p. 11). So Atwell developed a different approach to reading and writing: she treated her classroom like a workshop where students operate like real readers and writers, choosing their own books to read and topics for writing about. In addition to reading and writing, students spent class time getting feedback from other readers and advice from editors and deciding which pieces to abandon, which to perfect, and which to publish. Perhaps because it respected the middle school students' need for freedom and relevance, the approach worked. Atwell was impressed by her results: students who had previously resisted writing or wrote poorly began to write with the same quality that she had previously seen from only a few top students. But with the freedom to pursue their own ideas, Atwell found that every student produced significant pieces. She explains, "A workshop approach accommodates adolescents' needs, invites their independence, challenges them to grow up, and transforms the status quo" (p. 71).

Today, many English teachers consider Atwell's workshop approach to be the ideal, but at the same time, they acknowledge that some issues remain for teachers who adopt it. Because the primary content in workshop-type language arts classes is whatever students choose to read and write, there is minimal direct instruction in general and no systematic grammar instruction at all. Instead, grammar has relevance only in the context of a student's actual writing. Rather than waste students' time memorizing random rules, students focus only on the specific rules that are tripping them up as writers. In this way, students spend more time writing and improving writing and less time learning rules unnecessarily. And while this might seem to make sense, the question remains: do students actually improve as readers and writers in a workshop-type language arts program?

Shelley Harwayne (2001), a leading advocate of writing workshops, insists that they do, and she says that she takes pride in her students' "growing expertise in the conventions of language" (p. 326). And yet, her 298-page book dedicates just three pages to the many ways students *might* edit their work and the many ways teachers *might* remind them to do so (p. 327 – 328). Somewhat tellingly, in spite of their "growing expertise," most student's writing samples in Harwayne's book contain spelling and grammar errors. So did Harwayne just display a few anomalies? Other teachers suggest that she did not. English teacher Kelly Gallagher (2006) observes that while more frequent writing affected students' fluency as writers, "without explicit writing instruction their skills stagnate" (p. 9). Similarly, Harry Noden (1999) tried the more linguistic approach after finding that his students weren't applying what they were learning from grammar instruction to their writing, but he observed that the results were "disastrous" (p. viii).

Answering both the traditional and workshop approaches is the classical approach to language, which is one of the few educational philosophies that still embraces the systematic teaching of grammar to middle school students. This approach has roots back in 1947, when British author Dorothy Sayers called for a return to an emphasis on the classical liberal arts Trivium of grammar, dialectic (or logic), and rhetoric that she called "the lost tools of learning" (as cited in Hart, 2006, p. 120). Sayers argued that each of the three parts of the Trivium applied to students at different stages in their academic growth, and she saw children aged 9 to 11 as the ideal age to focus on grammar. She prescribed the study of grammar via Latin—or, for "those whose pedantic preference for a living language persuades them . . . Russian" (p. 112). Later, middle school students of about 12 to 14 would enter the Dialectic stage and move from the focus on grammar to formal logic, suggesting accordingly that readings "proceed from narrative and lyric to essays, argument, and criticism, and the pupil will learn to try his own hand at writing this kind of thing" (p. 115). In Sayers's model, middle school students would have completely mastered grammar, spelling, punctuation and be ready to apply all of this knowledge to logical exposition in writing.

The popular classical education homeschooling manual *The Well-Trained Mind* by Susan Wise Bauer and Jessie Wise (2009) outlines a similarly rigorous approach. Like Sayers, Wise and Bauer (2009) assume that by middle school, students will ably "read fluently and well . . . the basic mechanics of spelling, comma placement, capitalization and sentence construction should no longer act as barriers to expression" (p. 231-232). However, whereas Sayers saw fiction as too fluffy for the dialectic student, Wise and Bauer recommend an hour of free reading daily in addition to grammar, Latin, and logic (p. 347). The result of all this is a program that entails over four hours of language arts work daily, not including the prescribed logic and Latin, with which the program takes over five. In fact, *The Well-Trained Mind* calls for over nine hours of academic work daily. If parents want to schedule any recess or physical education, the day gets even longer.

When Kristen was in middle school, I read and reread *The Well-Trained Mind*, and I admired the authors greatly. The Wise family seemed to make the most of every minute of the day, listening to classical music while cleaning and reading so constantly that "while she polished shoes, Susan even read the newspaper that was under them" (p. 643). How I wanted to be as efficient! But when I tried to implement their program, it didn't work as well for us. There just weren't enough hours in the day to follow their program, and I discovered that the more I dictated what Kristen had to read and do every minute of the day, the less she seemed to accomplish. In the end, I concluded that the classical approach was just too oppressive; at least, so it seemed for my middle school student.

Fluency and Accuracy

So much disparity! It seems like one approach gets kids excited about reading and writing, but can't teach them to do so well; meanwhile the other approach addresses imperfection, but at the price of freedom. How can views clash so radically? Why can't educators agree? Where does do much disparity come from?

I believe that one of the main issues here is that most of the language arts programs available to homeschoolers are designed to correct the flaws of other programs, and so they tend to emphasize the aspect of language they perceive as most lacking in students. Workshop and whole language approaches sought to correct what was seen as an overemphasis on accuracy at the expense of fluency, and when those approaches failed to produce students who could read and write well, conservative educators called for reform that emphasized accuracy at the expense of freedom and fluency. And yet, both fluency and accuracy demand equal attention. A person who cannot express or comprehend communication with fluency will not be able to understand or be understood by others; a person who expresses or understands ideas inaccurately gets it all wrong. Emphasizing one over the other cannot help but result in an imbalanced ability to express and understand language.

I learned all of this firsthand when I moved to Guatemala in 1992. Before I actually moved to Latin America, I assumed that ten years of straight A's in high school and college classes in a variety of foreign languages would have prepared me to both speak and understand Spanish exceptionally well. I was wrong. I soon learned how humiliating it is to overhear the five-year-old girl with whom you are residing ask her mommy in perfect Spanish why you look like an adult but speak like a baby. Mind you, I tested out of the grammar portion of the ten-week Spanish brush-up program we were enrolled in: I knew the entire Spanish grammar. My vocabulary was expansive. And yet, my tongue had never gotten used to forming the words and speaking the language, and my ears had never been trained to decipher the rapid speech of native speakers. For all the words I knew and all the conjugation I could do, I had never built up any fluency in understanding or expressing a language other than my own.

In their book, *How Languages are Learned*, linguistics experts Patsy Lightbrown and Nina Spada (1999) discuss the practices that best facilitate language learning. Apparently, the main debate among language acquisition theorists is whether people acquire languages better through a systematic study of grammar and vocabulary or through actually using the language to communicate meaningfully. To answer this question, researchers have studied several approaches to language instruction that emphasize one or the other, and they found that instruction that focuses on only grammar fails to produce fluent speakers, while students who never study grammar never really learn to communicate accurately. Perhaps not surprisingly, Lightbrown and Spada conclude that language is not really an either-or kind of thing: "the challenge," they suggest, "is to find the best balance" (p. 153).

Finding Balance

So how does one find the best balance? You start by asking what fluencies are sought and what they look like in terms of reading, writing, speaking, and listening, and then by considering what accuracy looks like and how it may best be learned. Once you have an idea of what fluency and accuracy look like, you provide opportunities for students to develop both, keeping in mind the middle school student's need for relevance and freedom within a meaningful structure.

Fluency

Without an emphasis on fluency, most people never develop an affinity for language, and since so many students decide once and for all whether they consider themselves to be readers or writers in middle school, one of the most important goals for this program is that students develop an affinity to read and write—or, in other words, for students to like reading and writing. Unless they like what they're doing, they won't get into doing it, and they won't do it fluently. And, as I learned in Guatemala, fluency is essential to actual ability. Though I knew Spanish grammar and vocabulary, until I had trained my brain to think and my tongue to speak through constant practice, I would never have been able to communicate effectively. In spite of ten years of hard work, my knowledge would have ultimately served no purpose.

So what entices people to engage? For most people, it is meaningful activity that they have chosen for themselves. Maria Montessori (1967) writes, "An interesting piece of work, freely chosen, which has the virtue of inducing concentration rather than fatigue, adds to the child's energies and mental capacities, and leads him to self-mastery" (p. 207). Psychologists David Shernoff and Mihaly Csikszentmihalyi (2008) agree: they find that at least some student initiative and autonomy are necessary for meaningful learning experiences, and that teachers who organize enticing activities for students that pair academic intensity—that is, challenges at or just above skill level—with humor, enthusiasm, and playfulness engage students most in learning (p. 137, 138, & 143).

Students build fluency best when allowed to choose their own reading and writing projects, as students do in Nancie Atwell's workshop approach to language arts. Not surprisingly, students engage most willingly in tasks they find themselves to be especially good at. Nobody enjoys failing, so it's not surprising that all people feel attracted to activities that they do well, and they feel repulsed by and easily distracted from whatever activities they do poorly. In fact, Aristotle observed thousands of years ago that people attend best to work that they find most pleasing and become most easily distracted when their work seems less pleasant:

> People who are fond of flute-music cannot keep their attention to conversation or discourse when they catch the sound of a flute because they take more Pleasure in flute-playing than in

the Working they are at the time engaged on . . . who eats sweetmeats in the theatre do so most when the performance is indifferent. (p. 186)

Permitting students as much freedom as possible to choose their reading and writing projects increases engagement because they naturally choose interesting material to read and write about. Also, most students naturally choose projects that are either at or just above their ability level, because that is the level that feels most satisfying to them. And yet, parents do not merely assume that their students will push themselves toward growth. It's the parent's job to ensure growth by providing a modicum of structure: "The children in our schools are free," Maria Montessori writes, "but that does not mean there is no organization. Organization, in fact, is necessary, and if the children are free to work, it must be even more thorough than in ordinary schools" (p. 244). Thus 'free' does not mean 'disorganized': rather, parents carefully organize options to entice students, clarify reasonable expectations and requirements to ensure variety and progress, and offer helpful feedback and direction to help students when they get stuck.

Montessori's radical break with traditional school practices produced remarkable results among mentally retarded students, and she reasoned that her methods would have remarkable results with typically developing students as well, and my experiences with cognitively disabled, typically able, and intellectually gifted students lead me to agree. I have seen students who had given up on writing light up when told that they might develop their own projects about topics of their own choosing, so long as they put in the time and turn out the products. I have seen these same students produce projects of higher quality as well. It seems that caring about writing has a tremendous impact on quality.

Curiously, fluency takes more time to develop than accuracy. It results from regular practice and variety—you can't get fluent by memorizing one dialogue; you have to switch it up every day. When it comes to reading and writing, fluency is fairly simple: reading more results in reading faster, and writing more makes writing easier. A very little feedback and encouragement to try new reading and writing projects is generally all that's required to keep a student on the right track once on it. Fluency is all about doing time—and not just clocking the time, but actually engaging in reading and writing projects. More detail about organizing work and requirements that allow students maximum freedom and control over their projects and grades can be found in Chapter 3, which discusses the reading aspect of this program, and Chapter 4, which covers writing.

Accuracy

No one denies that students become more fluent readers and writers through extensive practice, but educators clash over the question of how students improve in terms of accuracy. Mainstream practices advocate training students to perform transferable skills such as editing and summarizing passages of writing, while advocates of the workshop approach suggest that all students need are occasional "mini-lessons" and a personalized checklist of errors to watch for. In contrast to both, classical educators insist that a systematic understanding of grammar and regular practice analyzing sentences are necessary. So are these different approaches all half-a-dime one, and a nickel the other? Could a parent just pick the one they like best, apply it, and achieve the same effect as with any other program?

The short answer is no. The various approaches reflect different priorities that ultimately affect what and how well students learn. It's important to understand that while fluency is essential in order for students to care about, engage in, and retain linguistic abilities, unless students receive systematic instruction in the various facets of accuracy as well, they will only get by in language arts; they will never really excel. When a pianist learns a new piece of music, inevitably some passages are going to be more difficult than others. When I was a piano student, my initial impulse was to rush through the hard parts, so I could get back to the parts that sounded good when I played them. I later discovered that I could not ignore the rough spots: unless I stopped and focused on them until I could play them perfectly and at the same tempo as the easy parts, I would never master the piece as a whole. That is why a workshop approach to language arts represents the best method for engaging students and improving fluency, but fails to help students develop accuracy.

In middle school, accuracy matters in terms of both reading and writing. As educational psychologist Diane McGuinness (1997) observes, students must be able to decode words accurately before they can speed up: "slow but accurate decoders [can] still comprehend what they read, whereas rapid, inaccurate decoders [can] not" (p. 275). Since by middle school, most students decode almost effortlessly, this aspect of accuracy will be considered prerequisite to this program; however, recommendations for struggling decoders can be found in Chapter 5.

Accuracy in this program refers mainly to the ability of students to spell and compose sentences. In middle school, students will conclude their systematic spelling studies and begin to take responsibility for applying what they know and researching in a dictionary words they don't. The main emphasis, however, becomes composing sentences accurately, truthfully, and well. Sister Miriam Joseph (2002) succinctly captures this order in her book, *The Trivium*:

- Phonetics prescribes how to combine sounds so as to form spoken words correctly.

- Spelling prescribes how to combine letters so as to form written words correctly.

- Grammar prescribes how to combine words so as to form sentences correctly.

- Rhetoric prescribes how to combine sentences into paragraphs and paragraphs into a whole composition having unity, coherence, and the desired emphasis, as well as clarity, force, and beauty.

- Logic prescribes how to combine concepts into judgments and judgments into syllogisms and chains of reasoning so as to achieve truth. (p. 9)

The abilities of spelling words correctly and composing and punctuating clearly truthful sentences are necessary for students who will soon be composing lengthier and more complex arguments. However, while middle school students should be writing truthful sentences and not pure nonsense and relatively clear ideas and not confusing mush, at this level, the emphasis necessarily falls on the ability to understand how to put a single idea—i.e., a sentence—onto the page with enough accuracy to be understood by a reader, not on the ability to craft the complex or powerful argument. In other words, accuracy in middle school refers to understanding how grammar works to make sentences both true and clear.

But how much grammar is really necessary? Some people believe that grammar and spelling are no longer necessary since most word processing programs come with grammar and spell checking functions. And it's true that, to some extent, these types of programs relieve some of the burden on writers to produce perfectly accurate prose. However, people who aren't sure of grammar principles or the variations in spelling inevitably have a hard time writing, even with the assistance of a computer.

The college students I tutor compose all of their essays on computers, and almost all of them struggle with issues of clarity, which, according to Sister Miriam Josesph is the "first requisite of style in expository writing," adding that "grammatical correctness is a prerequisite" (p. 263) That writers need to understand grammar to write well is evident from my experiences with writing students, whose writing is most awkward when students can't answer the question, "Can you identify your verb in this sentence?" Writers who don't understand the parts of speech tend to compose sentences that may be technically correct, but are sometimes vague, misleading, or awkward. Other times, I will ask a student about a sentence that is technically incorrect, and the student will answer, "Oh, I had to write it that way. The computer kept giving me that squiggly green line unless I did it that way." Students are often surprised to learn that they're actually smarter than their grammar checker.

The same is true of spell checkers: wild guessing at the spelling of words often leads to wildly inappropriate words appearing in documents where students have relied on the autocorrect feature of their word processor. Spell checkers tend to look for the closest match in spelling when a typist punches in a bunch of letters that don't add up to a word. Contrary to what people might think, spell checkers can't read minds so as to supply the word a typist intended. Nor can spell checkers figure out what is wrong with a sentence like this: "Eye trussed there are know miss steaks hear, four my come pewter is all weighs write" (O'Conner, 1999, p. 127). (Interestingly enough, my grammar checker didn't complain at this sentence either.)

Spelling matters. Grammar matters. Accuracy matters. And it falls to the writer to know enough about spelling and grammar and accuracy to be able to question when something he or she has written seems off. Professional writers rely on dictionaries and thesauruses to verify spelling and nuances in words when they're not sure of things, but they'd go nuts trying to verify everything they wrote. Every writer needs a foundation of basic knowledge as a prerequisite to writing.

Unfortunately, most middle school students today have only a fragmented understanding of grammar. This is because most language arts programs portray grammar as a set of rules to be applied to all writing, even though in reality, most of the rules are more like recommendations. Take the "rule" that no sentence should end with a preposition: absolute adherence to such rules results in sentences such as, "There are some things up with which one must not put!" Obviously, such rules are meant to be broken. But since students haven't been taught to think of grammar as set of interrelated principles that work together and sometimes cancel each other out, students don't understand how and when to break rules—as the real writers they read often do. The result is that students get the impression that grammar is really just a bunch of arbitrary and unnecessary trivia.

What most people don't understand is that grammar is not rules; it's a system: as Joseph T. Shipley (1977) explains, "Grammar may be defined as the system of principles . . . according to which words must be patterned in order to be understood" (p. 78). Unless a program explains how all of the words in a sentence work together to produce meaning through a systematic process of analysis, students aren't learning grammar. Most likely, they're learning (in theory) how to edit.

Most of the mainstream language arts curriculums marketed today address grammar by teaching students editing skills, which makes a lot of sense: if your goal is to get students to stop turning in work that is full of mistakes, you have to train them to become diligent editors so they can find and fix all the mistakes they make. To provide practice finding and fixing mistakes, you give them worksheets that explain specific issues such as comma placement or misplaced modifiers to show them what's right and wrong, and then you have them apply this knowledge to worksheet exercises that involve editing writing that contains lots of the specific kind of mistakes they're being taught to find and fix. Thus students not only learn what a modifier is, but they also develop the ability to edit them when they're wrong. Sounds logical, doesn't it?

The problem with these types of exercises is that people tend to remember what they see, and when people see different models of the same thing, confusion results. For instance, I pause when I try to spell 'occasional.' I know it has a double letter in there somewhere, and I just can't remember if it's the 'c' or the 's.' Since I've misspelled it often, whenever I need it, I try to visualize how it's spelled, but I see it both ways, right and wrong. Knowing that I tend to get it wrong, I reject the one I think is right, which means I usually choose the wrong one yet again. Thankfully, my spell checker helps me out on that one, but if I were to get confused on whether a word was spelled 'bear' or 'bare,' it wouldn't.

It is always confusing to have two competing models when only one can be right, and puzzling things out all the time gets so frustrating that some people just stop trying. I know I sometimes do. Some time ago, I met some parents who introduced their daughter as "Shawna" but immediately explained that the name was spelled like "Hannah" with an 'S' because 'Hannah' is a palindrome, spelled the same way forwards and backwards. While interesting, the information about how Shannah's name was spelled actually confused me. For the next year or so, I couldn't remember whether I should say "Shawn-ah" or "Sh-anna." I wanted to say "Sh-anna" because I kept seeing "Hannah" in my mind when I saw her, but I had a strange feeling that was wrong. In the end, to avoid annoying the girl and embarrassing myself, I avoided calling her anything at all.

Exposing students who are uncertain about how to spell or punctuate to models of inaccurate writing actually increases the likelihood that they will feel frustrated and confused and ultimately commit more errors in the future. Sadly, the students who struggle most with language tend to be the visual learners who are most likely to remember and retain the incorrect models they see, right alongside of or instead of the correct model. Since about one-third of all students are visual learners, teaching grammar by teaching editing actually impairs a large proportion of the student body.

In fact, every language arts program that claims to teach generic language arts "skills" such as editing compositions or inferring meaning from passages of text to teach reading comprehension does students a disservice. Education expert Ed Hirsch (1987) suggests that programs that emphasize skills are more or less a waste of time, since "researchers have consistently found that people do not develop general, transferable skills in problem solving, critical thinking, or in any other field" (p. 62). And yet, ever since educational reforms began emphasizing content standards, language arts curriculum packages have focused very specifically on teaching the skills that will supposedly help students do well on standardized tests. Teachers using these programs assign students pointless exercises when their time would be better spent reading and writing, affording students more meaningful practice and allowing them to develop knowledge, skills, and understanding more effectively. The reason educators currently favor these programs is that they assume that teaching targeted language arts skills is more efficient, but any program that is ineffective at teaching the skills they claim to teach can hardly be called efficient. Worse, a large portion of the students in schools are learning bad habits from them they'll have to unlearn with great effort later.

Students need systematic grammar instruction. And while the prominent model of classical education adopted by most homeschooling parents provides just this, the insistence on extensive sentence diagramming is unnecessarily tedious and time-consuming. Furthermore, I would argue that by breaking up language arts into grammar, logic, and rhetoric, classical educators overwhelm students' schedule with academic work, when in reality, more time should be allocated to the more appealing activities that develop fluency.

I say this not because I dislike all things classical. In fact, both of my daughters are inclined to read classic literature and study classical languages. Kristen independently elected to study Latin when she was fourteen and spent two years translating the writings of Catullus, Vergil, Ovid, and Seneca. She added Greek to her transcript her senior year and chose to attend St. John's College, one of very few colleges that prescribes a single classical liberal arts program for all students. Like Susan Wise Bauer, Kristen graduated from high school early (at sixteen) and did well on college admittance examinations. Meanwhile, Lauren, with five years of Spanish study under her belt going into eighth grade, has begun learning Greek, again, of her own accord. All things considered, I lean more toward the classical point of view than not.

The main issue with the classical education model familiar to most homeschoolers is that it splits the Trivium into three distinct stages, contrary to the intended nature of the Trivium. Mortimer Adler, who was one of the first (if not the first) educational leader to advocate a return to the classical model of education, felt that it was specifically the separation of the liberal arts into distinct disciplines that had led to their demise. What he meant by this was that, as universities became more and more specialized, grammar was subsumed by English composition, logic became part of philosophy, and rhetoric was taken up by communication courses. Adler contended that this separation of the Trivium led to the deterioration and disuse of the liberal arts among college students, who in reading, writing, and speaking lacked the Greeks' and Medieval writers' "integral unity and harmony" (as cited in Joseph, p. 284).

Contrary to the organization maintained by many homeschooling classical educators today, Sister Miriam Joseph, who studied the Trivium under Dr. Adler, points out that "because communication involves the simultaneous exercise of logic, grammar, and rhetoric, these three arts are the fundamental arts of education, of teaching, and of being taught. Accordingly, they must be practiced *simultaneously* by both teacher and pupil" (p. 7, emphasis mine).

While Adler's contention in 1935 was that the liberal arts had been consigned to distinct academic disciplines, his point was that the three liberal arts, properly understood, operated harmoniously. Indeed, Mortimer Adler's own prescription for K-12 education, *The Paideai Proposal*, describes a program that retains all three concurrently. Adler suggests that the ideal education comprises three distinct yet interconnected modes of teaching and learning that apply to all twelve years of education, with increasingly complex and difficult content, skills, and understanding year by year (p. 22). Adler maintains that students at all stages acquire knowledge, skills, and understanding, and he contends that students from K-12 learn best through a combination of didactic means, by which he means direct instruction through lecture or textbook, through being coached, drilled, and supervised as they practice skills, and through the discussion of ideas and values (p. 23). Adler depicts all of this in a diagram under which he writes in tidy caps, "The three columns do not correspond to separate courses, nor is one kind of teaching and learning necessarily confined to any one class" (p. 23).

The Out of the Holding Tank Model

So what is the answer? So far, I have suggested allowing students maximum freedom in reading and writing to develop fluency, and I've rejected all of the most commonly adopted approaches of educators for helping students to improve in terms of accuracy. So what's left? Is there any way to teach a student accuracy, without making language arts an insufferably tedious exercise?

What I'm going to recommend to you is actually a largely forgotten practice that is actually still used in France: training students to write correctly through dictation. Dictating sentences for students to transcribe affords them practice in listening, spelling, handwriting, capitalizing, and punctuating sentences; analyzing the sentences' grammar afterwards provides practice identifying parts of speech and seeing how they work to form meaning, and having students read back their sentences to make sure they didn't forget a word helps even struggling readers improve their reading ability. All of this work occurs simultaneously, making dictation an efficient way to get practice with all of the language arts.

By separating the Trivium into separate stages, the classical homeschool model increases student workload unnecessarily. By insisting on diagramming as the sole means of understanding grammar, classical educators make learning grammar unnecessarily unwieldy. True: diagramming simple sentences is easy enough, but as soon as you get into more complicated sentences with multiple qualifiers and dependent clauses, diagramming quickly becomes difficult to do neatly.

According to Wise and Bauer (2009), diagramming sentences reveals sentence structure, is hands-on, visual and kinesthetic, and prevents students "simply parroting back rules that [they don't] fully understand (p. 340). Dictation plus analysis does all of this and more: whereas diagramming involves arranging words on a page to show their relationships, transcribing dictated sentences involves writing grammatically and rhetorically effective sentences on paper in normal fashion, exactly as students do when they compose their own sentences. In other words, by transcribing sentences onto paper, students increase their ability to fluently translate the words in their minds into words on paper. Furthermore, dictation work involves listening, which is too frequently overlooked as an essential component of language arts programs. In fact, experts now recognize that one of the most important interventions for struggling readers and spellers is improving phonemic awareness, or attuning the ear to the subtleties of language. Finally, dictation allows students to have a say in what will be the substance of their sentence analysis work. Sentences can come from a favorite work of fiction or non-fiction, or you could dictate verses from a favorite poem or song; alternatively, you can invent sentences that incorporate words from a spelling or vocabulary program.

Following Adler's model of three interrelated modes of learning, the *Out of the Holding Tank* program is arranged in three interrelated pieces. The first piece focuses on accuracy in spelling and grammar through daily dictation exercises; the second is the writing program, in which students develop fluency in transposing their own ideas into writing. Finally, the reading program challenges students to take in new ideas that refine their thinking and help them develop more complex models of understanding. All of this takes roughly half of the time required by the program described in *The Well-Trained Mind*—unless, of course, your student chooses to spend more time reading and writing.

	Dictation Program	Writing Program	Reading Program
Goals	Students acquire knowledge about spelling, and grammar and practice handwriting effective sentence constructions	Students develop an affinity for writing for real-life purposes with increasing fluency	Students develop an affinity for reading for pleasure and for information with increasing fluency
Means	Daily dictation exercises (approximately 30 - 40 minutes)	Students choose writing projects and fulfill minimal requirements for polishing and publishing a number of products	Students choose and read material from parent-organized library in fulfillment of specific minimal requirements
Assessment	Mastery: the student moves on only when able to independently complete objectives with accuracy	Grading is based on student compliance; long-term evaluation is based on evidence of growth in variety and effectiveness of writing attempts	Grading is based on student effort; long-term evaluation is based on evidence of growth in breadth and depth of reading selections and book discussions

Interrelatedness is the key to the program's efficiency and effectiveness: as Montessori observed, in order to perfect one's ability to communicate, one must write down what one would say, for "analysis of the transient is impossible" (2008, p. 232). Thus learning to write down one's thoughts is a necessary preparation for learning how to communicate well, in speech or writing. Similarly, "if writing serves to correct, or better, to direct and perfect the mechanism of the articulate language of the child, reading serves to help the development of ideas, and relates them to the development of the language" (Montessori, 2008, p. 218). Because imparting knowledge, practicing skills, and discussing ideas apply to all three parts of this program, the integrity of the three liberal arts is preserved, even while it promotes fluency and accuracy in all four language arts.

The next three chapters outline each of the three parts of this program: Chapter 2 provides a fuller description of my dictation process and suggests a number of variations so that you can tailor your program to meet your student's needs for interest and growth. Chapter 3 describes the reading program and explains how you can ensure your student chooses literature that encourages intellectual progress. Chapter 4 details a program for writing that allows your student to write about topics that matter to him or her and teaches you how to respond to that writing as both a reader and an editor. Three appendices provide additional support to help you implement all three parts of this program. Finally, in Chapter 5, a discussion of variations in student learning preferences and aptitudes provides insights to help you individualize this program to best suit your student's current and future needs.

In contrast to the myriad objectives of state content standards, the goals here are simple: at the end of middle school, your student should love reading and writing and understand how to express ideas clearly and well. That's it. Here you will find no focus on isolated skills, no imposed reading, and no artificial creative writing assignments. Instead, I hope you will find that the program I've described is fun—yes, fun!—because it respects the ultimate purpose of language: to enable meaningful communication between people.

CHAPTER TWO

PRIORITIZING ACCURACY

THROUGH DICTATION

Language is a use-it-or-lose-it type of deal. That is to say, people forget languages they don't use. If a person studies a foreign language in high school but never uses it, they soon forget most of the words. My daughter Kristen, who had been nearly bilingual when our family lived in Mexico, all but forgot Spanish within a year of moving back to the United States at age seven. In fact, studies have found that the average college student forgets 50% of what they learn in courses within a year and 80% within two years. What people are most likely to retain is the knowledge they actually use regularly, in daily life (Tyler, 1949, p. 39). The same is true of grammar: people who do not think in terms of grammar or use its terminology soon forget its principles.

Even students who've had thorough preparation in language arts during the elementary years will need practice understanding the many subtleties of grammar as a system. The various disciplines of language arts—spelling, grammar, mechanics, vocabulary, usage—are subtle and often convoluted. Normal people don't speak with perfect correctness, and they'd sound pompous if they did. Most people speak in snippets of speech and run-ons. What's more, many contemporary writers of fiction, hoping to achieve a sense of authenticity in their writing, write in fragments and run-ons as well. So realistically, we are all surrounded by erroneous grammar on a regular basis. It's no wonder students have a strong sense for only some of the rules they've learned and are vaguely confused about the rest: so much inconsistency is confusing. That's why a consistent program that reinforces understanding language as a system is more helpful for retaining grammar knowledge than isolated grammar-related activities. Using English well and appropriately requires a great deal of practice across many applications.

"Can I Join You? I Really Need This."

I didn't know or think about such things when I began teaching my daughters at home. In fact, I was as ignorant as my kids when it came to grammar, though I didn't know it at the time. The truth is, I learned grammar with my kids. Before I learned grammar, I thought I knew enough grammar because I had gotten good feedback on the essays I'd written in college and seminary. My ignorance, however, left me with no tools with which to understand what was wrong with the essays Kristen wrote in seventh grade, and I resorted to re-writing many of her sentences as a result. Only after I began to understand how grammar worked could I teach my daughters how to communicate their ideas more clearly, without having to take over.

The process I eventually adopted is actually a combination of the teaching strategies I came across more or less by accident. Within about a year of homeschooling, I'd come to the conclusion that the many brightly colored, standards-compliant yet "fun" workbooks out there were neither efficient, nor effective, nor even all that much fun. What annoyed me most, however, was that I kept having to rip out entire pages of the workbooks because they were actually wrong.

By some happy circumstance, one of the first resources I acquired turned out to be a gem. I think I ordered Susan B. Anthony's *Spelling* worktext because it was cost effective—it identified appropriate spelling lists for grades one through six—but what I really liked about the book was Anthony's procedure of using dictation to teach spelling words. Instead of completing fill-in-the-blank type exercises, I dictated spelling words to Lauren, both in isolation and in short sentences. And while I couldn't just hand Lauren a workbook and go fold laundry or something, both Lauren and I found the dictation work to be kind of fun—especially when I took advantage of the time it took Lauren to write down her words to conjure up silly sentences. When we finished the book, neither of us wanted to stop doing dictation.

The other resource I came across was *Understanding and Using Good Grammar* by Genevieve Walberg Schaefer. The book clarified grammar principles using a process of underlining and bracketing and circling that showed how the various parts of speech work together to form meaning. The logical process Schaefer explained and the activity of double-underlining and bracketing parts of speech were somehow satisfying, and discovering what every word in a sentence was doing helped us understand grammar far more than the various comprehensive workbooks' erratic lessons about understanding which kinds of words are usually (but not always) nouns and exercises about dividing sentences into subjects and predicates (the purpose of which I still don't know).

When we finished Schaefer's workbook, Lauren and I agreed that we wanted to keep using her process to retain what we'd learned. I'd decided at some point to try using real works of fiction for dictation, and after a successful experiment with Roald Dahl's *Fantastic Mr. Fox*, I just kept going, figuring Lauren could learn punctuation from amusing dialogues, rather than from the boring stuff most workbooks are full of. One day, it occurred to me that we could combine Schaefer's process of grammatical analysis with the dictation we were doing.

Almost immediately, I felt like I'd really hit upon something. Suddenly, we were able to get all of our language arts work done in just about a half an hour of more or less gratifying work. We didn't need to rely on those annoying workbooks anymore, and the grammar and spelling in books we really liked helped us simultaneously review and expand our knowledge fairly naturally.

Writing out really good sentences and analyzing them made so much sense to me that I decided to offer a course for middle school students in our homeschooling community. To a certain extent, I was wary—how many kids would sign up for a class about grammar when they could take Tae Kwon Do or Lego Mindstorms? Yet somewhat to my surprise, a fair number of students signed up and seemed to actually like doing grammar with me. In fact, the first day of my class, a high school student passing our room paused in the doorway to watch me first dictate a sentence and then explain our grammar process. After a minute, she interrupted me. "Can I join you?" she asked. "I really need this."

Separate Writing Accuracy from Personal Expression

Accuracy absolutely matters, but it's important to separate the activities of writing to learn correctness and writing to express one's own ideas. This is not an artificial separation: if the student someday becomes a writer, he or she will keep the activities separate. Generating ideas requires a certain disregard for correctness in that the important thing is to capture the idea before it flits away—and since fingers fly slower than thoughts, it's something of a mad dash to get them down on paper before they're gone. Writers necessarily return to generated writing to consider whether the organization or phrasing could be improved upon and to seek out the inevitable glut of errors.

When a student generates a piece of writing that expresses his or her views, naturally the student will look for feedback for the quality of ideas—because that is what the student was thinking about when crafting the piece. No one generates writing consciously thinking, "and now I must add a direct object," and so on. Writers think and write ideas, and it is about these ideas that they seek and expect feedback. As a writer, this is how I think and feel, and I have yet to meet a student who didn't feel the same. When students receive feedback that primarily deals with numerous technical errors, they feel disappointed that their ideas failed to impress their reader. They also feel defeated as writers, because so many errors can only mean they write poorly. Responding to ideas with primarily negative feedback about accuracy turns writing into a distasteful activity for students who cannot help but make mistakes—they are, after all, still learning.

What college students say to me in tutoring sessions support this. Once, a student brought me an essay that was largely incoherent and scattered. Nevertheless, I realized that the young lady beside me had poured herself into the words on the page, so my first response focused on the quality of her ideas and which of them left me wishing for greater clarity. Then, I told her how she could do that: by developing a clear thesis statement and organizing three paragraphs in support of the thesis statement. In effect, I'd essentially told this young lady that her efforts required a complete re-write.

And yet, she responded to this advice, saying, "Thank you! You always make me feel so good about my writing!" The fact that I told her to basically re-write the entire essay didn't matter to her nearly as much as my encouraging response to her ideas.

In the language arts paradigm I am suggesting, you will focus on accuracy through daily dictation, which keeps the activity of writing prose separate from that of generating it. When students write dictated sentences, they develop good writing habits, and they have the opportunity to practice finding and correcting their own errors in writing without feeling criticized in the process. But dictation has several other benefits as well: it attunes students' ears to language, affords practice with spelling, handwriting, and language mechanics, teaches grammar and trains student to produce grammatically sound sentences through a no-risk, kinesthetic activity. Finally, the dictation process of writing and then reading back correct sentences helps struggling readers to improve their skills by following a process similar to the one used by the Ancient Sumerians who were among the first literate peoples to teach pupils to read and write:

> First, each child had to learn to prepare his own writing material, the clay tablet itself. Next, the "school brother," presumably a monitor, wrote out the day's exercises for each student individually. The student was then expected to copy the exercises and finally to recite them aloud. It is important to note that the writing always preceded recitation and that the student recited only what he had written. There was a direct connection between writing and reading. (McGuinness, 1985, p. 237)

With this process, students learn to write well by writing well-written sentences. Having practiced writing well and learned why good writing is structurally sound, students eventually apply the principles of grammar and punctuation to their own writing. The guesswork about what is correct and incorrect versus what is a permissible option for writing goes away, and students gain confidence about communicating their own ideas in writing.

"How Can a Zero Correct Anyone's Deficits?"

One of the worst experiences associated with education is failing an assignment that took a lot of effort to complete. Some students, knowing that pang of disappointment, learn to avoid trying, so as to be able to feign a carelessness about such failures: "It doesn't matter," they might say. "I wasn't trying anyway."

Can you blame them? Students who fail often have every reason to feel discouraged, and students who feel discouraged rarely engage in learning. That's why special education teachers learn to overteach—to not only give tons of opportunities for practice, but to also provide whatever extra support students need to be successful, over and over again, until they can confidently demonstrate skills independently. "Success is the key," writes special education teacher Patricia Oelwein in her book, *Teaching Reading to Children with Down Syndrome* (1995, p. 51). One of my favorite parts of her book is a heading for a section that says, "Make learning an almost errorless process" (p. 52). Her point is really very simple: students learn when taught, and they become discouraged by premature testing. Therefore, the best way to keep students learning is to minimize testing and just teach.

"Whenever we ask a question that we know the answer to," Oelwein explains, "we are testing the other person" (p. 57). In contrast, when you teach, you're imparting knowledge, facilitating discoveries, and providing opportunities for your student to learn. Testing requires students to answer correctly, sometimes after minimal opportunity to learn the material. Bear in mind that tests may be formal or informal: tests include not only graded quizzes and exams, but verbal quizzing and written worksheets as well. "What is meant by correcting exercise books?" Maria Montessori demands. "It means marking them from 0 to 10. How can a zero correct anyone's defects?" (1967, p. 245).

Some people might protest that with little or no testing, there's no way to be sure students have learned anything. However, formal tests are just one of many ways to assess whether learning has occurred. Other valid methods of assessment include collected evidence from performance tasks such as reading logs, work samples, and portfolios and informal checks for understanding such as teacher observations and conversations with the student (Wiggins & McTighe, 2005, p. 152). Of these, collected evidence serves teachers over the long term, while observation and conversation provide more immediately useful feedback to both student and teacher.

Meaningful work results when parents "survey the capacities and needs of [students] and arrange experiences that satisfy these needs and develop these capacities" (Dewey, 1939, p. 58). This means paying attention to what a student can do independently, what the student can do with prompting, and when the student needs explicit instruction to do something right the first time. Dictation work invites students to practice and thus reinforce acquired knowledge, gradually expand language understanding, and discover useful writing techniques—most of it in a scenario that maximizes opportunities for learning and minimizes opportunities for failure.

Dictation can be an errorless process for students when you carefully observe what your student can do, and provide support when necessary. Rather than peppering students with test questions, simply observe whether your student can independently punctuate correctly, needs prompting ("That sentence needs a comma") or requires explicit instruction ("There should be an introductory comma after the dependent clause that ends with the word, 'bridge'"). The student's level is evident by what he or she does. Instead of continually testing students on material which has been minimally taught, dedicate as much time as possible to teaching activities: first, impart information, providing any necessary supports so that students need never fail; next, prepare opportunities for students to apply the knowledge in various contexts, paying attention to increasing ability and reducing support when possible; and finally, eliminate all support, confirm the student's independence and mastery, and move on to the next lesson. Because independence is satisfying, you can count on your student to apply whichever rules he or she has committed to memory and learned to apply.

To halt learning opportunities in order to test students whose progress is already known by the teacher can only be described as unnecessary and inefficient. Maria Montessori, describing the gradual increase in understanding of a boy who first colors a tree trunk red and later brown says: "Thus we have the test of the child's intellectual progress" (p. 174). Increasing understanding is evidenced in the work the student does. For documentation, work samples suffice.

There is no reason to fixate on mistakes. When a student incorrectly identifies which grammatical function a word has, it is enough to invite the student to reconsider. In fact, it's not a bad idea to ask, "Are you sure?" occasionally, even when an answer is clearly correct. Students then learn to critically consider their responses and confidently defend answers they feel certain of. When they have doubts, they can freely admit them, and then the question can be discussed. There is no shame in not knowing every answer—and they will have seen from your model that sometimes, strange structures baffle you, too. They do me! Unusual sentences that defy the textbook models make great opportunities to discuss how and why the sentence works with your student.

USING LITERATURE FOR DICTATION

The procedure I follow for dictation is not complicated. Here, in a nutshell, are the basic steps:

1. Select a passage in a book and read it out loud to your student in its entirety.

2. Choose appropriate sentences to dictate and read them out to the student slowly.

3. Have your student read each sentence back to you before dictating the next sentence.

4. After dictating a page or so worth of sentences, analyze the grammar in each sentence.

5. Note any errors in mechanics and spelling, and assign these to the student as homework.

Choosing a Passage to Dictate

The first step in my process is choosing a book. You can use almost any published work for dictation, but I like to choose books that are either particularly well-written or that I know my daughter has particularly liked. I look for passages that are not too long—perhaps a page or two in length—and that either amuse readers with neatly crafted dialog exchanges or that use language particularly well. I don't focus too much on the words themselves. I'm more interested in the author's sentences than the words that comprise them. I do, however, prefer passages that contain more grammatically correct sentences than not.

Although you probably know this, you may not often reflect on the fact that not all sentences in a published book are necessarily grammatically correct. This is because the various kinds of writing fall across a spectrum that ranges from poetry on one side to exposition on the other. Poetry, which seeks to affect or inspire readers emotionally, relies on ambiguity and associations to do its work. As such, poetry rarely conforms to the standards of grammatical correctness. Exposition, on the other hand, seeks to argue and explain with clarity, and clarity comes from grammatically sound structures. Thus expository writing only rarely breaks the rules of grammar. Somewhere between the two extremes is fiction and opinionated non-fiction. Writers who seek to affect readers emotionally with lots of humor or pathos tend to write with more fragments and grammatically questionable structures, while writers who are more concerned with communicating a narrative with more clarity use a more spare writing style that falls closer to exposition.

Spectrum of Grammatical Correctness by Genre

Poetry or Poetic Writing	Amusing or Inspiring Prose	Most Fiction and Non-Fiction Narratives	Exposition and Academic Writing
Affects and inspires readers	Amuses and moves readers	Narrates a story or explains ideas	Explains concepts and argues positions
Shakespeare, Milton, Dante, Psalms and parables of the Bible	Mark Twain, Dave Barry, Gary Paulsen, P.G. Wodehouse	E.B. White, C.S. Lewis, Laura Ingalls Wilder, J.R.R. Tolkien	Aristotle, John Locke, Alexander Hamilton
Rarely follows the rules of grammar; figurative language results in ambiguity and prompts interpretation	Adheres to grammar rules loosely, breaking them fairly often for comic or some other effect; writing with lots of colloquialism and figurative language	Follows grammar rules regularly but not fastidiously so as to seem devoid of emotion	Rarely breaks rules of grammar; clear meaning evokes understanding

Of course, there is value in all of these kinds of writing; however, somewhat obviously, works on the left side of this spectrum do not lend themselves to grammatical analysis, and attempting to analyze the grammar of works by authors whose writing leans toward the left (like Mark Twain at his wittiest—and quite a bit of the irreverently humorous young adult literature available today) will likely only confuse your student.

Be aware that works of fiction and popular non-fiction sometimes contains sentence fragments punctuated as if they were complete sentences, and that this is considered acceptable. Nevertheless, it's important for students to distinguish between fragments and complete sentences, because in high school and college, most of the writing is expository in nature. If you come across a fragment in a passage you want to use for dictation, either don't include the fragment in the sentences you dictate, or make sure that your student is able to use what he or she knows about grammar to conclude that it is, indeed, a fragment.

The Dictation Session

I begin the dictation session by reading the selected passage out loud so that my student can visualize what is happening in the story. I tell my student, "I'm going to read this passage; don't worry about writing anything down yet." (If my student knows the story already, I might skip this step.) When I finish reading the passage, I say, "Okay, now I'm going to dictate sentences for you to write." I advise my student to skip every other line in his or her notebook, which will allow room for annotations when we analyze the sentence's grammar.

I normally excerpt the most suitable sentences for dictation, which at first means choosing simple sentences with nice, easy-to-visualize, active verbs. Sometimes, I dictate half of a sentence, especially if a clause contains an active verb that I know my student will find easy to identify. My initial priority is dictating clauses with vibrant verbs, since identifying the verb is the critical key to analyzing the grammar in any sentence. When I have selected a sentence (or an independent clause), I read the sentence in its entirety first; then I go back to the beginning and dictate the sentence more slowly, a phrase at a time. For example, I might choose a passage such as this one, which is from Jules Verne's *Around the World in Eighty Days*:

> **Phileas Fogg was not known to have either wife or children, which may happen to the most honest people; either relatives or near friends, which is certainly more unusual. He lived alone in his house in Saville Row, whither none penetrated. A single domestic sufficed to serve him. He breakfasted and dined at the club, at hours mathematically fixed, in the same room, at the same table, never taking his meals with other members, much less bringing a guest with him; and went home at exactly midnight, only to retire at once to bed. He never used the cozy chambers which the Reform provides for its favored members. He passed ten hours out of the twenty-four in Saville Row, either in sleeping or in making his toilette.** (p. 30)

Having read this much, I then tell my student that I am going to dictate sentences from the passage. Because the passage contains several long and complex sentences, I extract independent clauses because my student is just learning this process and I don't want to complicate matters. Because my student is learning not only how to compose proper sentences but also how to punctuate them, I announce punctuation marks as I dictate.

Since I see no point in catching students misspelling words they can't be expected to know how to spell, I spell any word my student would not reasonably know, such as unusual names or terms. I also spell any word a student asks me to spell. I'm not worried about students being lazy, since most students try to spell independently whenever they can. In short, treat questions about spelling as teaching opportunities—students feel less intimidated, and they learn more, too.

Here are the clauses I dictate:

"Number one. Phileas Fogg lived alone in his house. Phileas: P-h-i-l-e-a-s Fogg: F-o-g-g lived: Phileas Fogg lived. (Pause.) Alone in his house. Period." (When I dictate, I sometimes replace a pronoun with its noun for purposes of clarity.) After my student writes this down, I ask the student to read the sentence back to me. Assuming the sentence sounds like the one I dictated, we move on; if not, the student adjusts the sentence.

"Number two. He breakfasted and dined at the club, at hours mathematically fixed, in the same room, at the same table. He breakfasted and dined . . . . at the club . . . . comma; at hours . . . . mathematically fixed . . . comma; in the same room . . . comma; at the same table . . . period."

"Number three: He passed ten hours out of twenty-four in Saville Row. He passed ten hours . . . out of twenty-four. Twenty-four has a hyphen in between twenty and four. . . . in Saville: S-a-v-i-l-l-e Row. Period."

Normally, we do a page worth of sentences and then move on to the second part of the session, which involves analyzing the grammar in each sentence. The process always follows the same order:

1. Identify the verb (or verbs, if there are helping verbs or if the sentence includes compound verbs) by asking what is happening in the sentence; in other words, who is doing what?

2. Identify the subject by asking, "Who or what [insert the verb as written in the sentence here]?"

3. Identify the direct object by asking, "[Subject] [Verb] who or what?" If there is no answer to this question, the sentence has no direct object.

Taking the first sentence, "Phileas Fogg lived in a house," as an example, I would say, "In sentence number one, what happened? Who did what?"

The student would either say, "Lived," or answer incorrectly.

If the student answers incorrectly, I might say: "Try this: close your eyes. When I say, "Phileas Fogg lived alone in a house," who did what? What was Phileas Fogg doing?" (Yes, this tips the student off a bit, but that's okay; the student will catch on quickly enough.) When the student has identified the verb as "lived," I say, "Double-underline 'lived.' 'Lived' is the verb in this sentence."

Next, I say, "Who or what lived?"

Rarely do students miss this one; the student answers, "Phileas Fogg."

I say, "Underline 'Phileas Fogg.' 'Phileas Fogg' is the subject in this sentence. Now: Phileas Fogg lived who or what?"

The student may appear confused. There is no obvious answer to this question, but he or she may venture, "alone?" If so, I answer, "No, 'alone' is how he lived; it's not really 'what' he lived, is it? 'Alone' isn't really a who or what type of a word, is it? As it happens, this sentence doesn't have a direct object. Remember, not every sentence will have a direct object, but we always have to check for one, just in case. Since this one doesn't have a direct object, we can move on."

You cannot reiterate enough the importance of the subject, verb, and direct object in any sentence. Everything else in the sentence serves to modify, qualify, or add to the meaning asserted by these three essential ingredients. Think of them as the crust, sauce, and cheese of a pizza: these make a pizza a pizza; all of the adjective and adverbs are like the toppings that add to the pizza's essence. Just as a pizza always begins with crust and sauce, when analyzing a sentence, always begin with the verb and its subject.

4. To sort out what remains in the independent clauses, first consider whether there are any prepositional phrases. Prepositional phrases follow a nice, predictable pattern and take up a lot of space, so it's convenient to get them out of the way. Prepositional phrases are easy to identify once students are familiar with the prepositions themselves. Students who don't know their prepositions can use the "Cheat Sheet" in Appendix A until they learn to recognize a preposition when they see one. Students should mark prepositional phrases by placing a parenthesis before the preposition and another after the preposition's object. Above the preposition itself, students write 'prep' or simply 'p' and above the object, 'o.p.'

5. Once you have marked off all of the prepositional phrases, the remaining words must be one of three things: conjunctions, adjectives, or adverbs.

In an independent clause, the only conjunctions will be coordinating conjunctions like 'and,' 'but,' or 'or' – and any one of these will mean there are two of one of the other ingredients in the sentence (two subjects, two verbs, two direct or indirect objects, two objects of a preposition, two adjectives, or two adverbs). Since there are only three conjunctions and their function is simple, students grasp their logic easily. Have students mark them by underlining them with a wide zigzag line.

Adjectives describe nouns. They're usually not hard to spot because they normally precede the subject, the direct object, or the object of a preposition, but the real test of an adjective is its function. An adjective answers one of four questions:

- Whose [thing]?

- How many [things]?

- Which [thing]?

- What kind of [thing] is it?

Have students circle any adjectives. (Note that in this book, adjectives that your student would circle are in bold—circling text with a word processor is tricky.)

Adverbs describe verbs, adjectives, and other adverbs. Because they do so much, they're harder to identify, but like adjectives, adverbs answer one of four questions:

- When?

- Where?

- How?

- How much?

Have students bracket adverbs. Again, students may use the "Cheat Sheet" in Appendix A to remind them of the functions of both adjectives and adverbs until they memorize them.

So let's apply all of this to the remainder of the first dictation sentence. So far, the student has underlined 'Phileas Fogg' and double-underlined 'lived.' Now ask, "Are there any prepositional phrases?" The student, who may consult a list of prepositional phrases if necessary, will either answer that there are none, in which case you may prompt, "Are you sure?" After giving the student time to think, prompt him: "Look at the word 'in.' Is that a preposition on the list?" Once the student identifies 'in' as a preposition, ask, "Okay: Phileas Fogg lived 'in' what?" The answer will be obvious: "in a house." Instruct the student to put parenthesis around the phrase and label the preposition and its object.

In between 'in' and 'house' is the article, 'a.' Students soon learn two things that will make this 'a' easy to deal with: first, most words falling between a preposition and its object are adjectives describing the object (as is the case here). Secondly, all articles are adjectives that answer the question, 'which one?' Indefinite articles like 'a' and 'some' are very vague about which ones are indicated, while the definite article 'the' refers to a specific object that will be clear from the context of the sentence.

One word remains in the sentence. Since it is obviously not 'and', 'but', or 'or,' by process of elimination, 'alone' must be either an adjective or an adverb. If students aren't certain which it is, have them run through each of the four questions for adjectives and adverbs. Which question does 'alone' answer in the sentence, 'Phileas Fogg lived in a house?'" Begin with the adjective questions:

Whose Phileas Fogg lived in a house? 'Alone' does not make sense as the answer to this question, so we cannot conclude anything from this question.

How many Phileas Fogg lived in a house? Since 'alone' doesn't answer this, we move on.

Which Phileas Fogg lived in a house? Again, 'alone' doesn't answer the question.

What kind of Phileas Fogg lived in a house? Not quite: we can conclude that 'alone' is not an adjective. We move on to adverb options:

When did Phileas Fogg live in a house? 'Alone' doesn't answer this question.

Where did Phileas Fogg live in a house? Again, 'alone' doesn't work.

How did Phileas Fogg live in a house? Alone. Ah-ha. That's sounds right. 'Alone' answers the question of how Phileas Fogg lived. 'Alone' is an adverb, so we put brackets around it.

Sentence number one should now look like this on the student's page:

<pre>
                              prep   o.p.
Phileas Fogg lived [alone] (in a house).
</pre>

Now look at number three: **He passed ten hours out of twenty-four in Saville Row.** To analyze the grammar in this sentence, I would say, "What action is happening in sentence three?"

The student considers the sentence and suggests, "Passed."

I say, "Good. Double-underline 'passed.' Now, who passed?"

"He passed."

"Excellent; underline 'he.' Now: he passed who or what?"

If the student says, "ten hours," I would answer, "Give me just one word. What did he pass?"

"Hours."

"Yes. Write D.O. above 'hours.' We now have our subject, verb, and direct object; are there any prepositional phrases that you see?"

"Yes. 'In Saville Row.'"

"Good: put parentheses around the phrase. Which word is the preposition?"

The student answers, "In."

"And the object?"

"Saville Row." The student labels it, "o.p."

"Moving on: Are there any other prepositional phrases?"

The student answers, "Of twenty-four."

I might say, "Okay . . . the preposition is?"

The student says, "Of," and writes 'prep' above it.

"Of whom or what?"

The student answers, "Twenty-four." (No doubt you have seen the flaw already, but let's follow this through to its logical end.)

I ask, "Is twenty-four a what? If I said, "Hand me a twenty-four, would that make sense?"

The student says, "Not really, I guess."

"What does twenty-four tell us? What question does it answer?" The student might look confused; if so, prompt, "Look at your adjective questions."

The student replies, "How many."

"Which makes it an . . ."

"Adjective."

"Exactly. Now, in this sentence, what does twenty-four answer? Or, twenty-four answers how many of what: can you tell from the rest of the sentence?"

"Hours?"

"Exactly. So what has the author done with this sentence? Is it correct to end a prepositional phrase with an adjective?"

The student will probably say, "I don't know."

"Not usually. Usually, you need an object. So why do you think the author doesn't say, 'He passed ten hours of twenty-four *hours* in Saville Row'?"

"It doesn't sound as good."

"That's right. He already named the object, 'hours,' so it's kind of implied in the sentence. It would have been redundant to say it again." (Now, here is a lesson you will not find in most grammar books; using implication to complete grammatical structure pertains more to style than correctness.) "So: last word. What do you want to do with 'out'?"

The student looks at 'out' and realizes it doesn't seem to answer any of the adjective or adverb questions. I ask, "Could it be a complex preposition, so that it goes with the prepositional phrase: 'Out of twenty-four hours?'"

The student scans the list of common simple and complex prepositions, discovers that 'out of' is a common complex preposition, and moves the first parenthesis to include 'out.'

Sentence number four would now look like this[1] on the student's page:

D.O.   prep   prep   o.p.

<u>He</u> <u>passed</u> **ten** hours (out of **twenty-four**) (in Saville Row).

After analyzing each sentence, check over your student's work and note any errors in capitalization, punctuation, or spelling. Then, depending on whether the error constitutes a mistake the student should reasonably be able to fix or whether the error pertains to something you haven't covered yet, either explain what needs to be changed and why, or assign finding and fixing the mistakes as homework. I like to write the number of errors and their category on the bottom of the page so that Lauren knows what she's looking for; for instance, I'll write, "Find 3 misspelled words and add 1 comma." That way, Lauren has an idea what she needs to do, and she can usually do it quickly and without frustration.

An Advanced Example

Later on, students will be ready to work with more complicated sentences, such as this one from Kenneth Grahame's *The Wind in the Willows*:

---

[1] Except, of course, for the adjectives, which will be circled, not in bold.

> The Rat put out a neat little brown paw, gripped Toad firmly by the scruff of the neck, and gave a great hoist and a pull; and the water-logged Toad came up slowly but surely over the edge of the hole, till at last he stood safe and sound in the hall, streaked with mud and weed to be sure, and with the water streaming off him, but happy and high-spirited as of old, now that he found himself once more in the house of a friend, and dodgings and evasions were over, and he could lay aside a disguise that was unworthy of his position and wanted such a lot of living up to. (p. 201-202)

This is all one sentence, but the sentence contains many clauses. However, students who have learned to distinguish clauses and understand the components in a clause will not be overwhelmed by it; rather, they simply separate the monster sentence into clauses and phrases:

1. The Rat put out a neat little brown paw, gripped Toad firmly by the scruff of the neck, and gave a great hoist and a pull;

2. and the water-logged Toad came up slowly but surely over the edge of the hole,

3. till at last he stood safe and sound in the hall,

4. streaked with mud and weed to be sure,

5. and with the water streaming off him, but happy and high-spirited as of old,

6. now that he found himself once more in the house of a friend,

7. and dodgings and evasions were over,

8. and he could lay aside a disguise

9. that was unworthy of his position and wanted such a lot of living up to.

Broken up in this way, the sentence seems manageable: even a fairly unpracticed student could handle the first three clauses, which contain nothing but basic clause ingredients. The fourth section and beyond contain a number of verbal phrases, which I have not discussed yet, but by gradually introducing new grammar principles and practicing the skill of identifying all of the components in a variety of sentences, most students should be able to tackle an entire sentence like this by the end of middle school.

How to Start from Scratch

All of this dictation work, as you can see, consolidates what students have already learned about grammar and mechanics and spelling so far, and what students don't know, they quickly learn. However, there are two underlying assumptions operating here: first, that the student has a good enough grasp of spelling that he or she needs to ask for a word's spelling only when it is very rare or unusual, and secondly, that you yourself are familiar enough with grammar to guide your student through the more complicated structures.

In the first scenario—students lack strategies for spelling most words—you will need to implement a structured program that teaches the advanced spelling code alongside this dictation program. I like the *Megawords* series by Kristin Johnson and Polly Bayrd (Educators Publishing Service); others to look into include *Allographs II* by Diane McGuinness (Sea Gate Press) and *Patterns for Reading and Spelling Success* by M.K. Henry and N.C. Redding (Pro-Ed).

In the second scenario, you will need to learn grammar. If you're rusty or never learned grammar—and sadly, most adults today did not have the benefit of grammar instruction in school—you will need to learn grammar, either on your own or together with your student. One option is to acquire Genevieve Walberg Schaefer's *Understanding and Using Good Grammar*, which clarifies grammar principles in the same "logical, orderly progression" (1997, p. vi) described here.

In fact, one way to introduce grammar principles to your student is to dictate the sentences in *Understanding and Using Good Grammar* as a jump-start activity and then transition to dictating passages from other books later. The advantage students get from analyzing the grammar in real writing in addition to completing the exercises in a grammar workbook is that the sentences typically found in most grammar texts are so attuned to the rules of grammar that students never learn to what extent and in what contexts rules may be bent. The sentences in most grammar texts come complete with correct answers, but analyzing sentences from real writers sometimes forces you to figure out why an author chose to write a sentence a certain way—as with the implied 'hours' in Jules Verne's sentence about Phileas Fogg above.

Another possibility is to peruse the Dictation Helps I've provided in Appendix A. In it, I've included an order for introducing grammar principles as well as a few sample lessons, an abridged glossary of grammar terms, a parts of speech "Cheat Sheet" with lists of prepositions, conjunctions, and questions for discerning adjectives from adverbs, and even a few helpful comma rules. If you follow the order I've suggested for this program, you should be able to stay ahead of your students, or at least know when to say, "Just skip that phrase for now; we'll learn what to do with that later."

Length of Dictation Sessions

Dictation lessons should be regular but brief, since regularity ensures retention, and brevity precludes boredom. A half an hour of dictation work a day from a variety of literature genres and sources will give students a more thorough exposure to correct grammar structures and acceptable deviations than any grammar book can do. Once you and your student understand the process, dictation is neither tedious nor time-consuming.

Variations

Of course, works of fiction are not the only options for doing dictation. You can adapt this process to make it work better for you or to better meet your student's individual needs. For instance, if your student is working through a spelling or vocabulary program, you can reinforce those lessons with dictation exercises. The *Megawords* series by Kristin Johnson and Polly Bayrd emphasizes phonemic awareness by focusing on teaching students spelling alternatives, syllabication rules, and accent patterns. Though you can make up your own sentences, the authors provide several sentences for dictation at the end of each lesson.

Avid writers might enjoy taking a few lessons from Harry Noden's book, *Image Grammar: Using Grammatical Structures to Teach Writing*. Noden proposes teaching students grammar by showing them how specific grammatical structures result in effective writing; for instance, he explains that unusual adjective placement often improves a sentence's effect, as in this sentence from Sir Arthur Conan Doyle's *The Hound of the Baskervilles*:

And then, suddenly, in the very dead of the night, there came a sound to my ears, clear resonant, and unmistakable.

Compare this with Noden's more grammatically correct but less effective version:

And then, suddenly, in the very dead of the night, there came a clear, resonant, and unmistakable sound to my ears. (Noden, 1999, p. 9)

Finally, if your student is studying a foreign language and has mastered the principles of grammar in English, consider dictating sentences in the foreign language. Again, these sentences could be read out of a textbook or come from literature written in the foreign language. As with English, dictation sharpens the ear and hones the student's ability to understand the spoken language. In fact, Lauren and I just started doing dictation in Spanish this year. Lauren had built up a strong vocabulary in terms of visual word recognition, but she was struggling with comprehending the spoken language. Once we started doing dictation, we noticed the benefits almost immediately. Finally, instead of hearing a blur of words, she began catching prepositional phrases and recognizing frequently used terms that somehow she'd been missing before.

Analyzing the sentences of real authors teaches students that many effective sentences are neither perfectly correct nor really incorrect. Students get a feel for not only what is correct but what is acceptable, and by examining sentences of distinct styles, students learn how authors achieve the effects they do. Dictation thus helps students to form an opinion about what sort of writing style they'd like their own writing to most resemble, and discover the precise techniques that will help them achieve a similar effect through their own writing.

CHAPTER THREE

THE READING PROGRAM

When I was in junior high, I and everyone else in my English classes read books teachers assigned. We discovered mystery in *The Hound of the Baskervilles*, contemplated mortality in *I Heard the Owl Call my Name*, butchered our recitation of *Romeo and Juliet*, and had Pip's (and our own) shallowness pointed out to us in *Great Expectations*. I learned a lot, too.

Before junior high, I'd read most of the books in the Cooper Elementary School library (well, the ones that were not obviously written for boys) during the free time I'd earned by completing my far-too-easy reading packets early in the week. I then spent at least a quarter of my school day reading books I picked out for myself. Apart from the brutally cold Minnesota winters, which, thanks to growing up on a farm with a ridiculously long driveway that made getting to the bus a daily frigid nightmare, life was good.

But by the end of junior high school, I was a stranger to the school library. I never had time to go to the library to choose books, nor did anyone advise me what in the local public library might be good for a kid my age. Having read all the children's fiction, I tried reading a few of the books from the adult side, but the books were obviously not written for someone my age. I learned, after a few uncomfortable trials, that the adult section of the library was a minefield of inappropriate content. Uncertain, I eventually stopped trying to find books to read for fun and just read whatever my teacher assigned, most of it unenthusiastically.

Ultimately, junior high was when I learned to dislike reading—which was probably not what my teachers intended, and I think they would have been surprised to know it. I got A's in my classes: I did my work and wrote essays that expressed almost exactly what my teachers told me to write. Apart from preparing me for advanced drudgery in high school, what I mainly got out of junior high English was the conviction that reading was no longer for me.

The Problem with Assigning Books

Back then, I don't think anyone realized that when teachers assign a book, most students assume that given the choice, they probably wouldn't have selected it themselves—because they didn't. This perception becomes a self-fulfilling prophecy since people "tend to perceive and think about others and situations in terms of the ideas we have already formed about them" (Kirby, Goodpaster, &

Levine, 2001, p. 27). Perceiving the kinds of books teachers and curriculums assign as boring, students tend to find they are. Reading assigned books becomes something kids automatically assume they would rather not be doing.

Today, more and more educators are realizing that letting students have more choice in their reading selections has a tremendous impact on perceptions about reading. Even struggling readers feel motivated to read faster and better when reading involves freedom and fun. As English teacher Nancie Atwell (1998) observes, student choice "has a major impact on students' fluency, reading rate, and comprehension . . . Allowing readers to choose virtually ensures that, eventually, everyone will 'get into' books" (p. 37 - 38). One student in Atwell's class commented, "This year I learned I could actually enjoy reading if I picked the kinds of books I wanted to read. Before I always thought it was totally boring" (as cited in Atwell, p. 37). Some students find that previously assigned books they'd disliked at the time were actually quite good when they decided to give them a second try, which shows that part of the reason students perceive freely chosen books better is that freedom includes the ability to abandon a book that turns out to be terrible. And while it is true that some students will comply with just about any assignment you give them, every student reads the books they've picked for themselves faster and with more interest than books that have been assigned.

What middle school students really need is to find some kind of connection with books that convinces them that reading can be both pleasant and useful. This is where giving students options about what they're going to read is so important. Unless reading strikes middle school students as pleasant, they will only engage in it for the wrong reasons or not at all. Students who read only to impress or please someone else will stop reading when no one is watching. Even students who sometimes like reading will learn to discern the difference between the sorts of books they normally choose for themselves and the sorts chosen for them by a teacher or literature program. Meanwhile, students who normally prefer not to read run the risk of never discovering what literature has to offer them. Maybe they're not the type of person who gets a kick out of *War and Peace*, but it could be that *The Hitchhiker's Guide to the Galaxy* is just their style. Middle school is the time when you can hook a kid on reading for a lifetime.

Reading Goals at the Middle School Level

First and foremost, this reading program seeks to instill a love of reading in students by allowing them as much say as possible about what they're reading, where and when they choose to read, and how they go about reading. The only thing students can't negotiate is that they read—daily—for at least an hour.

Building Fluency and Expanding Repertoires

A second goal at the middle school level is building fluency as readers. Middle school students need to be able to decode words quickly, without expending a great deal of effort, and to subsequently understand whatever they've just read. Students who get bogged down, sounding out words or trying to figure out what words mean and then piece that meaning together really can't get into reading. This is why reading fluently is so important. Happily, with practice most students will be able to decode words faster and faster, until they're able to decode and comprehend text almost instantaneously, an ability that ideally all students will have achieved by the end of eighth grade.

A broad knowledge base is an often overlooked second aspect of fluency, but the more a reader knows, the easier it is to understand what a passage is saying. This is perhaps most obvious if you've ever had to read something written in a foreign language. Even if you know quite a few words—say, half of the words in a given passage—understanding only the occasional word results in a very sketchy idea of what the passage says. The same is true of passages in your own language: researchers suggest that a person must know the meaning of at least 90% of the words in a given passage in order to be able to puzzle out the remaining 10% (Hirsch, 2006, p. 60). But when students know most of the words on a page, they easily surmise the meaning of the rest, which increases their vocabularies. The more knowledge a student has, the easier it will be to read successively more difficult material. Thus fluency is more than speed; it implies that students expand their tastes, interests, and vocabularies every year by exploring a wide range of reading material.

When middle school students find a series of books that finally click with them, sometimes it's hard to convince them that other books can be just as good or that there are other equally worthy reasons to read. And while it's important to give students freedom to choose the kinds of books they love best, it's just as important to encourage them to sample new types of reading, which not only helps students discover new favorites, but exposes them to new ideas and vocabulary, expanding their knowledge base.

In fact, reading expansively is the best way to increase vocabulary. This might seem surprising, especially in light of the many curriculums available to teach middle school students more vocabulary. However, these programs have their drawbacks. Some curriculum designers, understanding people learn vocabulary best in context, combine vocabulary with literature studies. Unfortunately, these programs rely on assigning literature, which tends to decrease student engagement: they also treat literary works as a means to an end, rather than an end in and of themselves.

Other educators compile lists of unusual words for students to memorize. The problem with these programs is that learning a few select definitions for a word may give students a sense of general meaning, but no real a feel for the word's nuances. Ed Hirsch (2006) suggests that the way to build vocabulary is through many experiences with reading:

> The general sense of a word that a listener or reader gains from experiencing actual uses of the word is not a fixed and definite meaning but general meaning, possibilities and probabilities that get narrowed down through context. Each new exposure to the word in a new context can subtly alter that constantly accruing system of probabilities and possibilities. Researchers have found that we need multiple exposures to a word in multiple contexts to start getting a secure sense of its overtones and range. That is why word learning is inherently a slow and gradual process. We do not learn so many discrete words a day. Rather, we are learning small, incremental aspects of hundreds of words in a day . . . we have a remarkable innate faculty for learning word meanings in context. (p. 62 - 63)

Successful readers continually expand their reading repertoires and vocabularies. Because knowledge accrues slowly and gradually and via many exposures to words in context, students profit most from a program of reading that invites them to read expansively. Students increase fluency by reading many appealing books at a comfortable level of difficulty as well as by reading books that are slightly more difficult and distinct from the student's usual repertoire. It is not enough to read lots of contemporary young adult fiction or even the entire canons of Agatha Christie or Isaac Asimov. Students stretch their minds far more when they read expansively: plays written a hundred years ago, when people expressed themselves differently; non-fiction works that detail varied topics and concepts, short stories; novellas, and novels from many different authors, genres, and eras; and poetry, which compresses language and often employs vivid imagery with words that rarely appear in speech.

Preparing for High School

A final goal for middle school students is preparing for high school by gaining familiarity with a few classic literary works. Just as elementary students decode gradually longer and more difficult words, students in middle school need practice understanding and learning to appreciate gradually longer and more difficult literary works. First graders don't go from reading *The Cat in the Hat* to *The Hound of the Baskervilles* overnight; and neither do middle school students go from enjoying *The Diary of a Wimpy Kid* to appreciating *The Adventures of Huckleberry Finn* without increasing their stamina as readers somewhere along the way. As much as it's important for middle school students to learn to love reading, students who read only fun, fast-paced, entertaining tales throughout the middle school years simply won't be ready to appreciate the likes of Hawthorne, Dickens, and Shakespeare in high school.

How do students bridge that gap? So far I have recommended allowing students free choice in their reading material, and I reiterate that recommendation here. What prepares students for more challenging reading in high school is not imposing overly difficult reading on them in middle school but requiring students to sample a very few classic works of literature, providing struggling readers with alternatives to facilitate this if necessary. As before, students choose the classics they want to explore, and I've included a number of classic titles with the booklists in Appendix B for you and your student to browse. More details about alternative processes can be found in the section on facilitating success in this chapter.

Preparing for high school is not the same thing as performing high school level activities that are beyond a middle school student's capability. Middle school students simply aren't ready to analyze or interpret literature independently. The programs that suggest they do typically outline an expert's interpretation or analysis and expect students to then parrot back the position as if it were their own. Such work misrepresents true literary analysis, which involves a reader either exploring some idea he or she found fascinating or arguing a position about a book that he or she feels passionately about.

"Humor can be dissected," E.B. White once wrote, "but the thing dies in the process" (as cited in Zinsser, p. 215). Dissecting books is much the same. Trying to get ahead by previewing the literature activities appropriate to high school actually deters students from enjoying books, improving fluency, and expanding their tastes, interests, and knowledge base as readers. Of course, that does not mean that middle school students are not ready to discuss literature in a real and important way. It is just one thing to talk about whether you liked a book or not and attempt to nail down which qualities in it made it good, and quite another to turn a good book into a language lesson wherein every unfamiliar word must be diligently defined, every incident of foreshadowing examined, and every hidden symbol found and exposed in all its meaningful glory. These are the activities that turn most people off reading.

The Consistent but Shifting Nature of Goals

These goals are consistent, yet evolving. That is, whereas a sixth grade student should be mainly building up speed as a reader, by eighth grade, that same student should be choosing more classic works of literature in preparation for high school. That doesn't mean that the eighth grader never chooses fluency-building fun books, just that goals revolve in importance as students move through the program, as shown in the chart on the next page:

	6th Grade	7th Grade	8th Grade
Primary Goal	Build fluency by reading many appealing books	Expand tastes and interests by reading from diverse genres	Prepare for greater complexity by reading more classic literary works
Secondary Goal	Expand tastes and interests by reading from diverse genres	Prepare for greater complexity by gaining familiarity and reading classic literary works	Build fluency by reading many appealing books
Tertiary Goal	Prepare for greater complexity by becoming familiar with classic literary works	Build fluency by reading many appealing books	Expand tastes and interests by reading from diverse genres

Organizing the Reading Program

How do you get your student to independently choose books that will help him or her to grow? In the movie, "Field of Dreams, a farmer named Ray Kinsella (played by Kevin Costner) hears a voice repeatedly telling him, "If you build it, he will come." So the farmer turns his cornfield into a baseball diamond, and ball players magically appear and play ball on the field. To get students to read edifying books, you organize appealing options, maximize student choice, and nudge your student in the direction of growth with a very minimal set of requirements. In other words, if you build it, he (or she) will come. Here's a breakdown of the steps involved in implementing this program:

1. Identify and acquire appropriate and appealing literature.

2. Clarify options and requirements for students with a written checklist.

3. Limit requirements for written work.

4. Provide helpful feedback and encouragement.

IDENTIFY APPEALING LITERATURE TO ENGAGE STUDENTS

Parents organize work for and with students. By involving students in the tasks of identifying and acquiring appealing and appropriate literature to meet course goals, you not only give students a say in what books they'll read, you also invite them into a conversation where the vocabulary of literature—terms like pacing and plot, perspective, and so on—are necessary and useful. Instead of having to superimpose lessons about genres on students, you can bring genre into your discussion of which books your student likes to read—which, for most normal people, is the only reason to ever think about genres anyway. More about literary language can be found in the section below on functional feedback, and you'll find a list of useful literary terminology as well as annotated booklists that identify books by genre in Appendix B. The remainder of this chapter focuses on the task of gathering literary works for your home-based reading program.

Acquiring Books

If free choice is the way to get kids to love reading, the public library might seem like the perfect solution for homeschooling families: not only are books free (so long as you remember to return them on time), you'd be hard pressed to find a better selection. Nevertheless, there are a number of problems with relying on a public library for a homeschool reading program. For one thing, middle school students, dependent on parents for a ride to the library, can't always get to one when tey're ready to choose a new book. Furthermore, selecting books to read weeks in advance can be tricky. Young readers can't always predict what they're going to want to read next, especially if they're trying to expand their reading territories and explore new kinds of books. Of all readers, they're least able to predict that after *Where the Red Fern Grows*, they're going to need a good laugh.

More significantly, the public library can be problematic for parents who are concerned about the content and values portrayed in the books their students read, because the young adult section in most public libraries these days carries many books that are simply inappropriate for middle school students to read.

The young adult section of most libraries and bookstores is a hodgepodge of some of the most appealing books for pre-adolescent and adolescent readers, a smattering of classic literature generally deemed enriching for teenagers, and a growing number of books specifically written for older, worldlier teens that many parents consider inappropriately violent, vulgar, or profane. The question for parents is: How do you tell the difference?

Understanding Young Adult Literature

The answer to that question involves a little background knowledge. First, of all, parents should understand that there are actually two definitions floating about for YA literature. In one view, YA is anything that someone between the ages of 12 to 18 should or could read; it includes everything from historical fiction to science fiction, classic and contemporary, from *Harry Potter* to *Silas Marner* (Stephens, 2007, p. 34). Most libraries and bookstores categorize books this way, which is why a pre-teen can peruse the YA section of the library and stumble across a book with an interesting title and an appealing cover, flip it open to see if it looks any good, and discover blatantly pornographic or profane content inside.

The other view sees YA as more of its own genre with characteristic features that include teen protagonists with strong voices, often in first-person POV, so that the writing seems as if a teenager wrote the story himself and speaks directly to the reader. Main characters are often self-degrading, flippant, sarcastic, or even irreverent, in keeping with the humorous tone of most of the more popular YA books. YA story lines intrigue readers with situations that are relevant to adolescents, and plots are generally fast-paced. In addition, YA authors often employ linguistic or structural tricks such as using lots of sentence fragments ("Which I hate."), repeated words ("run run run run run"), or onomatopoeia ("Splash!") (Stephens, 2007, p. 35). Finally, YA lit books take stances on issues and deal with them much like authors of literary fiction for adults. In fact, as far as I can tell, YA literature actually is literary fiction, just for teens.

Literary fiction is distinct from other fiction genres such as mystery, fantasy, romance, or mainstream fiction in that all of these genres tend to be plot-driven, and themes in these books derive from the plot. In contrast, literary fiction is generally weak in plot and richer in description, symbolism, and character development. Authors of literary fiction consider it very wrong to impose morals on anyone else, so they avoid any semblance of moralizing while purposefully depicting scenes that portray injustice in order to inspire a sense of moral indignation in readers. People who appreciate literary fiction find this subtle way of inculcating values more powerfully affecting than the more didactic approach taken by many classic authors; people who don't appreciate literary fiction find the tactic calculated and manipulating.

In the same way that writers of literary fiction subtly weave themes of injustice through their writing to convict readers, writers of YA lit design stories to raise awareness about what they see as the real issues facing teens today. Some YA books take a sort of "forewarned is forearmed" stance by telling stories that involve teens experimenting with sex and drugs and suffering the consequences; other times, the books operate more psychologically, affecting readers powerfully, increasing their repertoire of experiences, and helping them to embrace their own sense of personal identity. Often these books involve characters dealing with challenging situations such as broken families, societal pressures, sexual orientation, drugs, depression, abuse, and so on (Stephens, 2007, p. 35 & 41). Because these authors strive to depict teens as authentically as possible, many YA lit books portray teens disrespecting anyone in authority, using "edgy" language fraught with obscenities, and engaging in immoral behaviors either right under a neglectful parent's nose or far away from a parent who obviously doesn't care that their teen runs wild. Apparently, many of these authors assume that most teenagers come from broken homes with no morals or caring parents.

Shockingly, some of the most offensively inappropriate YA titles win prestigious awards. In 2007, the American Library Association awarded the Michael L. Prinz Award for Excellence in Young Adult Fiction to John Green's *Looking for Alaska*, a book about an awkward boy who goes to a boarding school where he meets a girl named Alaska. Though the book is mainly about the boy's coming to grips with Alaska's suicide, many adults have found the explicit sexual content to be so shockingly inappropriate that they have protested its inclusion on YA shelves. Even the author himself has stated that he would never allow his own twelve-year-old to read the book. That being the case, one would think that the book would not be easily accessible to twelve-year-olds, but as it happens, it is. Out of curiosity, I looked for *Looking for Alaska* in my own local library here in Alaska, and I found a well-worn paperback copy. Nothing on the cover—certainly not the big silver award—would have alerted me as a parent to the nature of the content within.

How did we get to a point where a book most people consider pornographic could be shelved right next to a gentle and delightful story like *The Wind and the Willows*? Up until about fifty years ago, all books were designated as either for adult readers or for children. In fact, many of the classic books assigned to kids in middle school today were once intended for adults, which explains why so often students find classics works such as *Great Expectations* tiresome: the story is not meant to entertain so much as enrich them, and the theme, which is indeed enriching, comes only after having plodded through a fairly slow-moving plotline made up of less-than-riveting events. Such books are written by authors who have gained some deep insight over time about the lessons and insights that one ought to have in youth but don't; youth being the time of life when people are least wise, since wisdom generally comes with age. Unfortunately, youth being youth, they're usually not quite ready to appreciate the depth of that insight on their own and need adults to explain why the great insights in such works are so great. Once explained, middle school students might understand the point, but they usually don't feel as compelled by it as they might if they were to read the same book in about twenty or thirty years.

Many classics, however, were written specifically to entertain children. And this makes sense, since it was assumed for a long time that serious men read only serious matter with titles like "Political Economy" (Mark Twain's short story of the same name makes light of such overly serious twaddle), while women were perceived as less intellectual creatures who read primarily romances, which, since Victorian values were pretty prudish, were absurdly mushy gushy and would rarely rate even a PG-rating by today's standards. Both views, of course, were extreme: men like to be entertained as much as women, and women enjoy intellectual stimulation as much as men. But the extreme views led to very defined genres and audiences, and so with men and women largely accounted for, what was left was fairly obvious: wonderful adventures for children.

Don't let the moniker fool you: classics written for children are hardly easy reading. *The Swiss Family Robinson*, for instance, was written as a more kid-friendly retelling of *Robinson Crusoe*—only as it turns out, the book has more difficult words in it than Defoe's original. Of course, Johann David Wyss didn't likely try to write a harder book; what he actually did was include a wider variety of adventures. The unintended consequence of all those amazing adventures was lots and lots of vocabulary—and, since generations of families enjoyed the stories, they didn't notice the harder reading. A few other classics written mainly for younger audiences include *Heidi* by Joanna Spyri, *The Adventures of Tom Sawyer* by Mark Twain, *Black Beauty* by Anna Sewell, *The Wind in the Willows* by Kenneth Grahame, and *The Princess and Curdie* by George MacDonald, and the list goes on.

Then, about a hundred years ago, perspectives began to change. Shortly after World War I, authors began to explore the realities of the war and the waste of life it had caused. This angst is evident in books by authors like Ernest Hemingway and John Steinbeck, whose stories were considered exceptionally realistic but often very grim and sometimes profane. A number of the books that were most highly acclaimed by the literary community were in fact offensive to many Americans, and works like *A Farewell to Arms*, *Catch-22*, *The Catcher in the Rye*, and *Of Mice and Men* were sometimes protested by parents when these were assigned in schools, and in some places, they were actually banned for profanity or inappropriate content.

Of course, most normal people don't particularly enjoy wallowing in angst, so the post-WWI era also marks something of a golden era for many more lighthearted and uplifting genres. Among the most lighthearted authors of the time was the British humorist P.G. Wodehouse , whose Jeeves and Wooster stories narrate the silly adventures of a bumbling aristocrat and his much more intelligent manservant. Other authors at this time entertained people by writing in other genres. Agatha Christie hooked millions on mystery; J.R.R. Tolkien essentially invented the epic fantasy; Isaac Asimov, Ray Bradbury, and Robert Heinlein re-invigorated if not reinvented science fiction; and Americans Margaret Mitchell and Harper Lee set new standards for quality historical fiction with *To Kill a Mockingbird* and *Gone with the Wind*. To this day, it can be generally said that works in these genres are more generally uplifting and optimistic than literary fiction, which remains typically dark and brooding.

Only a few series written for children during this period (such as the Nancy Drew and Hardy Boys mysteries) still appeal to young readers today. Perhaps because the "quality" literature of this era were all so starkly and unapologetically realistic, the morally pure and cheerful protagonists in children's literature began to seem more and more saccharine and unrealistic, especially to adolescent readers. In 1967, one teenage reader named S.E. Hinton inadvertently staged a literary rebellion of sorts when she penned *The Outsiders*, a book that is generally considered the first young adult novel.

The Outsiders featured a teenager as protagonist and described in the protagonist's first-person voice the difficulties he encountered as a parentless, lower-class youth.

The late sixties and early seventies were tumultuous times for America, and many young adults joined protest movements and fought for the end of military inscription, for civil rights, or against poverty and female oppression. An unforeseen backlash of this culture of rebellion was a society-wide trend toward the dissolution of the American family. Divorce rates soared in the mid-seventies and children experienced unprecedented levels of psychological strain, whether due to family troubles, peer pressure, uncertain identities, or economic position. These issues because premises for many of the most successful young adult writers in the 1970's, when young adult literature was gaining popularity. More and more serious literary writers focused on the psychological state of teens in troubling situations. Books like Robert Cormier's *The Chocolate War*, Judy Blume's *Forever*, and Beatrice Sparks's *Go Ask Alice* all tackled serious teenage issues, all gained tremendous popularity among teens, all provoked controversies—and all remain controversial to this day.

At the same time, something of a literary divide began to grow. As "serious" young adult literature became more serious and controversial, a number of authors rose up, as before, to provide less controversial alternatives for young readers. Authors like Scott O'Dell and Jean Craighead George wrote gripping tales of survival and adventure, John Fitzgerald wrote in a first-person voice of his precocious older brother's amusing, Tom-Sawyer-esque adventures, and Roald Dahl wrote fantastic tales with wit and endlessly unexpected twists. Still other authors, such as Robert O'Brien, Richard Adams, and Madeline L'Engle, conveyed serious themes through anthropomorphic fantasy and science fiction. More recently, genre authors began to see frequent doses of humor as a key ingredient in their light-hearted young adult stories. For instance, John Erickson's *Hank the Cowdog* mysteries, the aforementioned *Diary of a Wimpy Kid* adventures, and Dave Barry and Ridley Pearson's pseudo-science fiction *Science Fair* all infuse heavy doses of humor to tell their stories.

Distinguish Values from Taste

Every parent is going to have a different idea of what's appropriate for his or her kids to read, but it's important to have a clear idea about what types of literary content offends your family's values, and distinguish these from the kind of books that simply don't appeal to your personal taste. Personally, I prefer books that are somewhat slower paced and have strong themes; I'm not offended by fast-moving or silly books; I just don't particularly like them. On the other hand, I try to avoid books that contain a lot of profanity or graphically depict violent or immoral situations because such things offend my sense of values. I'd much prefer my daughters to ponder what is beautiful and good and true than contemplate all that is ugly and false in the world. These are the values that guide me as I consider books for my daughters—but I try not decide whether or not to get a particular book simply because it doesn't appeal to my personal taste.

Not long ago, my daughters got excited about James Patterson's *Maximum Ride* books, and they told me I had to try them, they were so good. Well, I hated them. I still do. I hate the tone and the humor and the pacing. I'm a George Eliot kind of girl, for heaven's sake. And yet, my brief perusal didn't turn up anything that really offended my sense of values, so I let the girls have their mind candy fun. Why not? Every now and then, I curl up with a mystery by Elizabeth Peters—it's really the same kind of thing.

I think a lot of parents have struggled with whether or not to give in and get their kids books that are just plain silly or crude. For whatever reason, a lot of middle school students can't get enough humor about bodily noises. I know some parents who read to their kids when they were little, assuming that doing so would instill excellent literary taste in their children, only to have their middle school students prefer books with lots of burping and farting jokes. To this, all I can say is, hey, it's middle school. Students can't help being immature. The good news is, they grow out of it.

So don't worry too much about tastes that reflect a bit of immaturity. But do take a close look at the books your student finds most appealing and decide if they're actually offensive to you ethically or morally, or if they're really just not your taste. If it's just a matter of taste, and if you really want your student to truly enjoy reading and build fluency as a reader, you might have to be willing to compromise a bit about the kinds of books you're willing to supply.

Determining Appropriateness

So how do you determine which books are appropriate for your student and which are not? Probably the easiest thing to do is check is when the book was published. Books that were originally published more than one hundred years ago are generally inoffensive. Books intended for young readers that were published more than fifty years ago are also pretty tame by most standards, although a few books from this era that are often recommended for middle school students have been challenged. However, if a book from this era has generated any controversy, by now the fact will be common knowledge, and you can find out about it with a quick search online. Wikipedia usually includes any information about a book being challenged right after a book's synopsis.

Books published less than fifty years ago are a bit more complicated, but one generalization I have observed is that books that are clearly a specific genre such as historical fiction, mystery, action/adventure as well as most fantasy and science fiction are less likely to be problematic than books that deal with "issues." Now, some books about serious topics may be written tastefully, but if you are concerned about appropriate content, consider books about subjects like broken families, absent or abusive parents, drug abuse, suicide, dating, rape, pregnancy, prostitution, depression, or self-mutilation all to be red flags that suggest you need to take a closer look at exactly what the book says and how.

Be especially aware of nuances in realistic YA fiction: a book about basketball is not quite the same as a book about a basketball player who is dealing with a specific issue. I learned this as I was researching YA for this book. Looking for books I could recommend for students interested in sports, I found and borrowed three books from my local library: *Game* by Walter Dean Myers, *Take Me to the River* by Will Hobbs, and *Pop* by Gordon Korman.

Although I'd never read or particularly wanted to read about sports before, I loved *Game*. The action Myers described during the basketball games was so vivid, I think I enjoyed reading about basketball even more than I like watching real games. The second book I read, *Take Me to the River*, was almost too action packed for my taste, and I found the rising tension a bit contrived, but that's all neither here nor there since apart from that, the book seemed perfectly appropriate.

Then I pulled out Korman's *Pop*, which is about a football player whose parents had recently divorced, precipitating a move to a new town where he encountered a former NFL football player suffering from Alzheimer's because of the many hits he'd taken playing ball. It sounded interesting, and the first chapter set it up well enough. Before long, though, the book became iffy for me. The protagonist Marcus kept running into a cheerleader named Alyssa who used Marcus to make her former boyfriend jealous, saying things like, "I could jump his bones in the parking lot and you'd have nothing to say about it!" (p. 18). Later, she invites Marcus to a party and leads him into a closet—nothing too graphic there—but the insinuations are constant: when Marcus suggests just being friends, she answers, "With benefits?" (p. 115). I don't know if kids in middle school would understand such a reference, but reading a line like that in a book like this might lead them to try and find out. All in all, I kept getting the impression that Korman writes Alyssa into his book for an element of realism that makes *Pop* more distinctly YA, as opposed to children's literature.

Interestingly, Walter Dean Myers gives his protagonist a loving, supportive family and no girlfriend. His book developed more convincing characters for me than Korman's, whose characters actually seem more stereotypical (the slutty cheerleader, the jealous jock, the unavailable mother)—in spite of Korman's attempt to authentically explore an issue: football injury induced Alzheimer's.

Genre-wise, although all three books were shelved as YA, I would say Myer's *Game* combines action with coming-of-age, Hobbs's is mainly adventure, while Korman's *Pop* is issue-oriented YA lit.

Ultimately, if you can't tell whether a book is appropriate for your student, it's up to you to investigate it more. You can page through promising books in a bookstore or check them out from a library; additionally, you can tell a lot about appropriateness by checking out what other people have said about a book online. Online reviews on sites like Goodreads or Amazon will normally include at least a few mediocre or negative reviews that warn parents about the most blatantly inappropriate books. But don't assume a book is fine just because it has lots of five-star reviews—a lot of people honestly think that teens have seen and done it all anyway. Remember, people in this country hold widely divergent values. The most helpful reviews to look at are the ones rated two and three stars, because these are the ratings that normally go along with the posts from concerned parents who take the time to warn others about objectionable content in an otherwise popular book.

But I don't want to give you the impression that all contemporary YA books are bad or scare you into acquiring only hundred year old books for your reader. In fact, there are a lot of books out there with really wonderful and relevant lessons for young people today. Remember, many of the authors of books for this age are motivated to help these kids develop strong values, and they write highly entertaining, appropriate, and readable stories to help struggling readers especially build fluency and give bookish kids more options. There really is a lot of great stuff out there—you just want to be aware and avoid the few books that lurk inappropriately within the wider YA category.

Stocking Books for a Home Library

At the end of the day, the best way to provide your student with easy access to appropriate and appealing literary works is to stock a home library. A home library doesn't require a huge number of books, but the collection you offer your student should genuinely allow for selection. If your library contains fifty titles and you expect your students to read thirty of them by the end of the year, that's not really allowing students to choose what they want to read, it's just allowing them to reject what they really don't.

If you are truly allowing students the freedom to choose, they need a lot more latitude. A reasonable size for any initial collection is approximately whatever number of books your student might normally read in a school year times ten. So a student who might be expected to read thirty good books in a year would need a library of three hundred titles, while a student who is more likely to read ten should have the option of choosing from about a hundred. Because your student retains these books as options in subsequent years, your initial investment will be the largest. After that, you'll only need to refresh the library's stock by about 10 - 20% each year. New acquisitions will reflect the student's increasing competence and expanding tastes and interests as a reader.

The books in your library should all appeal to your student, but as you go about acquiring titles, consider the program's three goals: you want your student to love reading, to explore new ideas, and to sample a few classics. Therefore, you'll want to design a library that facilitates each of these goals. This translates into a fairly straightforward formula: simply take the total number of books you plan to acquire (the quantity of books your student will likely read in a year times ten) and divide it by three. Then plan to acquire books so that approximately one-third of the library's makeup is as appealing as possible to your student, one-third is appealing in general but maybe not specifically representative of your student's current taste or interests, and one-third represents classic works that hold some appeal. So the basic breakdown is actually very simple:

- 1/3 books that will appeal, period

- 1/3 books that challenge students to explore new topics and genres

- 1/3 books that are classics that appeal to your reader

Now, you might be wondering about that first 1/3. Does "books that will appeal, period" mean fluff like comic books like *Calvin and Hobbes* and chapter book mind candy like *Upchuck and the Rotten Willy*? Some parents might cringe that their student likes such books at all and would never consider allowing them to read such empty brain calorie books for 'school.' But as you'll soon see, this program is designed so that you get your goals met and your student gets the freedom to choose whatever he or she wants to read. And if you're truly giving your student the green light on reading what he or she likes, and if *Upchuck and the Rotten Willy* is it, then I would say that a supply of books with *Upchuck*-like characteristics is, for now, the ticket to your student feeling like reading is fun and worth doing. But don't worry: the remaining goals for the program involve expanding tastes and preparing for the harder work ahead, so the requirements you give your student for this course will ensure that *The Dork Diaries* and *Captain Underspants* books are not ALL your student reads.

Inexpensive Options

Acquiring books for your student will obviously cost something, but it need not be as expensive as you might think. Here are a few of my favorite sources for great but cheap books:

- Swap meets—if your local homeschool co-op or community doesn't have one, ask if you can sponsor one. Books, of course, are free.

- Thrift stores – my favorite thrift stores organize books neatly so I can peruse just a few sections quickly and easily. Books cost anywhere from a few cents to a few dollars.

- Rainbow Resource Center (www.RainbowResource.com) discounts most of its stock, which includes most of the Newbery award winners and many classics.

- Dover Publications (www.DoverPublications.com) also sell many classics appropriate for middle school readers. See especially their Evergreen Thrift series. Books sell for as little as $2.00.

- Large, quality used bookstores can be a good source for finding both classics in good condition and more contemporary books at a discounted price.

- Amazon (www.Amazon.com) is my source for everything else. It's where I go first (to see what's available and read reviews) and last (where I buy new books that I can't find cheaper elsewhere). Sometimes, you can get used books for as little as $4 (a penny for the book plus $3.99 for shipping).

ENSURE GROWTH BY CLARIFYING REQUIREMENTS

"Field of Dreams" is, alas, a fantasy. If you build a home library, I really can't promise you that your student will magically show up and play ball. In fact, I'm pretty sure that, if your student is normal, he or she will be happy to comply with picking out books to read; they just won't necessarily be the ones you'd like him or her to choose. Most people, given the choice, read whatever seems most appealing at the time—and rarely is that something outside one's own comfort zone.

On their own, students will shortchange themselves, so it falls to you to set a few requirements that will ensure gradual progress. These requirements clarify how many and what kinds reading projects students should undertake, what options they have for completing projects, and any written responses or products you need for documentation.

For instance, you might require the following:

1. Choose anything on the designated bookshelf and read for at least one hour daily.

2. Read books from at least five distinct genres, including at least one non-fiction title.

3. Read or listen to at least two classic works (published more than 100 years ago).

4. Read at least two modern classics (published more than 40 years ago).

5. Find two poems you like well enough to memorize and recite.

6. Keep a reading log that lists the author, title, genre, page count, classic status, and your rating of each book you read.

If you tabulate those requirements, you'll notice that this list technically requires a student to read just six books in a semester, which is really not all that much, especially when you consider that options will include not only full-length novels but short stories, essays, and drama as well. But what you'll find is that many students, perceiving themselves to have freedom to read more or less as they like, will actually surpass their requirements: they get to the end of the checklist and just keep reading.

In fact, the list above is exactly what I've required of my daughter Lauren for the last two years (sixth and seventh grades), and she exceeded her requirements both years. Last year, she read 52 books. She read books from ten distinct genres, including ten classics, and twelve modern classics. Included on her reading log are authors like Isaac Asimov, Charles Dickens, Jack London, L.M.M. Montgomery, William Shakespeare, and J.R.R. Tolkien. What's more, she rated eighteen of the classic books four or five stars (out of five)—which reflects a higher average rating than what she gave books that were not classics. Interestingly, she re-read a contemporary fantasy she'd read the previous year—and her rating for the book dropped, which shows that her taste in books are improving with more exposure to truly great books. After two years of being required to sample classics, Lauren actually prefers more sophisticated literature.

Because you want to give your student as much freedom as possible, you would ideally determine and require the absolute minimum number of books your student needs to read in order to ensure progress, but some students need a few more guidelines. For instance, some students intend to complete or even exceed their requirements, but somehow forget and don't quite finish by the end of the semester. These students aren't necessarily rebelling; they just didn't expect time to go so fast. These are the students who need more specific requirements. Not only do they need a checklist telling them what they need to complete, they need that list broken down and due dates attached to required elements:

1. Read anything on the designated bookshelf for at least one hour daily.

2. Include at least five distinct genres, including at least one non-fiction title.

3. Read or listen to at least two classic works (published more than 100 years ago).

4. Read or listen to two modern classic works (published more than 40 years ago).

5. Find two poems you like well enough to memorize and recite, and recite one by the end of each quarter.

6. Keep a reading log that lists the author, title, genre, page count, classic status, and your rating of each book you read.

7. Complete at least one specific requirement on the checklist every other week.

8. Submit your reading log to me every week for my approval.

To prevent confusion, provide your student a list of your requirements in writing. Students can keep track of what they've completed on their reading logs or you can provide a checklist that includes spaces for them to fill in the titles that meet their requirements. A sample reading log template and a few tips for filling one out can be found in Appendix B.

Facilitate Success through Alternative Processes

Obviously, students can only improve their ability to decode words by reading regularly, so it's true that every student will need to complete at least some independent reading; still, decoding words is just one process by which students can achieve the program goals. Appreciating literature, expanding knowledge and interests, and preparing for more difficult literature in the future may all occur through alternative processes, such as listening to unabridged versions of literary works (whether recorded or read aloud) and, to a lesser degree, viewing video adaptations of literary works.

Although many classic literary works tell great stories, their texts are often slow-paced and contain unfamiliar vocabulary. These factors slow down readers, sometimes so much so that the texts seem incomprehensible. As Ed Hirsch (1987) explains, students who are preoccupied with decoding unfamiliar words and ideas often can't make sense of the words they're reading at all: "Slowness of reading beyond a certain point makes assimilation of complex meaning impossible. The limits of short-term memory do not allow the integration of 'unchunked' material" (p. 56 - 57). As a result, a slow or inexperienced reader might find complicated literature too difficult—but that does not mean that the same student can't access classic literature at all; it only means that the student will find it impossible to simultaneously decode and understand.

Take away the decoding part, and a student can concentrate solely on understanding the literary work that would otherwise be unreachable. Insisting on decoding as the only process by which students access literature unnecessarily limits opportunities for slower readers to accumulate positive, quality experiences with literature when realistically, people are not limited to the written word for learning language. Think about it: before people learn words by reading them, they learn them by listening. It is not for nothing that so many of the students who turn out to be good readers in early grades are the students whose parents read to them as toddlers and preschoolers: those are the kids whose vocabularies and general knowledge of the world have been increasing for years, facilitating reading comprehension.

It's important to help slower readers access quality literature by reading to them or by allowing them to listen to unabridged audio versions of literature that is beyond their ability to easily decode. Slow readers aren't necessarily less intelligent than their peers, but unless they access information somewhere, they will fall behind other students simply because they have less opportunity to access knowledge through reading. Because the very knowledge these students are not getting through reading is exactly what helps people read faster and better in the first place, Hirsch prescribes "reading aloud and discussing challenging material . . . that is well beyond their ability to decode with understanding" (2006, p. 27).

Alternative processes make engaging with literature more flexible and more accessible to all students. A student who enjoys a quiet, sedentary hobby such as drawing or cross-stitch can comfortably listen to an unabridged audio version of a classic book—many of which are available for free on-line—and engage in two pleasant activities at one time. Another optional process for engaging meaningfully in literature is watching video adaptations of literary works. Although watching a performance is not the same kind of activity as either reading or listening to literature (which are parallel activities that the mind processes in essentially the same way), video adaptations can familiarize students with the essential plot, characters, and theme of a classic while enhancing the student's general knowledge as well. In fact, as Mortimer Adler and Charles Van Doren (1972) point out, playwrights don't write for readers, they write for actors. As a result, when you read a play, you only get part of the story (p. 223). Watching plays actually provides a more complete and meaningful experience than just reading them. Also, watching video adaptations of classic literature increases students' interest in classics and provides them with a preview that facilitates reading, but don't rely on this exclusively, as students won't get the same exposure to rich language as with other options.

Give Students Control over Grades

In public schools, grades can mean lots of things. An A used to mean that a student had achieved significantly more than the course required, while a C meant that a student had performed adequately and passed the course. Today, grades sometimes reward good behavior as much as academic performance. When I was in high school, one of my teachers kept docking me points for falling asleep in class, which I thought was rather unfair since I could hardly help my teacher being so very boring. In any case, you should be aware that what grades mean is not always the same in different schools. Sometimes, an A means successful participation in a course, while a C means barely scraping by; other times, an A means top of the class while C means average.

Since homeschool families rarely compare their students with peers, they tend to see grades differently than public school teachers. For many, grades reflect the quality of performance on tests. You get an A on all of the tests, you get an A for the course. But if that is the case, how do you determine the quality of your student's reading? Some independent reading programs include tests so that teachers can point to objective evidence that a student has earned a certain grade. For a while, that's how I graded my girls' reading. I'd found two curriculums that offered quizzes and tests for lots of different books. That way, I figured my girls could choose their own books, and I'd have a way of knowing how well they were reading them.

Only later did I see the flaw in that strategy: the tests were basically trivia questions designed to make sure my students had actually read the books. Of course as a homeschool parent, I didn't need a test to tell me that; I only needed the tests for the grades I could record as proof that we'd done literature. But apart from the grade, the tests served no real purpose for us. No one needs to memorize trivia about books, and actually, my kids didn't even score as well on the quizzes as they ought to have, especially since they'd read and really enjoyed the books. Curious, I tried taking a few myself, and I realized what was wrong: most people don't pay attention to trivial details in the books they're reading. They pay attention to the plot and maybe a few details that particularly strike them as interesting, but the details that strike them aren't necessarily the ones that strike quiz-makers.

That's why I decided that the best way to do grades for my reading program would be to let my daughters control their own grades. I decided to go back to the old-school grading mentality wherein a C means acceptable—that the student had met the requirements for passing the course. In this case, the requirements for the course are spelled out in the student's checklist. A student who completes the requirements but nothing more gets a C. Overachievers get a B or A, depending on how significantly they exceed requirements, and underachievers get a D. Students who simply don't try get an F.

Grades for the Reading Program

A = the student surpasses expectations significantly by reading and responding to the equivalent of two books in addition to the number of books required or by reading two books representing greater challenge, or any combination of these

B = the student surpasses expectations slightly by reading and responding to one book in addition to the number of books required or by fulfilling requirements with at least one book reflecting significant challenge

C= the student reads and responds to the required quantity and quality of books

D = the student reads and responds to fewer than the required quantity of books required but does complete some of the required work

F = the student fails to read and respond as required

The beauty of this grading system is that students have complete control over their own grades, and the choice is theirs, whether they will meet requirements or exceed them. And that's why I recommended that you design your requirements so that they reflect the least amount of work you will accept from your student. By requiring the least amount of work, you allow your student to freely choose to excel, because excelling is entirely possible. When you require work that really reflects excellence, you're actually asking too much of students, which feels daunting and oppressive. That's when students are most likely to drag their feet or rebel. But most students love overachieving. After all, who doesn't love crushing a goal?

LIMIT REQUIREMENTS FOR WRITTEN PRODUCTS

None of the goals for this reading program require students to do written work about the books they read. Most of the writing associated with books is unnecessary. Written exercises designed to improve vocabulary or reinforce understanding about literary elements make reading feel like work and apply valuable time to activities that serve no real purpose since understanding what's going on in books that appeal happens naturally, or at least, with very little interference. Also, according to English professors Harold Vine and Mark Faust (1993), "providing background information, lists of vocabulary words, purposes for reading, and follow-up questions to enable students to read texts" cause students "to label them as school reading and to dissociate such activities from real reading" (p. 93). Of course, if students choose to write about books in fulfillment of one of their writing products for the writing part of this program, great! They can write a plot summary, book review, write a fan fiction or design a game based on the book—if they like.

What students do need to do is log their reading. Completing a reading log doesn't take long to do, provides some useful practice classifying books, and allows students to attach personal ratings. These ratings serve as a record of students' developing tastes and interests. This might not seem like a big deal, but over time, tastes change. At the beginning of sixth grade, students will usually be choosing books from a very limited range that reflects fairly unsophisticated tastes; by the end of eighth grade, those tastes will have expanded and become more sophisticated. The gradual shift in tastes as well as the gradually increasing level of difficulty in the books your student chooses is your proof that your student is learning and growing as a result of this reading program. So a reading log requires minimal effort, but has lasting value. A template for a reading log and helps for classifying and rating books can be found in Appendix B.

Another use for the reading log is to gauge whether you need to adjust the requirements you give your student. If your student isn't exceeding goals or is meeting only some of them, ask your student what's going on. Maybe your student needs you to be more flexible about the processes you permit—would watching a classic on DVD make that requirement more attractive? Or maybe you decided that your student was such a good reader, five classics seemed more appropriate than two, but then your student, having read the entire *Percy Jackson* series in a week, underestimated how long *The Adventures of Huckleberry Finn* would take. Obviously, when you're the teacher, you can adjust your program if something about it is off—in a sense, how you design requirements doesn't matter, so long as they help your student reach his or her goals.

PROVIDING FEEDBACK VERSUS ENSURING COMPLIANCE

In public school systems, teachers record grades based on a student's performance on tests. Teachers test students by giving written quizzes or formal tests, orally quizzing students, assigning book reports or requiring students to write "friendly letters" about the books they read. In a typical middle school reading program, these tests check two things: first, they ensure that the student actually read what they claim to have read, and second, they gauge reading comprehension. Unfortunately, not only does all of this testing add a negative association to what should be a pleasurable activity, it's entirely unnecessary.

Homeschooling eliminates the need for ensuring compliance. Unlike public school teachers who need objective proof that twenty or thirty students aren't pulling the wool over their eyes, a parent teacher can observe the progress of each of his or her students. Rather than having to check up on students, homeschool teachers can simply check in.

Contrary to what many people might think, reading is not a solitary venture: books are written by people, to affect or instruct people, and to invite interaction between people—between authors and readers and between readers and other readers. When reading matter is good, people can't resist sharing it. Case in point: when you read a really funny comic strip, don't you normally invite anybody in the vicinity to read it and laugh at it with you? Reading ideas that please us in some way almost always motivates us to connect with another human being. And as a homeschool teacher, it makes sense to take advantage of that innate urge to share good books and use it to check in with your reader.

Checking in has a completely different feel to it than checking up on students. Rather than asking, "Did you *really* read?," you ask questions like these:

- What are you reading right now?

- How do you like it?

- What's good about it?

- What don't you like about it? Do you think it's time to ditch it and try something else?

- Do you think I'd like to read it?

These are the kinds of questions adult readers ask each other about the books they read. Maybe not as regularly or purposefully as you will, but certainly, when two readers get together, they're bound to touch upon literature at some point in the discussion, and I can almost guarantee you that they never ask questions like "Did you make any reading connections with the text?" or "What clues did you find in the book as to the author's meaning?" or even, "Can you support your inferences with evidence from the text?" Now, it may be that the answers to these questions emerge in conversations about really good books, but readers volunteer such information—they don't demand it of one another. When people ask questions like these, they feel like tests—because they are.

Checking in with students with natural questions like the ones in the bullet list above serves another purpose: when you talk about books you can sneak in the terminology of literature that applies to the discussion at hand. Educated people use specific terms to talk about literature: protagonist, antagonist, plot, theme, conflict, climax, dialogue, description, perspective, voice, genre. These terms enable efficient discussion about books. For instance, say your student says that Gary Paulsen's *Woodsong* is pretty good and further explains that it's really funny in parts and other times, well, you'd just have to read it. A vague response like this is the perfect opportunity to work in a few literary terms. "So is it funny because of all the dialogue?" The student would immediately know to say, "No—it's not like that. Most of the time he's alone with his dogs. It's about the author and his dogs." "Oh," you could answer. "So it's funny because of the author's *voice*—the way he talks about his dogs. Is it written in the first person?" Rather than overtly teaching and testing these terms, students take them in as they take in all useful vocabulary: in their rightful context. A glossary with useful terms for talking about books can be found in Appendix B.

INDIVIDUALIZE THE PROGRAM

How do you customize a library for your student's unique reading level and tastes? How do you know which books will help your reader stretch out in terms of ability and interests? What kinds of books are even appropriate at this level?

Organizing and implementing the most appealing and appropriate program for your student will involve understanding something about the way your student learns. Chapter 5 provides a more detailed description of several personality types and their effects on motivation; it also discusses the effects of learning styles on the way students learn. In addition, you'll find suggestions for students who struggle with reading. Finally, Appendix B includes a questionnaire for students to complete as well as some suggestions to help you and your student identify appealing books for your program.

Before closing this chapter, I want to emphasize that, if you want your student to achieve the goals identified by this program, you need to be a reader, too. Reading for fun, expanding your reading repertoires, and appreciating great literature is not just for kids—these are activities that help everyone grow. The more you engage in the same activities you require of your student, the more your student will buy into the idea of reading as a worthwhile activity, and the more both of you will get out of this reading program.

CHAPTER FOUR

THE WRITING PROGRAM

In the writing portfolio I've kept of Kristen's writing is a five-paragraph essay describing a kiwi. I discovered the essay several years after the fact, as Kristen and I sorted through her papers to determine what to throw and what to keep before she left for college. When I showed the essay to Kristen, she assured me that she'd had no choice in the matter: her sixth-grade teacher had specified that the class was to dedicate a paragraph to each aspect of the fruit: color, shape, texture, and so on.

"But this is terrible," I said, gazing at the sparsely written paragraphs.

"Oh, I know," Kristen agreed. "But seriously: how much can you write about the shape of a kiwi? It's roundish. Elliptical, if you will."

I couldn't believe anyone would make students write an essay about such a topic. "Were all of your writing assignments like this?"

"Most of them. I remember I got excited about one of the prompts we got around Christmastime, but I couldn't remember some of the words to 'The Night Before Christmas,' and my teacher wouldn't let me go to the library to look them up, so I just wrote something lame and turned it in."

I was actually impressed by the quantity of writing Kristen had generated the semester she attended public middle school. Unfortunately, most of it was like the kiwi essay: more or less inane. I sighed and set the essay with the rest, in the toss pile.

Sadly, inane writing assignments are not confined to the realm of public schools. For whatever reason, they seem to be ubiquitous in language arts in general, and they're especially prevalent in middle school. As a writing tutor, I've noticed a pattern. College and high school students normally come to me for advice on their essays, more or less resigned to having to write academic essays. But middle school students tend to balk, especially when assignments call for creative writing.

Frankly, I'm never surprised when a student rebels: creative writing doesn't make sense. It doesn't really even exist. There are no professional "creative writers" out there. There are poets and novelists and playwrights and journalists, and some of them write imaginatively and skillfully. But the kind of stuff called for in creative writing prompts typically yields inane mush when demanded of unskilled and unmotivated young writers faced with prompts like "Write a story from the perspective of an insect;" "Create a myth explaining the seasons;" or "Pretend you are Juliet and write a journal entry about your feelings about Romeo's perfect nose." What the creative writing folks don't seem to realize is that no one "creates" anything good on demand. Literally speaking, 'to create' is to make something out of nothing, and as Allan Bloom (1987) observed, so far the only Person who has ever made something out of nothing is God (p. 180).

Command performances for creativity almost never result in writing of any quality because inventiveness and ingenuity necessarily come from within. This is not only true of middle school students: few professional writers of fiction or poetry can produce quality writing on demand, and you can usually tell when writing reflects another person's agenda. Take Michael Crichton's *Lost World* as an example: it lacks the brilliance of its prequel, *Jurassic Park*, which was fantastic: the premise, based on actual genetics and chaos theory; the plot and its twists, the pacing, appropriate to the story; the characters, so real in their complexity; the theme—the whole thing was brilliant. But *Lost World*, written after *Jurassic Park* had netted big bucks in the movie theaters, was so-so. It was almost as if someone said to Crichton, "You've got to write a follow up—and find a way to bring back Malcolm—I know he died, but people loved him." So he did, but *Lost World* never felt as compelling as *Jurassic Park*—to me, nor, based on its reviews, to anyone else.

Pre-designed creative writing assignments actually oblige students to write poor, specious compositions. This poor writing is not just the result of inability; as Nancie Atwell discovered when she decided to complete the assignments she was giving her students, even an experienced writer performs poorly when confined:

> My assigned poetry was formulaic and cute . . . my assigned narratives never went beyond the first draft; I wrote them at the breakfast table the day they were due. My assigned essays consisted of well-organized and earnest clichés. But the worst was the assigned daily journal entry . . . . I either had nothing to say or so much to say that ten minutes just left me frustrated. (p. 11)

There is a tremendous difference between putting your ideas down on paper because you want to and performing for the sake of a grade. I'm sure the theory behind creative writing prompts is that kids need teachers to tell them what to write and that without some structure and guidance, kids either won't write, they won't write the right way, or they'll write the wrong stuff. By what, exactly, is the wrong way to write? Which of the ideas kids want to write down are not worthy of being set down and recorded in print?

Good writing comes from within; it is what you want to say, on paper. William Zinsser writes, "Any method that helps you say what you want to say is the right method" (p. 5). Of course, Zinsser is referring to all sorts of things when he talks about method, but two essential ingredients in any method are technical skill—that is, the ability of a writer put a sentence down on paper intelligibly, so that the reader can grasp what is meant by the words on the page—and the writer really wanting to say something: "What holds me," Zinsser says, referring to his interest in someone else's writing, "is the enthusiasm of the writer for his field" (p. 5).

Good writing results when people have something to say. In fact, this is how I came to be a published author. One day while I was waiting for the carpet-cleaning guy to arrive, I sat down and wrote a poem about my friends' daughter. Her disabilities were severe and life-threatening, and I kept wondering why God would create her that way. Suddenly, a poem came to me that seemed to provide some resolution, and I felt an urgent need to write it down before I forgot it. Back then, I was a busy mom of three small children, and I rarely had time to write or even think about writing, much less think of myself as a writer, but the words came to me, and so I wrote them down. When I finished, I instinctively knew what I'd written was good. Rather naively, I sent it to a few publishers (I had no idea how hard it is to get published), and an editor at Eerdman's Books for Young Readers liked it. When I wrote it, I had no thought of publication of course; I only wrote the poem because I had something I needed to say, and as it happens, needing to say it was what made it good.

Goals for Any Middle School Writing Program

Certainly, not every student is going to see the need to write. No doubt most students will need some kind of inducement—not because they have nothing to say, but because they've yet to develop a habit of putting what they have to say down on paper. Poems and stories and ideas for blogs or even books don't come to people who have no inclination to write; they come to those who have learned to recognize the benefit of preserving and communicating their ideas.

An Inclination to Write for Personal Reasons

Developing the habit and inclination to write is a bit like developing a taste for a good diet and regular exercise. Initially, it might seem to a person that Twinkies and Doritos and exercising only when it seems fun is a good idea. But sooner or later, a body starts to protest such poor treatment; it deteriorates and rebels, and it becomes clear that healthier habits merit the discipline is involved in maintaining them. So it is with writing: initially, the effort it takes to write daily seems a bit like eating Brussel sprouts and doing jumping jacks. Some lucky kids realize almost immediately they actually like Brussel sprouts and jumping jacks; others get used to them in time. After a while, however, the habit sets in, benefits become clear, some special talent appears, and a will to write evolves. Knowing that ideas are for honing, preserving, and sometimes sharing, inspiration comes, and with it the motivation to put pen to paper productively.

Habit Formation

Middle school is the time to help students form that habit. Elementary students lack the physical ability to write fluently; not only are vocabularies and spelling skills still developing, but the speed with which younger students can transpose ideas onto paper dissuade them. Even students who enjoy writing stories at these ages often find that their efforts never measure up to their original vision. And that's okay; certainly, there's no reason to discourage a kid who likes to write from writing. By the time students are in high school, though, they're too old. Not in age or ability, perhaps, but time is really running out by high school for playing around with writing. High school students have work to do: they need to master writing so that they can get a job or get into college. High school writing is not about a life-enriching habit so much as a functional life-skill. There's a huge difference. Now, high school students who've already developed the habit and inclination to write anecdotes and poems and skits and stories can certainly continue to do so in high school, possibly as an elective. Realistically, though, the kind of academic writing students need to learn in high school doesn't come from within; in high school, students need to learn to write to academic prompts such as the ones they'll get from college professors. Middle school is really the time when kids will either develop an inclination to write for personal reasons or not.

Playfully Serious Experimentation

Normal people write down their ideas for all sorts of reasons, and this is why it's good to encourage students to explore writing in a variety of genres. When I was in middle school, I wrote to relieve my boredom, somewhat ironically, during English class. I remember writing a pseudo-soap opera of sorts chronicling the rather ridiculous adventures of my own little group of friends. I'd write it during my English class and pass it on during break so that my friends could read it and relieve their boredom during theirs. (In retrospect, I'm a bit surprised I never got in trouble for this behavior, because as I recall, I didn't pay a whole lot of attention to what my teacher was saying. I can only assume my teacher thought I was taking notes.)

Middle school is a great time to encourage students to experiment with writing playfully. Students get immediate satisfaction from playing with words, writing puns and parodies, skits and sketches. My girls and their friends love to collaborate on skits and song lyrics and various parodies, and they get immediate positive feedback writing witty banter to friends via e-mail or the little online social network our youth pastor set up for the kids at church. Positive feedback motivates students to expand their abilities to writing anecdotes or short, humorous narratives to publish in print or through personal blogs.

Middle school is also a great time to experiment with writing poetry. All too often, language arts programs that impose poetry give students the impression that poetry is about using language sublimely, something that comes naturally to a few and eludes the rest. The reality is that poetry can serve a real and important function for middle school students, because poetry is the writing form that allows people to explore the lingering questions they have about life. A person doesn't have to be a poet to write poetry, just someone who feels deeply about some personal experience. Of course, as Shel Silverstein and other poets prove, poems can also be a way to play with words and make people smile. But once a person understands what poems are for and what they might look like, poems often come, unbidden.

There are still other reasons to experiment with writing: students in middle school write to relate to other people, to preserve their thoughts and express their opinions, to offer practical tips or advice, to amuse others, and even to show what they know. With a student-centered approach to writing, what matters to the students themselves on any given day is "the primary content of the course" (Atwell, p. 71). All of this writing matters to students, and given the freedom to pursue what they see as relevant helps middle school students engage in their projects, care about quality, and thrive as real writers.

FACILITATE SUCCESS THROUGH MANY OPTIONS

The more limited students feel about writing options, the less they ownership they will feel for what they write. Instead of writing what they have to say about a topic they care about, they will be attempting to say what you want them to say about a topic you care about. Remember Kristen's kiwi essay? She could not have cared less, and her essay could not have been much worse—and it wasn't her fault. Since the essay was on-topic and ticked off all the teacher's criteria ("paragraph about shape, check!"), the essay earned a decent score in spite of being quite awful. But such writing is pointless to students. Like dogs in a show, students are asked to jump through little hoops for applause and maybe the prize of a good grade.

What keeps students from writing? Writing coach Ralph Fletcher polled reluctant writers to find out what held them back most as writers. Asked to complete the sentence, "When we write at school, I wish we were able to . . . ," the most common response was, "Write what I want" (as cited in Tyre, 2008, p. 156). When you allow students to write as real writers with real purposes and actual audiences—and by this, I mean not just you, not just an imaginary audience, and not just some potential, sometime-in-the-future-when-you're-a-famous-author audience—writing becomes an opportunity for personal expression, functional communication, and purposeful play.

You'll need to introduce this idea to your students, especially if your student has not had this kind of freedom before. Students who are used to writing to prompts might feel uncertain, as if there really is a prompt, and you're just not telling them, like some of the athletes who participate in Special Olympics with my son and me. When we practice swimming for races, the young ladies line up at the wall and wait for the signal. When Coach Jackie shouts, "Go!," the swimmers just stand there expectantly. Then, one of the girls will venture to ask, "Go?" And Jackie reiterates, "Yes. Go!" Only then do the girls start swimming. They obviously know what 'Go' means, they just want to be sure that 'Go' was really the signal to start swimming.

At the beginning of the semester, explain what options students have for writing, what your expectations and requirements are for the course, and where they may go for help when they get stuck. Most importantly, students need clear ideas about what kinds of projects you consider acceptable. The list below will give you and your students some idea of the variety of projects they might attempt.

- **Collected Thoughts** include books of favorite quotations and excerpts from other sources, top ten lists, wish lists, bucket lists, journal entries, and reflection essays.

- **Poetry** can include poems that rhyme, poems with counted syllables such as Haiku, free verse, ballads, parodies, and song lyrics.

- **Informative Writing** includes notes and messages; rules and regulations; advice; how-to articles; cookbooks; textbooks; reporting of sports, current, or special events; profiles; and feature articles.

- **Opinionated Writing** includes book, movie, restaurant, hotel, service or product reviews; blogs; op-eds; commercial scripts, persuasive speeches; tributes; or eulogies.

- **Narrative Writing** includes autobiographical memoirs and anecdotes, fairy tales, fables, fan-fiction, short stories, chapter books, skits, plays, and novels.

- **Correspondence** includes notes of sympathy, congratulation, and thanks; letters to pen pals or long-distance friends or family members; letters of inquiry or complaint; fan letters; and personal or family newsletters.

- **Writing with Graphics** includes comic strips, graphic novellas, picture captions, picture books, greeting cards, posters, brochures, pamphlets, and websites.

- **Playful Writing** includes generating puns, acrostics, tongue twisters, palindromes, zeugmas and even playing board games such as Scattergories or Balderdash.

An annotated list of possible writing projects, models, and suggestions for inspiration can be found in Appendix C.

So far, I have not mentioned what you might think of as academic essay writing, and there is a reason for this. Whereas a goal for middle school students is to find personal reasons to write and to find satisfaction in writing well, the whole point of academic writing assignments is to satisfy an academic authority or teacher, usually by answering an academic prompt.

Now, there's nothing wrong with academic writing. In fact, in *Grading with a Purple Crayon*, I recommend that a high school composition course consist primarily of academic writing. The reason I can recommend so much freedom here is that students who have had the benefit of three years of solid grammar and writing practice should have no problem developing the ability to write for academic reasons in high school, making writing for academic purposes unnecessary at the middle school level. Furthermore, high school students who have developed a habit of writing for personal reasons during the middle school years often continue to do so in their leisure during high school.

That being said, a student who enjoys writing might actually prefer writing academic essays in fulfillment of requirements for courses such as health, science, or history. If so, I see no reason why essays would not be acceptable as one of the student's polished products from one category of writing. I would not, however, permit the student to complete nothing but academic essays.

LIMIT REQUIREMENTS

As with the reading program, freedom comes from minimal requirements. What is the least amount of writing a middle school student should produce in a semester? Remember, a full half of the writing work in this program is daily dictation. This part of the program is more concerned with students developing an inclination to experiment with various kind of writing as well as with polishing and publishing a few of their self-appraised most successful attempts. Students may attain all of these goals by completing a very few requirements. For instance, consider this checklist:

- Generate (plan, write, or draw) or polish (revise, edit, format, or publish) writing projects for ½ hour daily.

- Produce writing projects from at least three distinct writing categories.

- Select three pieces to polish and submit for preservation in your writing portfolio. Of the three, one should incorporate some graphic element, and one must exceed one page of text in length.

- Find a real audience for at least one project.

- Keep a writing log of the projects you attempted, polished, and published.

It doesn't look like much. In fact, this checklist only requires a student to produce something like five page-long polished projects over the course of a semester, but since students are required also to account for their time and record the projects they attempt, the list adequately addresses the habit-forming issue since students must generate and produce writing daily. Students have maximum freedom to experiment and choose the projects they want to dedicate the most time to; parents get the assurance that students are working toward important, life-enhancing goals.

The Accuracy Aspect

A necessary component of any writing program must address the conventions that are appropriate to a piece of writing. Not everything a student generates necessarily requires exhaustive editing and revision—because not every piece of writing is meant to be preserved or published. Professional authors purposefully abandon pieces, leaving them completely unedited and unrevised, because they know when something isn't living up to its promise and doesn't merit the time and energy it would take to perfect it. What you're asking your student to do in this program is experiment, and experiments by their very nature are speculative; in fact, fewer pan out than do. Good writers abandon experiments that don't seem to be working and ideas for which they've lost enthusiasm, and they dedicate lots of time and energy to the ones that hold the most promise. Students make the most efficient use of their time when they do likewise.

Different levels of perfection pertain to the various kinds of writing, even when the writing is intended for a real audience. For example, notes may be written for a real audience—that is, they're written to communicate with a real person—but what adult edits and revises the scribbled note on the fridge asking another family member to let the dog out? I'm thinking very few. By contrast, every adult with any sense at all would revise and edit, get a second opinion, and then revise and edit again the cover letter and resume they intend to use to apply for a dream job—and in the same vein, every writer revises and edits and, yes, revises and edits again any piece of writing they're submitting for publication. Somewhere in between these extremes is the amount of attention a person gives conventions in semi-formal writing, such as a thank-you note. More than once, I've tossed a flubbed thank you note in the trash and started over, but I've also gone ahead and sent thank-you notes that I had fixed by striking a misspelled word and penning it in neatly above the botched one.

As you can see, accuracy matters most with certain kinds of writing. People who write a lot don't obsess with accuracy as they write, but they do try to write as correctly as it occurs to them to, because they know that writing sentences that are irrational, incorrect, or illegible just means a lot more revision later. That much should be obvious, even to students, but if it's not, remind them to always write as correctly as they can. At the same time, inform students that only the projects they'll submit for their portfolio or decide to publish need to be revised, edited, and formatted to the absolute best of their ability.

Submitting Work for Publication

A final goal for this program is for students to submit at least some of their projects for publication. By this, I don't necessarily mean professional publication by a press—although there's no reason to exclude the possibility—but rather, that at least some of the writing students do must find an audience, however large or small, that is not YOU. Writing must serve a more immediate purpose for students than "Someday when you are in college, you will need to be able to write well." As Nancie Atwell asserts, "Middle school students look for in school what matters in life; they don't look at school as a place to *get ready for* what matters in life" (p. 67, emphasis in the original).

Once out of school, most people do not write in order to get ready to write; they write to communicate, express, entertain, or inform. So, too, middle school students write for a purpose, and while they need permission to label some if not most of their efforts as mere attempts that they can give up on when they fall flat, what really convinces students that writing serves a meaningful purpose is seeing an occasional project through to publication and feeling the satisfaction of knowing that they have affected someone else in the world.

At the middle school level, publication may not look like HarperCollins picking up their story and marketing it as the latest YA hot pick of the year, but never have more realistic opportunities for disseminating writing been available to students. Say a student writes text and draws pictures for a picture book. He can easily scan the pictures and import them into a Word document, format and print the document with a high quality printer, and use a bookbinding kit to produce a nearly professional picture book to present to someone as a gift. If the book gets really good feedback from family and friends and if money is no object, he or she can even look into publication through a vanity publisher that works with young authors, such as StoryJumper or KidPub Press, both of which will format, publish, and make books available for purchase online for a fee.

Of course, most of what people write is not intended for broad audiences but narrow ones. I'm not writing this book under the illusion that it will sell millions of copies; I write for the homeschoolers I know and like: a small but worthy audience. I've actually written several books with just a single person in mind. An audience doesn't need to be big to be real.

One opportunity for publication that has always been available to kids is writing letters or newsletters to relatives or friends; alternatively, students today can design their own website and publish weekly blogs. Poems adorned with artwork can be framed or turned into greeting cards; short stories, tributes, and memoirs can be sent as gifts to long-distance relatives and friends. More public options for publication include submitting a piece to a local or online newspaper, contest, or magazine. Appendix C contains even more suggestions for publication.

Clarify Expectations for Regular Writing Sessions

How often and for how long, when and where students write, ideally, should be up to them—after all, real writers work out a writing process that they find helps them to be most productive. Realistically, however, students are not professionals; they're still maturing, which means they're going to need some expectations outlined for them.

How do you ensure that students write regularly? You clarify expectations for regular writing, keeping in mind your student's individual preferences and tendencies. Some students need little or no definition for how much time you expect them to commit to writing nor do they need help coming up with projects—they have projects in mind already and will be thrilled to be permitted to work on them instead of wasting time on someone else's agenda. These students will have gotten ideas for writing from the books they read; the main feedback they'll need from you is your response as a reader. Permitted to explore and produce, some students will not only fulfill expectations, but exceed them.

Other students, however, will need more guidance: they'll need your expectations and their options very clearly laid out from the beginning, and they'll appreciate some direction in terms of the types of projects they should consider doing. Don't worry about inhibiting freedom if students want input about how to proceed; what inhibits freedom is when you design the project for your student to complete. Students who don't know what to do need you to know them well enough to nudge them in a direction where they are most likely to find inspiration. For instance, a student who likes historical fiction clearly appreciates finding meaning in the past. Such a student might welcome the suggestion to look for inspiration in a family picture album or to consider writing a memoir, autobiography, biography of another family member, or a tribute. Another student might be fascinated with astronomy. Such a student might be encouraged to consider various options for writing informatively: he or she might consider designing a PowerPoint presentation, a poster, feature article, or even something unusual, like an advice column for astronauts stranded in space. Invite your student to brainstorm with you. The important thing is for the student to commit to something that sounds like a project he or she can envision and wants to take on.

Students who need a lot of direction often want details spelled out in writing. They'll want to know specifically how much work to complete or how much time they need to clock. The checklist of requirements should assure them that the quantity of attempted projects matters less than the time spent generating them. The checklist clarifies the expectation that students write for a minimum half an hour daily, and for students who like to follow such guidelines to the letter of the law, you might want to emphasize the word 'minimum.' You might also want to let your student know that it's okay to write for an hour two or three days a week instead of half an hour every day. Again, what matters most is what works for students.

Some students may even want to know at what time they must do their writing. Here, you may want to get their input, since writers typically have a time of day that works best for them. My ideas flow best early in the morning; my daughters like to write late at night. For uncertain students, however, you might want to designate a time when you're available to answer questions.

Finally, many students appreciate having models to work from—not to imitate, but to get a picture in their heads of the sort of thing they're attempting. I've included a few examples of various writing projects in Appendix C, but realistically, there's no way any one source can demonstrate all of the variety of project types and writing styles that students might find worthy of imitation. Look for models of good writing in the books you collect for your home library, which hopefully reflects the kind of writing your student finds most appealing and will be most eager to imitate. Also, consider looking for models of successful projects on the Internet. Websites that publish student writing will also have samples of what others have done.

Middle school students find it easier to develop productive reading and writing habits if you prohibit the use of recreational electronics during the school day. In my home, I have found it helpful to designate a timeframe for "school" (in our house, "school" is from 7:30 a.m. until 4:00 p.m.) and a list of acceptable school-day activities for when the day's "official" work is done. Once my girls finish language, math, social studies, and science, they are free to choose their own activities. Since lit-boxes are off-limits, they may freely choose to play outside or play a board game, exercise or participate in sports activities, practice musical instruments, bake cookies, clean their bedrooms (never a popular choice for some reason), daydream, read, or write. So long as they fulfill their reading and writing requirements, I tell them that I don't care how they fill that time, and so far, that policy has never backfired—the girls have both independently opted to exceed requirements for both reading and writing every semester.

Adjusting the Requirements for Gradual Growth

Remember, you want to design requirements to reflect the *minimum* you will accept from your student. Requiring work from three categories allows students the most freedom you can possibly give them while respecting your need to see them attempt projects that reflect variety and growth. Students who are drawn to projects like comic strips and top ten lists will have to attempt something longer, while students who prefer writing long narratives such as chapter books and novels are forced to explore other genres as well. The chart below shows how gradually increasing expectations challenge students to take on slightly more ambitious projects each year.

	6th Grade	7th Grade	8th Grade
Habit Formation	Students complete and submit a writing log documenting time spent working on writing projects	Students complete and submit a writing log documenting time spent working on writing projects	Students complete and submit a writing log documenting time spent working on writing projects
Inclination to Experiment	Students produce writing projects from at least three distinct writing categories	Students produce projects from at least three distinct writing categories, at least one of which they have not attempted previously	Students produce writing projects from at least three distinct writing categories, at least two of which they have not tried before
Growth	At least one polished exceeds one page in length; polished products reflect the student's knowledge in terms of vocabulary, genre, and correctness	At least one polished product exceeds two pages in length; polished products reflect learning in terms of vocabulary, genre, and correctness	At least two polished projects exceed two pages in length; polished products reflect higher quality in terms of vocabulary, genre, and correctness

PROVIDE HELPFUL FEEDBACK

Picture this scene: a twelve-year-old student gets an idea for a story. The story strikes the student as wonderfully clever, so she sets out to write it. She spends several hours writing her idea down, and while she's not unaware that the story as written is not quite the same as her original vision, all in all, she's pleased. A few bits she's particularly fond of, and at least a couple of lines she's sure will make you laugh. She arrives at a stopping point and decides to show it to you.

So she does. She gives you a small sheaf of notebook papers with ragged edges to read, and she tells you that she wants your opinion. Then she hovers. While you quickly read and sometimes skim the story she spent approximately ten hours writing, she watches your face. Do you like it? Will you laugh at that one line? Do you get the beauty of the vision? Finally, you get to the last page and flip it over. Back to the first page. Done. You look up.

"Well?" she asks. "What do you think?"

"It's good," you say cursorily, nodding in affirmation of your own statement.

"You like it?"

"Yeah, it's good," you say again. And then, you do the unthinkable: you flip to page three, the page with the really good line that she wrote and re-wrote and tweaked until it was just perfect, and you point to the line just above it, and you say, "There are just a few little things . . . . like here: see this comma?"

Oh, dear. I wish I could say that I myself would never be the 'you' in that story, but of course it is entirely autobiographical. I can't tell you how many times I have responded not as a reader but as a nit-picking teacher. And my Lauren's response, every time, was one of deep disappointment. Finally, one day it hit me: Lauren wanted me to respond to her story as a reader. And so the next time she had a story she was pleased with and brought it to me to read, I tried it. When she asked me if I liked it, I didn't just say, "Yeah," I told her which parts I liked best.

Lauren was elated.

Now, I sometimes mention that there are a few things she could do better and that if she gets to a point where she wants to improve her writing, that I would be happy to let her know what she could do better. She's okay with that.

When a writer shares a piece of writing with you, he or she is always taking a huge risk. Writers put a little tiny piece of themselves down on a piece of paper. That's why it's so important to know what kind of response your writer is looking for when he or she brings a piece of writing to you for feedback. Is your student looking for a reader's reaction? Not a teacher's reaction, necessarily, just a reader, any reader. Then put on your reader hat and respond as a reader, and understand that what writers want to know is not merely whether you give their work a thumbs-up or a thumbs-down; they want to know what you liked, and they want to know specifically which part you like especially. What made you laugh? What made you feel sad or scared or disgusted or impressed? What word choice really made you go, "Nice!"

It's okay to have some not-so-awesome feedback, too. If something confused you, that's worth pointing out. Time and again, I've found that students don't mind feedback like, "You've got some really good ideas here that deserve to be brought out more clearly" or "I think I would actually appreciate you project more if you cut out some of the clutter and let the best parts really shine." Just make sure that your feedback suggests ways to go about improving their work, and doesn't imply that a project your student is still excited about is irredeemably hopeless.

Polishing Work for the Portfolio

If your student says, "Okay, I've decided I want to polish this piece and try to publish it, but I'm not sure what to do next," your responses need to be a bit more exact. Put on your editor's hat and point out two or three things that would most help the piece connect with any other reader. Rather than give your student the specific words that you think will make the writing better, however, limit yourself to pointing out the specific spots in the piece that are not working for you and ask your student to come up with ways to improve them. For instance, consider the following questions:

Correctness

- "This word is making me think you mean [x]. But is that what you mean? Is there another word that would say this a little better?"

- "I can't tell where this sentence ends and the next one begins. Can you clarify that for me?"

Clarity

- "I don't understand what you're trying to say during this part right here."

- "This sentence confuses me—what are you trying to say with it?"

Coherence

- "I get a little lost in this part. Is there something missing?"

- "I'm not sure how this part fits with the rest of the story. How does it connect?"

- "I almost feel like this part would go better in the beginning (or at another part of the piece). What do you think?"

Limit yourself to three suggestions for improvement, and remind your student to take time to re-read his or her own writing and find a few things to improve before you offer any suggestions. Many students find it helpful to read a piece out loud—this helps students catch the occasional misplaced or missing word, and prevents you from being the mistake-police and lets you be someone to bounce ideas off of. Then, when you suggest that a certain part of a project is a little murky, your student can sagely nod and say, "Yeah, I kind of thought so myself."

After your student has considered and possibly applied all of the suggestions for improvement, accept the revised piece as a sample of your student's best writing at this stage of his or her writing career, even if the piece isn't perfect. Put it in his or her portfolio and keep it as the priceless artifact it is.

Publishing Writing

On the other hand, if your student intends to publish a piece of writing, tell your student that you're putting on your copyeditor hat. Copy editors are quality control for authors; they catch misspelled words, typos, errant punctuation, and basically anything that might be considered a mistake in order to prevent embarrassment and to help readers get the most out of a quality piece of writing. Now, when you don that copyeditor hat, make sure you only edit out errors and don't get carried away. Sometimes, it's hard to leave something in that you think would be better written another way, but unless there's an actual error, an editor has to respect the writer's choices.

As a copy editor, you can either identify mistakes for your student to correct or actually suggest the corrections he or she should apply to the final copy. Which you choose depends on your student's ability to correct mistakes and whether he or she will likely find the task frustrating or merely a bit annoying. Personally, I would go ahead and volunteer correct spellings for poor spellers, assuming they're addressing their spelling issues through another program, but some people might feel that students learn best by correcting their own mistakes.

Some teachers have students keep lists of the conventions-related rules to use on future assignments. I like Nancie Atwell's copyediting process:

1. She identifies up to three conventions that need improvement in the piece.

2. She explains up to two of the rules behind the conventions.

3. She has the student add the new rules to a personal proofreading list.

4. She expects students to double-check future assignments for items on the proofreading list before asking for help. (p. 251)

My process as a copyeditor is a bit different; I'm more likely to explain and ask my student to correct about half of the issues and, depending on the audience, pen in the corrections for the rest myself. I do this because (a) I don't want to exasperate my student, but I also don't want her to be embarrassed when she finds errors in a published piece later, (b) I'm not worried that she doesn't understand the importance of making corrections since she does some of them here and all of them when doing dictation work, and (c) it seems unreasonable to me to expect a middle school student to have mastered all of the writing conventions professional writers have. Students do, after all, have the rest of high school to practice making corrections, and, if you will forgive the cliché, "Rome wasn't built in a day."

In a sense, who does the corrections really doesn't matter, since goals for the writing part of this program aim more at the student's inclination to write, while the dictation work focuses on accuracy. Also, bear in mind that accuracy will always lag somewhat when students are generating writing as opposed to transcribing the words of others. Accuracy in ability to perfect personal projects will improve gradually, in part because once a piece of writing is very familiar, errors become more difficult to see. I'm forever catching errors in my own writing—things like 'of' where I mean to type 'or,' and other obvious things like that. Tics like these are why professional writers have copy editors; it's not because they don't know how to write. The important thing here is that any writing being submitted for public viewing be as clean as possible so that the student can feel proud of his or her work.

LET STUDENTS CONTROL THEIR OWN GRADES

As in the reading program, students must exceed the minimum requirements in order to earn an A or B for this course. How they choose to exceed requirements—by experimenting with more kinds of writing, by exceeding the page count for polished projects, by exceeding the total number of projects they polish, or by publishing more than one product—is up to them. But notice that the

---

Grades for the Writing Program

A = the student documents daily writing and exceeds requirements by submitting two or more polished products to the writing portfolio than required or by exceeding requirements substantially in length; the student publishes two or more products

B = the student documents daily writing and exceeds requirements by submitting more than the required number of polished products to the writing portfolio or by exceeding requirements for project length; the student publishes two or more products

C= the student documents daily writing and submits the required quantity of polished products for the writing portfolio; the student publishes one product

D = the student documents daily writing and submits the products for the writing portfolio; however, the student fails to polish products, publish products, or meet the requirements for variety, quantity, or length of projects

F = the student fails to write or document writing as required

grades students receive for the writing portion of this program has nothing to do with any subjective opinion about the quality of their writing attempts (except that the polished products must in fact be polished); rather, grades have everything to do with students' willingness to try.

MEASURE GROWTH

While grades reflect effort, you should also be able to tell whether or not this program has brought about growth. What does growth look like in a middle school student who has successfully completed a writing course? The answer comes from the course objectives, and it is against these objectives that growth is measured.

- To what degree did the student choose to engage in writing without being coerced or nagged to do so at the beginning of the program? To what degree does the student choose to engage at the end of the grading period?

- To what degree did the student experiment with various kinds of writing at the beginning of the program? To what degree does the student experiment at the end?

- To what degree did the student find a real audience for his or her writing at the beginning of the program? To what degree does the student format and publish writing at the end?

- To what degree did students identify and correct errors in writing at the beginning of this program? To what degree does the student identify and correct errors at the end?

Ultimately, the way to measure growth is simple: you compare the written work your student was able to complete at the beginning of sixth grade versus the products completed at the end of sixth grade, seventh grade, and eighth grade. To see how and how much your student has grown, simply pull out your portfolio of his or her work. The products your student could produce as a sixth grader will have their own charm, but three years of writing and analyzing dictated sentences, reading across a wide range of genres and topics, and experimenting with various writing projects will, by the end of eighth grade, result in apparent growth that both you and your student should be able to see, appreciate, and chart.

Chapter Five

Understanding Differences and Individualizing the Program

The organizational work of parents entails not only permitting free choice and enticing students to take whatever constitutes the next step in terms of educational progress, but also taking the student's unique learning preferences, gender, and aptitudes into account. Psychologist William Glasser (1988) suggests that whether students get into reading and writing often has to do with whether these activities satisfy any personal need for freedom or fun, belonging or importance (p. 15). He also notes that, by middle school, students have developed an opinion about how they feel about language arts and whether they themselves are good or bad at it (p. 38). Some students will have already discovered pleasure in reading and writing and be willing to attempt projects, knowing their efforts will garner them praise. Other students will have come to associate reading with boredom and writing with failure. To them, the activities of language arts hold no reward, intrinsic or extrinsic. The only reason they're given for doing their work—and to them, it is most definitely work—is that someday they will need these skills in order to go to college and get a job. Reading and writing become means to an end that a large number of students simply care nothing about.

Taking Individuality into Account

All students bring with them a unique set of strengths and weaknesses, and certainly some students are more apt to succeed in school. Still, Mortimer Adler (1982) insists that "there is no uneducable child . . . there are only children that we fail to teach in a way that befits their individual condition" (p. 45). With Adler, I believe that all children benefit from a tailored program that acknowledges their uniqueness and maximizes the degree to which students see activities as inherently rewarding. "The answer," Adler suggests, "lies in adjusting that program to individual differences by administering it sensitively and flexibly in ways that accord with whatever differences must be taken into account"(p. 44). Students are all different many ways: "in native ability, in interests and inclinations, in temperament, in every taste and aptitude for learning, in home upbringing, in economic status and opportunity, in ethnic and racial heritage, and so on" (p. 42). This is where parents have an advantage over public school teachers: not only do parents know their own children's history and personality better than anyone else, they are unencumbered by the task of analyzing the individualities of twenty or thirty other students as well.

But beyond knowing that their child is lovably one-of-a-kind, parents do well to understand a bit about educational psychology, which explains how different students' minds work and what motivates diverse individuals to engage most in learning. Adler goes so far as to suggest that the effectiveness of the teacher's efforts "depends on the teacher's understanding of how the mind learns by the exercise of its own powers, and on his or her use of this understanding to help the minds of [their students] to learn" (1982, p. 61). A student's learning preferences, style, gender, and aptitude all affect how he or she may best be taught and the kinds of activities that will most encourage learning.

Learning Preferences

Learning preferences, educators Jane Kise and Beth Russell (n.d.) argue, affect students' abilities to learn in the same way that right or left handedness affects the ability to write. Although people generally prefer writing with one hand or the other, most people actually can write with either hand, if made to do so. The reason people prefer one hand over the other is that using the preferred hand facilitates work and increases the ability to perform well, while using the non-preferred hand impedes work and requires more thought. Kise and Russell emphasize that acknowledging a student's learning preferences can facilitate more successful learning experiences, but need not be taken as a learning limitation. Rather, once you understand your student's learning preferences, you can organize the kind of work that will entice your student to engage, and once he or she has experienced success, you can discretely challenge him or her to try activities and options that lie outside that preferred personal comfort zone.

Learning preferences derive from individual temperaments, or personality types. In their book, *Please Understand Me*, psychologists David Keirsey and Marilyn Bates (1984) describe four basic personality types: the Epimethean, Promethean, Apollonian, and Dionysian. These four temperaments hold important implications for what meaningful engagement looks like for different types of students.

EPIMETHEAN: THE 'LIVES–TO–PLEASE' STUDENT

The first temperament is Epimethean or, in Meyers-Briggs terms, the SJ personality. People with an Epimethean personality type long to belong to a group; what motivates them is serving and pleasing others (Keirsey & Bates, 1984, p. 40). Unfailingly responsible members of any group, they will be the ones who follow all the rules and do their duty (p. 41). Needless to say, Epimetheans are among the most compliant, easy-to-teach students; however, their desire to please means that these students like frequent assurance that they're on the right track. They also feel more comfortable when they know exactly what's expected of them. Clear, written instructions in the form of a checklist or learning contract make these students feel secure and confident as they work toward goals.

Epimethean Readers

Epimetheans tend to prefer books that value truth and heritage such as historical fiction and mystery stories, that feature characters that they feel are like them in some way, whether in terms of heritage or situation, and books that involve characters doing the right thing. Although Epimetheans are often willing readers, it's important to suggest books that are neither too long nor too difficult because Epimetheans want more than anything to please, so they're sensitive about performing up to whatever standard you set. Help Epimetheans feel confident and positive about reading by stocking a library with books that are either at or slightly above their actual reading level.

Epimethean Writers

Since Epimetheans look to please, they may defer to you when it comes to determining what kind of writing projects to undertake. Design your program so that students have a clear sense of what you want to see by making requirements explicit. For instance, rather than simply requiring a few polished writing projects from distinct genres each semester, you might need to specify the nature of the projects:

> This semester, to earn a C, you must turn in at least three projects that have been revised, edited, and appropriately formatted, including:
>
> - One thoughtful or opinionated piece, such as a poem, a reflection, or a review
>
> - One narrative piece, such as an autobiographical or imaginative story
>
> - One informative piece, such as a report, a how-to piece, or a newsletter
>
> In addition, you must submit six writing projects in draft form (unrevised and unedited).
>
> To earn an A or a B, you must exceed these requirements by producing, polishing, or publishing additional projects.

PROMETHEAN: THE INTENSELY SELF-DIRECTED STUDENT

A second temperament is the Promethean, or NT. Prometheans long to understand; what motivates them is intellectual competence (Keirsey & Bates, 1984, p. 48). Unlike Epimetheans, Prometheans don't care as much about impressing other people or seeking outside approval; they are motivated more by their need to understand why the world is as it is (p. 53). Prometheans prefer to explore their own ideas rather than follow a teacher's, and the more freedom they have to study whatever intrigues them, the better they learn; however, since Prometheans' curiosity tends to be all-or-nothing, they need help setting priorities so that they don't neglect important but less personally intriguing subjects (p. 118).

Promethean Readers

Prometheans will read just about anything, fiction or non-fiction, classic or contemporary, so long as it doesn't strike them as contrived, predictable, formulaic, or inane—and of all types, Prometheans are most likely to pass judgment on the books they read. Prometheans tend to be precocious students with strong vocabularies; they typically love wit and wordplay as well as intricate plots with clever twists. In terms of tastes, Prometheans often prefer fiction that involves strong themes, as is often the case in coming-of-age stories, fantasy and science fiction, and in your book discussions, ask your Promethean questions about a work of fiction's plot and theme. These students also gravitate toward non-fiction books that allow them to explore the topics and concepts that are intriguing them at a particular time. Give Prometheans a say in what their library looks like and allow them to pick what to read and when, and they will basically educate themselves.

Promethean Writers

Prometheans will appreciate having the freedom to hone their knowledge about whatever intrigues them through writing about it. Requirements should permit and encourage students to use writing as a tool to understand topics better. These students benefit from requirements that call for fewer writing projects but of greater length and complexity. For instance, instead of requiring a Promethean to submit ten products (as in the suggested requirements for the Epimethean above), requirements might require a minimum of three polished projects of distinct types totaling a minimum of ten pages of writing for a C grade, with additional pages necessary for the A or B grade. Since Prometheans value competence, they will appreciate writing about the topics that intrigue them most, since this not only increases their competence as writers but hones their knowledge as well.

APOLLONIAN: THE IDEALISTIC, "MAKE A DIFFERENCE" STUDENT

A third temperament is the intuitive feeling Apollonian, or NF. Whereas Epimetheans yearn for belonging and Prometheans crave competence, Apollonians long for meaning; they live to make a difference (Keirsey & Bates, 1984, p. 58, 60). And they do: although only 12% of the population are Apollonians, so many of them are writers that they have a disproportionate influence on society (p. 60). Apollonians are people people: they "seem to have a natural talent for relating socially, both to peers and to adults" (p. 118). More than any other group, Apollonians love languages and identify with characters in stories (p. 118).

Apollonian Readers

Many Apollonians are naturally gifted readers who are most likely to appreciate the kinds of books English teachers (who also tend to be Apollonians) love to assign: richly written fiction in which a protagonist gains insight, often through tragic circumstances. Almost all of the Newbery Honor books fit this description and many classics as well. In tailoring a library for an Apollonian, think in terms of challenging your student to explore new genres and sample more classics than the average student. In the discussions you facilitate about fiction, think in terms of a work's tone, theme, and any literary devices the author uses such as symbolism, foreshadowing, and figurative language, since no one appreciates a well-crafted metaphor more than a word-loving Apollonian, nor delights more in descriptive imagery. Some people speculate that Shakespeare was an Apollonian.

Although many of the classics that were written for adults are going to be pretty difficult for a sixth or seventh grader, you might want to stock books like *Black Beauty*, *Treasure Island*, and *Heidi*, which are great stories written at a slightly more difficult reading level and slower pace than most contemporary YA fiction. Advanced readers may even appreciate classics such as *Little Women*, *Great Expectations*, *Jane Eyre*, or *Moby Dick*. Classics like these, as some of the most enduring stories that readers have found meaningful for generations, are among the books that Apollonians typically cherish most.

Be aware, however, that some Apollonions love images more than words. These Apollonions fit the description of visual-spatial learners discussed below. Visual-spatial Apollonian readers are typically gifted but slow bloomers who may initially prefer comic books and graphic novels to text-heavy books. These students benefit from a library that permits them to indulge their taste for images with a combination of graphic fiction and non-fiction as well as a selection of non-intimidating but imagery rich, descriptive fiction.

Apollonian Writers

Apollonians love to craft images with words. Expose them to poetry and require them to produce at least a few poetry products, and the results will amaze you. Word-loving Apollonions are most likely of all types to independently decide to attempt a long fiction project such as a novel, so design requirements that allow for a project to take a lot of time to complete. A good set of requirements for these students might involve a minimum number of pages of draft-quality work plus a number of short, polished pieces (such as poems). Image-loving Apollonians are likely to be enticed by the prospect of tackling a graphic novel or picture book for children; however, these students may also gravitate toward poetry, which permits much expression with an economy of words. One resource that you may find particularly helpful in helping Apollonian writers to shine is

Image Grammar by Harry Noden. Intended for English teachers, the manual describes Noden's process for helping students paint pictures with words using specific grammatical structures.

DIONYSIAN: THE 'LIVE-FOR-THE-MOMENT' STUDENT

Finally, there is the Dionysian temperament, or the SP. Dionysians yearn for freedom above all else; they are motivated by their own impulses (Keirsey & Bates, 1984, p. 31). Because they naturally act on impulse, Dionysians improvise and perform well in crises (p. 32); they also make "excellent team player[s]" (p. 108). Of all groups, Dionysians have the hardest time with long-term goals and set routines (p. 33). Dionysians, who make up about 38% of the population, are most likely to be labeled hyperactive in traditional school settings (p. 39). They can't stand being constricted or restricted and feel much more comfortable when they have opportunities to move about freely, be spontaneous, and play, although they do need quiet time as well (p. 107-108). Dionysians settle down to read and write much more willingly when their needs for activity and involvement have been met.

Dionysian Readers

Dionysians tend to be actors, not thinkers. That doesn't mean they're not intelligent, just that for an Dionysian, an action is its own end; it "cannot serve a purpose or be instrumental in achieving a goal" (p. 31). That aversion to performing for anything but immediate gratification translates into Dionysians feeling oppressed by most of the reading they're normally expected to do in school settings, whether it's practicing decoding words in order to learn how to read or reading to find the right answer or to learn vocabulary or to get some kind of deeper meaning out of the symbolism in a poem or story. Of all the types, Dionysians are most likely to develop an interest in reading later than other students. Long, challenging, "rich" books exhaust Dionysians. Dry, informative books bore them, and deep, meaningful books depress them. Dionysians need fun.

The best books for Dionysians are going to books that are exciting, suspenseful, fast-paced, and frequently funny. Dionysians appreciate protagonists in fiction that are action-oriented and do their duty with honor, which are values that resonate most with this personality. Comic books and graphic novels also sometimes appeal to these readers. Non-fiction books should be of immediate interest and text should be supported by ample graphics such as books from Kingfisher or Dorling Kingsley. As Dionysians build fluency, consider looking into opportunities for participation in age-appropriate drama. Acting speaks to the Dionysian need to perform and have an audience. Finally, allowing students to draw or doodle while listening to audio versions of appealing classic texts helps students with less reading stamina increase their vocabulary and accumulate experiences with literature.

Dionysian Writers

Dionysians write most willingly to amuse or entertain others. As Keirsey and Bates point out, "The more game-like the task, the better. The less an activity seems like mere preparation for something later, the better" (p. 107). Comic strips and captioned art (hand-drawn or photographic) may be appealing means of expression for some Dionysian students; for more text-based writing projects, steer Dionysians toward shorter projects with actual audiences and opportunities for feedback such as top ten lists, how-to articles, book, movie, and restaurant reviews, and correspondence. Dionysians will find collecting amusing quotations more satisfying than, say, writing reflections or thoughtful memoirs.

Kiersey and Bates point out the "seeming paradox" that Dionysians, for whom every action serves its own purpose, often become exceptional performing artists:

> The virtuosos of art, entertainment, and adventure. The great painters, instrumentalists, vocalists, sculptors, photographers, athletes, hunters, racers, gamblers—all need the skills which come only from excited concentration on an activity for long periods. No other type can mobilize what virtuosity takes: untold hours of continuous action. (p. 35 – 36)

Dionysians crave freedom, so design requirements that maximize freedom in terms of which kinds of writing projects they'll take on and how extensive they need to be, but be willing to make suggestions to point a Dionysian in the direction of a project that might appeal. Dionysians need clear instructions, structure, and consistency. More than other students, Dionysians may need help seeing the relationship between their actions and the consequences of their actions, so you may actually be doing them a favor to clarify that participation in sports or other preferred activities are contingent on completing required academic work first. Reasonable requirements for Dionysians might include many short, polished writing projects—perhaps ten per semester—that they can share with others. Dionysians will be more enthusiastic about writing if you require fewer expansive writing projects.

Learning Styles

Another distinction among students involves learning styles. In 1988, educational psychologists Richard Felder and Linda Silverman observed that students get bored, become distracted, and generally perform poorly when teachers' preferences for presenting information "seriously mismatched" the learning styles of students (Felder & Spurlin, p. 103). Although the studies involved four dimensions, Silverman eventually identified two main learning styles: auditory-sequential and visual-spatial.

Audio–Sequential Learners

According to Linda Silverman (n.d.) audio-sequential learners prefer the logical, step-by-step progression of learning typically embraced by educators. Since "the strongest modality for audio-sequential learners is audition," these students tend to remember what they hear and read, memorize information easily, and generally excel in language-related activities (p. 4). As you can imagine, audio-sequential students do well in school whether or not teachers have any particular knowledge of learning styles (Silverman, p. 24).

Visual–Spatial Learners

Teachers often misunderstand visual-spatial learners. Visual-spatial learners process ideas differently: they "need to see a concept in order to understand it" (Silverman, p. 2). Mazes, maps, numbers, and puzzles intrigue visual-spatial learners; they enjoy building things and working puzzles. They tend to be late bloomers who have trouble with reading, spelling, and handwriting (Silverman, p. 24; Lovecky, 2004, p. 163). Many have histories of recurrent ear infections and poor phonemic awareness (Silverman, n.d., p. 15). Not surprisingly, these students "prefer visual representations of presented material such as pictures, diagrams, and flow charts" (Felder & Spurlin, 2005, p. 103).

Visual-spatial learners have significantly different ways of learning. Whereas rehearsing information and doing drills benefit most learners, they don't help visual-spatial learners. Silverman compares their learning to a work of art: "When an artist has developed an image for a painting, it is there, complete and permanent. It does not need to be rehearsed or practiced; it does not improve with drill or review" (as cited in Lovecky, p. 161).

According to Silverman, about one-third of all school children have visual-spatial preferences (as cited in Lovecky, p. 160). Interestingly, while thirty-three percent of fourth-grade children scored at or below proficiency on the 2011 National Assessment of Educational Progress reading tests, by eighth grade, that percentage drops to twenty-four ("Below Basic, Basic, and Proficiency Spectrum," 2012). One can speculate whether these percentages reflect the visual-spatial learner's late blooming tendency, but the data seem to support Silverman's suggestion that visual-spatial learners' preferences are more often neglected in schools.

Visual-spatial Readers

For a visual-spatial student, stock a library that includes a variety of books that are rich in imagery as well as books that might not include a lot of pictures, but stimulate the imagination and help students visualize events. Students can learn elements of fiction from comic books and graphic novels and many non-fiction topics can be explored in illustrated reference books from publishers like Usborne, Kingfisher, or Dorling Kindersley; for students with strong visual-spatial preferences, consider stocking as much as one-third of your home library with highly visual types of books—they're the ones that will appeal most. At the same time, remember that all of the learning preferences in this chapter are continuums, not either-ors. Most students with some tendency toward visual materials will also appreciate books that are mostly or entirely text but that encourage students to visualize events such as the many imaginative fiction works available for upper elementary and YA readers—especially action, adventure, science fiction and fantasy stories.

Visual-spatial learners are more likely to remember information when they have the big picture first, so watching a video adaptation of a classic like *The Three Musketeers* or even a contemporary hit like *How to Train Your Dragon* can facilitate comprehension for a student who might otherwise find reading slow going. This need to have a big picture holds implications for how visual-spatial learners grasp other academic subjects like history and science as well. Most textbooks present topics sequentially and in as much depth as possible, and they usually require students to memorize vocabulary and pass tests on the information before moving on, but visual-spatial learners can't make sense of information before they have a sense of the whole. It's like they need to develop mental file folders for subjects before they can file information away in them.

Allowing these students to survey academic subjects at more basic levels first and then choosing topics to investigate in greater depth can help them understand and retain more. For example, Great Source's visually appealing *ScienceSaurus* handbooks survey life, physical, and earth science at both the 4 – 5 and 6 – 8 levels, the main difference between the two being the amount of detail. A visual-spatial learner might get more out of surveying the 4 – 5 handbook, which provides a rapid overview of material, and then exploring the material in more depth later—or even choosing a few particularly interesting aspects of the material to study in depth. Either way, having a big picture first and adding detail later helps these students retain more about the topics they're learning.

In terms of the reading program, let visual-spatial learners choose their own books and follow their ideas wherever they go, but design your reading requirements to expand their tastes beyond their preferences and become more well-rounded readers. As Felder and Spurlin (2005) point out, you only further hamper a visual-spatial student when you cater entirely to his or her preferences, because realistically, the world will not. What understanding learning styles should help you do is adjust your student's program so that it is more balanced and thus more comfortable overall. Visual-spatial learners should have opportunities to learn in their preferred manner, but they must also develop the ability to operate in a primarily auditory-sequential world (p. 105). Happily, this program suggests requiring all students to explore reading and writing across several genres and categories, effectively permitting every student to choose preferred activities and projects as well as to expand their skills by engaging in less obviously attractive options.

Visual-spatial Writers

Visual-spatial students remember the pictures they see of words better than most people, so avoid editing exercises that depict misspelled words, misplaced punctuation, and faulty capitalization at all costs—these exercises only engrain incorrect patterns in these students' minds. Doing dictation and copying favorite quotations from books are both excellent ways for these students to gain a clear picture of correctly spelled and punctuated writing.

Visual-spatial students come in two varieties: the image-loving Apollonian and the artistic Dionysian. These writers often struggle with fine motor issues, making handwriting difficult and keyboarding skills particularly valuable; somewhat surprisingly, however, many Dionysian visual-spatial students are remarkable artists. Artistically inclined visual-spatial students may especially appreciate Scott McCloud's book, *Understanding Comics*, which is a graphic textbook that explains how comic books and graphic novels work.

Students seeking direction for writing projects will appreciate suggestions that involve imagery in some way. You might challenge students to write descriptions of artwork or explain how the frame in a graphic novel effectively tells a story; conversely, students might reverse the project and create a graphic representation of a passage from a favorite fiction work (Annett, 2008, p. 164). Also, you might suggest students attempt projects that combine text and graphics: comic strips, graphic novels, posters, brochures, picture books, illustrated instruction manuals, PowerPoint presentations, websites, or graphic organizers as means of categorizing or classifying information. For students who need to memorize information for other courses, you could suggest a project in which they would design flashcards incorporating pictures as mnemonic devices. For instance, to remind themselves of the differences between 'there' and 'their,' a student might draw a picture of an arrow pointing to a building labeled 'there,' and another picture of people in front of a house with an arrow pointing to the people, indicating that the house is theirs, labeled 'their.' Don't, however, worry about making students study the cards they design; remember, these students get little out of repetitive drilling. Students actually learn the material through designing the cards.

Visual-spatial learners need models of finished projects to help them visualize their own (Lovecky, 2004, p. 169). Often, these students need help breaking a large project down into the various steps that contribute to the finished project. Checklists can help keep these students on track; alternatively, students might make a writing project of designing a flowchart that can help them be more independent with their own writing projects. A helpful computer program for graphically organizing information like this is Inspiration software.

Gender Differences

Another important learning difference is gender. Originally, I wanted to avoid referring to gender-related learning issues, especially since some people consider any reference to gender as inappropriate stereotyping. I decided to include this section, however, because recent statistics suggest that more and more boys in America are struggling academically.

Boys as Readers

Whereas once boys outscored girls academically, recent findings suggest that educational practices designed to help girls achieve equality have effectively reversed the situation so that boys are now being outscored by girls. The 2004 U.S. Department of Education Trends in Educational Equity of Girls and Women Report affirms that "the large gaps that once existed between males and females have been eliminated in most cases" (as cited in Tyre, 2008, p. 281). One school district in Illinois recently conducted a study examining scholastic performance by gender and found that not only had junior high girls achieved higher grade-point averages than boys in all eleven subjects, but boys compared worse for every year the students were in school (Whitmore, 2010, p. 19). These results suggest that current education practices favor girls.

Factors involved in the demise of boys in public schools probably include both environmental and biological factors. On the environmental side is the recent push to ensure that all students in a given grade achieve a specific, one-size-fits-all level of proficiency. According to Diane McGuinness (1985), psychological studies have found that differences in learning rates among normal children span approximately five years, but currently, "American schools are organized according to chronological age with a variation of only two years in a classroom" (p. 20). Biologically, boys are predisposed to learn through physical exploration and rely on visual input for direction. Contrary to what most people would expect, "a strong reliance on the visual mode is often antagonistic to progress in learning to read" (McGuinness, 1985, p. 70). This predisposition, plus the fact that boys tend to develop later than girls academically, may account for higher percentages of boys falling behind and staying behind girls in school (p. 21).

Could boys' aversion to reading be culturally influenced? That is, is culture giving boys the message that boys ought to be playing with cars and trucks and that reading is for girls? One psychologist decided to find out. Rather than getting caught up in questions of nature versus nurture that confound the issue, psychologist Sandra Scarr studied what each gender finds easy to learn, since "what is 'easy to learn' is most rooted in biology and least influenced by environment" (McGuinness, 1985, p. 118). She found that girls in general found reading easy and were less affected by environmental factors like how interesting the reading material might be than boys. Boys, on the other hand, had more difficulty with the auditory and motor skills important for reading; as a result, most boys found reading hard, and their ability to read was most affected by environmental factors such as how interesting reading material was and whether anything more interesting was happening in the vicinity.

The good news is that many of the suggested remedies for boys are easily implemented at home.

1. Let boys develop reading skills at their own pace. Also, since feeling like a failure often diminishes the motivation to try, try not to refer to your son's reading abilities as problematic in his presence.

2. Let boys read what appeals to them. According to Richard Whitmore (2010), "Interviews with successful boy readers revealed they often became hooked on comic books early and then transferred that interest to broader literature by sixth grade" (p. 205). Since boys are visually oriented, books with lots of graphics appeal especially to boys. Also, as publisher Steve Hill says, "Boys are not into feelings, people skills, or personalities. They're very much into things. Tanks and guns and buildings and submarines and airliners. They like to know how things work. They like the details" (as cited in Whitmore, 2010, p. 52) Author Jon Scieszka agrees: "Boys like books that are about stuff—science books about pyramids and grasshoppers. And books of just facts, random facts, like the *Guinness Book of World Records*" (as cited in Tyre, 2006, p. 150). Boys also like stories with male protagonists that courageously do the right thing, as well as books that are funny and involve humorous adventures.

3. Help boys develop auditory discrimination by listening to audio-books and reading stories out loud, together. Also, transcribing excerpts from dictation builds auditory skills and facilitates reading skills.

Boys as Writers

If boys struggle with handwriting, let them use computers for writing projects that are mainly text. Also, since boys prefer visual representations, projects with graphics often appeal to them.

In terms of content, it's important to remember that many boys are not always as tuned-in to touchy-feely topics that many girls enjoy exploring. Ralph Fletcher says, "Be prepared for them to tackle dangerous topics replete with violence, mayhem, and gore" (as cited in Tyre, 2008, p. 158). One teacher I know here in Alaska observes that a large percentage of the writing he sees from boys involves guns in some way.

Not long ago, a teacher asked me what I thought of a writing sample a middle school boy had produced. In it, the boy had personified Death. "Don't you think this is pretty dark?" the teacher asked me, clearly concerned. I told her that it didn't. The boy's mother had told me that he was in complete shutdown mode with his writing, and I think the Death piece had been the last piece he'd written. To me, his choice of topic made perfect sense. The boy was, in his own special way, saying, "You're killing me here!" The next creative prompt he got, the writer in him played dead.

Learning Aptitude

According to Diane McGuinness (1997), "every child or adult who isn't mentally retarded or deaf can be taught to read if given proper instruction" (p. 12). In her book, *Why Our Children Can't Read*, she examines "twenty years of data from brain-imaging studies and electroencephalographic (EEG recordings)" and emphasizes that "people diagnosed 'dyslexic' have no damage to any part of their brain" (1997, p. 118). She writes,

> If a child scores badly on a reading test, he or she has a reading problem and needs to be taught. There is no evidence from any of the studies or any of the tests that most poor readers have anything wrong with them, except the inability to read an alphabetic writing system, and this in turn is related to a difficulty in accessing the phonemic level of speech. In other words, children with reading problems have a hard time "ungluing sounds in words." (1997, p. 122)

If your middle school student is still finding decoding difficult and has to work at understanding what a passage means, read Diane McGuinness's book. It will help you understand the issues involved and convince you that poor readers are the products of poor reading programs. Then, seek remediation. Poor readers need to get up to speed fast, "otherwise, [students who by middle school have internalized the fact that they have a reading problem] become discouraged and apathetic" (p. 311). McGuinness recommends one-on-one tutoring and suggests that a good program should take no more than sixty hours. Two remediation programs that McGuinness approves are Lindamood-Bell Clinics, the availability of which may be an issue if no clinicians operate near you, and *Phono-Graphix*, which is a program that you can purchase online and implement yourself. A third highly recommended resource, *Reading Reflex*, was developed by Diane McGuinness's son and his wife, Carmen and Geoffrey McGuinness.

Another helpful practice for struggling readers is Guided Repeated Oral Reading. Recommended by learning disabilities researchers and clinicians Brock and Fernette Eide (2006), this procedure involves reading a passage out loud to your student and then having your student read the passage back to you as many times as necessary to master reading the passage fluently (p. 358). One of the nice things about this process is that it can be incorporated into the daily dictation routine.

Increased exposure to auditory language is another way to help a struggling reader improve fluency. Since books contain more words than people typically use in speech, listening to audio versions of books or having books read to them out loud helps students increase their vocabulary, which in turn helps them to understand more words and read better in the future (Hirsch, 2006, p. 60). Eide and Eide (2006) also suggest that attending plays and watching vocabulary-rich documentaries and films can help students broaden vocabulary and build reading fluency (p. 358).

Finally, another way to help struggling readers improve fluency in reading is by practicing writing (Eide & Eide, p. 359). Though this may sound counterintuitive, Maria Montessori believed that writing should precede reading, and that by reciting the letter sounds and later slurring these into words, children learned to read naturally (McGuinness, p. 237). Diane McGuinness explains why this works:

> We now have considerable evidence that the fostering of any skill, no matter how much it may seem to be an internal process (like silent reading), is acquired more rapidly and efficiently if there is motor involvement. Writing develops the connection between the visual symbols and the fine-motor system. Recitation involves the oral-facial musculature and provides feedback to the auditory system. (p. 237)

Adjusting the Reading Program for Struggling Readers

Beyond the primary goal of gaining an inclination to read, every student's personal goals in reading will depend on where they're at in terms of reading skills. Initially, the goal for all readers is to read well, with accuracy and fluency. Many students basically accomplish this goal in elementary school, but not all. Students who continue to struggle need focused practice with decoding as well as regular opportunities to explore highly entertaining reading material. So does this mean that since these students are behind, that they have to put in double the effort, or that they just won't be able to work on some of the more ambitious goals, such as preparing for high school?

Absolutely not. There is no reason students who struggle with decoding can't work toward the exact same goals as other middle school students so long as those goals are appropriately prioritized at each stage of the program and alternative processes are permitted to facilitate success. If you look at the table on the next page, you will see that none of the reading program goals are eliminated; rather, requirements involving expanding tastes and interests are postponed, while alternative processes such as viewing video adaptations and listening to audiobooks make gaining familiarity with classic works accessible. By the end of eighth grade, students following these requirements each semester will be familiar with more than twenty classic works, and more if they exceed their options.

Such a student's individualized middle school reading program will look like this:

	6th Grade	7th Grade	8th Grade
Primary Goals	Practice decoding; participate in a reading remediation program	Build fluency by reading appealing books	Expand tastes and interests by reading from diverse genres
Secondary Goal	Build fluency by reading appealing books	Accumulate positive experiences with classic literature	Build fluency by reading appealing books
Tertiary Goal	Accumulate positive experiences with classic literature	Expand tastes and interests by reading from diverse genres	Accumulate positive experiences with classic literature
Sample Semester Checklist	Read at least six books of your own choosing Watch at least two video adaptations of a classic literary work	Read books from at least four distinct literary genres Listen to unabridged versions of and read along with at least two classic literary works Watch at least two video adaptations of classic literary works	Read books from at least six distinct literary genres, including at least one work of non-fiction Listen to unabridged versions of and read along with at least three classic literary works Watch at least two video adaptations of classic literary works

Adjusting the Writing Program for Struggling Writers

According to Eide and Eide (2006), as many as one in five children have serious difficulties in producing neat and accurate writing by hand (p. 277). An appropriate solution for this issue is using a computer for the majority of writing assignments; however, a computer will not solve every problem for students who write slowly. One issue for many slow writers is that they forget ideas before they can transpose them onto paper. Taking notes for the student while discussing writing plans can help in this regard; alternatively, students can record their ideas using a small digital recorder and play them back as they write.

Because certain situations require the ability to write neatly by hand, Eide and Eide (2006) recommend that students also practice handwriting from fifteen to thirty minutes a day (p. 396). Conveniently, this is about as much time as the dictation work for this program requires. However, you may also want to consider implementing a multisensory handwriting program such as *Handwriting Without Tears*; for students with severe and persistent issues, the authors recommend consulting an occupational therapist (p. 397).

An Individualization Caveat

This chapter has provided you with several means of individualizing your student's program. Designing a tailored program will result in a program that initially entices the student to engage and hopefully experience success with the various course objectives. Never forget, however, that the goal is not to produce comfortably complacent students who are incapable of adapting to new situations, but students who continually improve their language skills, expand their personal repertoires as readers and writers, and appreciate increasingly sophisticated literary experiences. Therefore, the information here should help you envision both a starting point—your student's preferences—and an end goal: your student's growth.

References

Adler, M. & Van Doren, C. (1972). *How to read a book: The classic guide to intelligent reading.* New York: Simon & Schuster.

Adler, M. (1982). *The Paideia proposal: An educational manifesto.* New York: Simon and Schuster.

Aesop. (1985). Aesop's Fables. New Jersey: Watermill Press.

Annett, D. (2008). Implementing graphic texts into the language arts classroom. *Minnesota English Journal.* p. 150 – 179.

Aristotle. (1998). *Nicomachean ethics.* Trans. D.P. Chase. Mineola, NY: Dover Publications.

Atwell, N. (1998). *In the middle: New understandings about writing, reading, and learning.* Portsmouth, NH: Boynton/Cook.

Baum, L. (1993). *The wizard of Oz.* Great Britain: Wordsworth.

Below basic, basic, and proficiency spectrum. (2012) Learning Stewards, A 501(c)(3) Non-Profit Organization. Retrieved from www.ChildrenoftheCode.org

Bloom, A. (1987). *The closing of the American mind.* New York: Simon & Schuster.

Dahl, R. (1992). *Boy and Going Solo.* England: Puffin Books.

Dewey, J. (1938). *Experience and education.* New York: Simon & Schuster.

Eide B. & Eide F. (2006). *The mislabeled child: How understanding your child's unique learning style can open the door to success.* New York: Hyperbion.

Felder, R. & Spurlin, J. (2005). Applications, reliability, and validity of the Index of Learning Styles. *International Journal of Engineering Education. 24* (1) p. 103 – 112.

Gallagher, K. (2006). *Teaching adolescent writers.* Portland, Maine: Stenhouse Publishers.

Glasser, W. (1988). *Choice theory in the classroom.* New York: HarperCollins.

Grahame, K. (2008). *The wind in the willows.* London, England Puffin Books.

Guarino, D. (1989). *Is your mama a llama?* New York: Scholastic.

Hart, R. (2006). *Increasing academic achievement with the trivium of classical education: Its historical development, decline in the last century, and resurgence in recent decades.* Lincoln, NE: iUniverse.

Harwayne, S. (2001). *Writing through childhood: Rethinking process and product.* Portsmouth, NH: Heinemann.

Hirsch, E. (1988). *Cultural literacy: What every American needs to know.* New York: Vintage Books.

Hirsch, E. (2006). *The knowledge deficit: Closing the shocking education gap for American children.* New York: Houghton Mifflin.

Hoban, R. (1964) *Bread and jam for Frances.* New York: Harper Collins.

Joseph, M. (2002). *The trivium: The liberal arts of logic, grammar, and rhetoric: Understanding the nature and function of language.* Edited by Marguerite McGlinn. Philadelphia: Paul Dry Books.

Kiersey, D. & Bates, M. (1984). *Please understand me: Character and temperament types.* Del Mar, California: Prometheus Nemesis Book Company.

Kirby, G., Goodpaster, J., & Levin, M. (2001). *Critical thinking.* Boston, MA: Pearson Custom Publishing.

Kise, J. and Russell, B. (n.d.) Are they really problem students? Bridging differences through understanding. Retrieved from www.personalitypathways.com.

Korman, G. (2006). *Pop.* New York: Balzer & Bray.

Lightbrown, P. & Spada, N. (1999). *How languages are learned.* Oxford, England: Oxford University Press.

Lovecky, D. (2004). *Different minds: Gifted children with AD/HD, Asperger syndrome, and other learning deficits.* Great Britain: Jessica Kingsley Publishers.

McGuinness, D. (1985). *When children don't learn: Understanding the biology and psychology of learning disabilities.* New York: Basic Books.

McGuinness, D. (1997). *Why our children can't read and what we can do about it: A scientific revolution in reading.* New York: Simon & Schuster.

Montessori, M. (1967). *The absorbent mind.* New York: Dell.

Montessori, M. (2008). *The Montessori method.* Radford, VA: Wilder Publications.

Noden, H. (1999). *Image grammar: Using grammatical structures to teach writing.* Portsmouth, NH: Boynton/Cook.

O'Conner, P. (1999) *Words fail me: What everyone who writes should know about writing.* Orlando, FL: Harcourt Brace.

Oelwein, P. (1995). *Teaching reading to children with Down syndrome: A guide for parents and teachers.* Bethesda, MD: Woodbine House.

Schaefer, G. (1997). *Understanding and using good grammar.* Portland, ME: Walch.

Shernoff, D. & Csikszentmihalyi. (2008). Flow in schools: Cultivating engaged learners and optimal learning environments. Retrieved from www.cedu.niu.edu/~shernoff/Shernoff%20and%20Csikszentmihalyi%20C011.pdf

Shipley, J. (1977). *In praise of English: The growth & use of language.* New York: Times Books.

Silverman L. (n.d.) Identifying Visual-spatial and auditory-sequential learners: A validation study. Retrieved from www.visualspatial.org/files/idvsls.pdf

Stephens, J. (2007). Young adults: A book by any other name . . . : Defining the genre. *The ALAN Review. 35* (1) p. 34 – 42. Retrieved from http://scholar.lib.vt.edu/ejournals/ALAN/v35n1/stephens.html.

Tolkien, J. (1978). *The hobbit.* New York: Ballantine.

Tyler, R. (1949). *Basic principles of curriculum and instruction.* Chicago, IL: The University of Chicago Press.

Verne, J. (2007). *Around the world in eighty days.* U.S.A. Dalmatian Press.

Vine, H. & Faust, M. (1993). *Situating readers: Students making meaning of literature.* Urbana, IL: National Council of Teachers of English.

White, E. (1952). *Charlotte's web.* New York: Scholastic.

Wiggins, G. & McTighe, J. (2005). *Understanding by design.* Upper Saddle River, NJ: Pearson Education.

Wilder, L. (1933). *Farmer boy.* New York: HarperCollins.

Wise, J. & Bauer, S. (2009). *The well-trained mind: A guide to classical education at home.* New York: Norton.

Zinsser, W. (2001). *On writing well.* New York: Harper Collins.

APPENDIX A:
DICTATION HELPS

This section provides a few helps for you as you get started doing dictation with your student.

An Order for Grammatical Analysis and several preliminary lessons orient you to grammar concepts and the process for identifying parts of speech in syntax. Give your student time to practice each new principle, and when you no longer need to prompt your student of each word's function in a sentence, you'll know it's time to move on to the next level of analysis.

Cheat Sheets: Several of the items serve as "cheat-sheets" which your student may keep handy as you analyze sentences. This is not cheating; it's a form of teaching. Students needn't be stumped as to whether a word is a preposition or not when they can just check. Eventually, the cheat sheets will all become obsolete as students memorize the grammar terms and internalize concepts.

Finally, a **Glossary** provides a brief explanation for each of the eight parts of speech plus a few additional terms that students will need as they examine the make-up of grammar.

A few tips:

Don't rush through levels or worry that your student isn't moving through grammar principles quickly enough. The most valuable and applicable lessons come first, so no amount of practice with the beginning lessons can do them harm, and if students never learn absolute phrases, they will hardly notice, as absolute phrases occur rarely anyway.

Be consistent, but not rigid. Grammatical analysis doesn't apply to all writing in quite the same way: poems, for instance, follow other rules than those of syntax. Feel free to take a break from the focus on grammar to examine how poems or punctuation in dialogues work.

Don't worry if you don't know all of the grammar in a passage. Either omit confusing parts while dictating or skip them while analyzing the sentence. Simply say, "Don't worry about that part; we'll learn it by and by." So long as the essential core is decipherable, the exercise has value.

Follow the logical process and trust that the logical answers are the right ones. Be aware that a subject can be a phrase—a subject might be as long as some sentences!—or that the subject can follow the verb on occasion. If you start with your verb and answer who or what does it, you can't go wrong.

BASIC GRAMMATICAL ANALYSIS PROCESS

1. To start, work with simple sentences or independent clauses.

2. Begin by identifying the main verb(s) and any helping verb(s) by asking "What is the verb in this sentence? What is the subject doing?"

3. Identify the subject by asking, "Who or what [insert the sentence's verb here]?"

4. Identify any direct object by asking, "[Subject][verb] who or what?"

5. Identify any indirect object. This item is rarely necessary, and if there is no direct object, there will be no indirect object either. However, if there is a direct object and there is another noun in the sentence that does not follow a preposition, ask, "[Subject][verb][direct object] to or for whom or what?"

*Note any conjunctions and identify any compound subjects, verbs, or direct objects as you go.

6. Identify any prepositional phrases by marking them off with parentheses.

7. Identify any adjectives by circling them.

8. Identify any adverbs by bracketing them.

ADVANCED GRAMMATICAL ANALYSIS PROCESS

1. Break compound, complex, and compound-complex sentences into independent and dependent clauses. (Leave noun clauses and adjective clauses intact within their respective independent clauses.)

2. Begin by identifying the main verb(s) and any helping verb(s) by asking "What is the verb in this sentence?" If the student needs a hint, ask, "What is [the subject] doing?"

3. Identify the subject by asking, "Who or what [insert the sentence's verb here]?"

4. Identify any direct object by asking, "[Subject][verb] who or what?"

Note: when a subject, direct object, or any other object is a verbal phrase, treat the entire phrase as if it were one word.

Also, note any compound subjects, verbs, direct objects, or direct objects and their respective conjunctions as you go.

5. Identify any indirect object by asking, "[Subject][verb][direct object] to or for whom or what?"

6. Identify prepositions and their objects.

7. Identify adjectives, circling participial phrases and adjective clauses as units.

8. Identify adverbs by bracketing them, but analyze dependent adverb clauses.

ORDER FOR INTRODUCING GRAMMAR PRINCIPLES

I. Preliminary Lessons: Basic Grammar Concepts

    A. Subject, Verb, and Direct Objects

    B. Prepositional Phrases

    C. Adjectives and Adverbs

    D. Indirect Objects

II. Dictation Work Levels for Grammatical Analysis

    A. Simple, Transitive Sentences

    B. Compound and Complex Sentences

    C. Distinguishing Linking Verbs, Progressive Verbs, and the Passive Voice

    D. Understanding Phrases and their Functions

        1. Prepositional Phrases

        2. Participial Phrases

        3. Infinitive Phrases

        4. Gerund Phrases

        5. Absolute Phrases

    E. Understanding Dependent Clauses

        1. Adverb Clauses

        2. Adjective Clauses

        3. Noun Clauses

Preliminary Lesson I: Subject-Verb-Direct Object

Directions: Follow the process for analyzing a simple sentence.

1. Herbivores eat plants.
2. Clowns juggle scarves.
3. Cats chase mice.
4. Heroes fought wars.
5. Scholars read books.
6. Architects design buildings.
7. Orphans deserve help.
8. Consumers purchase groceries.
9. Shakespeare wrote tragedies.
10. Professors explain concepts.

Let's take the first one as an example:

1. Ask: "What is the verb in this sentence? What is happening? Who is doing what?"

If the student needs a hint, ask, "What are the herbivores doing?"

2. Once the student identifies 'eat' as the verb, say, "Yes: 'eat' is the verb for this sentence. Double-underline the verb. Next: Who or what eats plants?"

3. Once the student answers correctly, say, "Yes: 'herbivores' is the subject; underline the subject. We have the subject and the verb; now, 'Herbivores eat' who or what?"

4. Once the student answers correctly, say, "Yes: 'plants' is the direct object. Write 'D.O.' above the direct object. Now you have the subject, verb, and direct object of the sentence; these three are the most important parts of any sentence. Always determine these first in any sentence."

D.O.

The sentence should now look like this: *<u>Herbivores</u> <u><u>eat</u></u>* plants.

If your student should need more practice with simple sentences like these, invent more. To construct simple sentences, it helps to use a list of spelling or vocabulary words and choose either nouns or verbs as your starting point. When you start with a noun, ask, "What does this noun do?" Shoot for precise and interesting verbs so that students can easily identify them. Even better, build sentences from verbs. With a verb, simply ask, "Who or what [verb]s?" "Who or what garnishes?" "Who or what bungles?" "Who or what plods?" Remember, not every verb takes an object. Horses plod, but they don't plod anything. Practicing a few intransitive sentences like this is a good idea.

Since these simple sentences contain nothing but the three grammar functions, many students will find them fairly easy, so don't linger on them too long. Once students have the concepts in mind, the next few parts of speech will only make the process that much more interesting.

Preliminary Lesson II: Prepositional Phrases

Directions: Give your student a copy of the list of prepositions on page 125 and follow the process for determining the verb, subject, and direct object; then look for prepositional phrases.

1. Birds gather worms at daybreak.
2. Writing in cursive takes effort.
3. At dinner we use forks.
3. People wear pajamas for sleeping.
5. Men at labor use pickaxes.
6. Children wear sandals in summer.
7. Coffee in mugs retains heat.
8. I eat Wheaties for breakfast.
9. Students learn arithmetic in school.
10. On Sunday, we attend church.

Let's take the first one as an example:

1. Ask: "What is the verb in this sentence? What is happening? Who is doing what?"

If the student needs a hint, ask, "What are the birds doing?"

2. Once the student identifies 'gather' as the verb, say, "Yes: 'gather' is the verb for this sentence. Double-underline 'gather.' Next: Who or what gathers worms?"

3. Once the student answers correctly, say, "Yes: 'birds' is the subject; underline the subject. So we have the subject and the verb. Now, birds gather who or what?"

4. Once the student answers correctly, say, "Yes: 'worms' is the direct object. Write 'D.O.' above the direct object. Now you have the subject, verb, and direct object of the sentence. Once you have these, look for prepositional phrases. Do you see any prepositions in this sentence? Check your list of prepositions if you're not sure."

5. When the student correctly identifies the preposition 'at', ask "At whom or what?" to elicit the object of the preposition.

6. When the student says, "At daybreak," say, "Yes: 'daybreak' is the object of the preposition, 'at.' 'At daybreak' is a prepositional phrase. Put a parentheses around it and label the preposition 'prep' and the object of the preposition, 'o.p.' And you're done."

                                                                       D.O.   prep   o.p.

The sentence should now look like this: <u>Birds</u> <u>gather</u> worms (at daybreak.)

Once students understand the concept of a prepositional phrase, they will begin to notice them easily, making it easier to deal with the more difficult task of discerning adjectives and adverbs.

Preliminary Lesson III Adjectives and Adverbs

Directions: Give your student the "Cheat Sheets" with the lists of prepositions and questions for adjectives and adverbs. Follow the process for determining the verb, subject, direct object, any prepositional phrases, adjectives and adverbs in the sentences below.

1. The fox lured the foolish fowl to his den.

2. Prunes certainly aid digestion.

3. Many colleges charge exorbitant fees.

4. Politicians often debate about ridiculous matters.

5. Pigeons once carried messages for humans.

6. A peculiar odor filled the air.

7. Oddly, carnivores consume cannibals.

8. Stacy has an allergy to pistachios.

9. Harold hired a temporary worker for the holiday season.

10. The orchestra played the symphony beautifully.

11. Pirates rarely fret about their reputations.

12. The male gymnast practiced his routine on the apparatus.

Let's take the first one as an example:

1. Ask: "What is the verb in this sentence? What is happening?" Or, "Who is doing what?"

2. Once the student identifies 'lured' as the verb, say, "Yes: Double-underline 'lures.' Next: Who or what lures?"

3. If the student says, 'The fox,' ask him or her for just one word. The student will say, "Fox." Say: "Yes: 'fox' is the subject; underline 'fox.' Now: "Fox lured who or what?"

4. Again, if the student says, "the foolish fowl," ask him or her to narrow the answer down to a single word. Once the student responds, "Fowl," say, "Yes: 'fowl' is the direct object. Write 'D.O.' above 'fowl'. Now: do you see any prepositional phrases? Check your list if you're not sure."

5. By now, the student will probably volunteer the entire prepositional phrase, 'to his den,' but if not, ask, "'To whom or what?" to elicit the preposition's object, 'den.' Once again, say, "One word" if the student says, 'his den.' Once the student has identified 'to his den' as a prepositional phrase, say, "Put parentheses around 'to his den' and label the preposition and object.

> Note: Students typically want to include adjectives that clearly apply to a subject or object when they first analyze sentences in this way. However, it's important for students to distinguish between nouns and adjectives. As a result, you will need to ask them to reduce their answer to one word for subjects and objects, eliminating articles and adjectives whenever students include these in their responses, unless two words are clearly meant to represent one thing, as in 'hot dog' or New York City. Also, occasionally, you may happen upon a subject phrase in which multiple words express a single idea, as in "Replacing faulty electrical wiring can be dangerous." Treat these phrases as if they were single words.

6. Ask the student if there are any more prepositional phrases. Once the student confirms that there are none, have the student consider each of the remaining words against the functions of adjectives and adverbs. For whatever reason, I have found that working back from the end of the sentence toward the beginning facilitates this process. The first unmarked word in this sentence, moving backward from the end, will be 'his,' which falls between 'to' and 'den.' Students will find it helpful to note that by far the majority of words that come between a preposition and its object are adjectives. Have your student consider whether 'his' answers any of the questions for adjectives." Point to the list of adjective questions if necessary. When the student says, "Yes: whose." Say, "Good. 'His' answers 'whose,' so 'his' is an adjective. Circle it."

Continuing backwards, the next unmarked word, 'foolish' answers "What kind of fowl?," making it an adjective, and 'The,' which is an article, always answers, "Which one?" Students will quickly learn that they can circle every article.[2]

This particular sentence contains no adverbs; however, on subsequent sentences, retain this order: work through the adjective questions first and only then consider the adverb questions. This facilitates the analysis process since most sentences contain more adjectives than adverbs.

Allow your student to use a "cheat sheet" with a list of the questions for identifying adjectives and adverbs until these are firmly engrained in his or her mind.

D.O.   prep   o.p.

The sentence now looks like this: **The** <u>fox</u> <u>lured</u> **the foolish** fowl (to **his** den).

---

[2] Students should circle adjectives; however, for ease of formatting, adjectives in my examples appear in bold.

Preliminary Lesson IV: Indirect Objects

Directions: Give your student the list of prepositions, conjunctions, adjectives and adverbs. Then follow the process for determining the verb, subject, direct object, any prepositional phrases, and finally adjectives and adverbs in the sentences below.

> At practice yesterday, Ted threw Jim the ball.
> The doctor prescribed William some strong medicine.
> My sister showed me about a billion pictures of her new baby.
> The pastry chef gave her dough a sprinkle of flour.
> Madge told Mildred all the boring details about her family vacation.
> The evil minion gave the cute puppy a kick in the ribs.
> The supposedly nutritious energy bar gave Shane a terrible stomachache.
> The senior editor offered junior reporter a raise and a promotion.

Process for Analysis

1. Taking the first sentence as an example, ask: "What is the verb in this sentence? What happened? Who did what?"

2. Once the student identifies 'threw' as the verb, say, "Yes: double-underline 'threw.' Next: Who or what threw?"

3. Once the student says, "Ted," say, "Yes: 'Ted' is the subject; underline 'Ted.' Now: Ted threw who or what?"

4. Most students will see the obvious flaw in answering, 'Jim', but if your student says 'Jim,' ask, "Ted threw Jim?" The student, hearing this, will correct his or her answer and say, "No: Ted threw the ball." Say: "Yes: 'ball' is the direct object. Write 'D.O.' above it. Now: you already noticed another object, Jim. Jim is the indirect object in this sentence. The indirect object in a sentence receives the direct object. Did Jim receive the ball in this sentence? If so, write I.O. above Jim."

5. "Next: Do you see any prepositional phrases?" By now, the student may volunteer the entire phrase, 'at practice' and probably know to put parentheses around it and label both parts.

6. Finally: walk your student through discerning whether each of the remaining words are adjectives or adverbs using the questions on page 126 as a guide.

The sentence now looks like this: (At practice) [yesterday], <u>Ted</u> <u><u>threw</u></u> Jim **the** ball.

prep o.p.   I.O.   D.O.

At this point, your student should be able to identify the subject, verb, and direct object as well as any indirect objects, prepositional phrases, adjectives, and adverbs in any sentence. You can now use this process to analyze any of the simple sentences you dictate from your student's favorite books.

LEVEL 1. SIMPLE, TRANSITIVE SENTENCES

First, make sure your student understands all of the potential ingredients in an independent clause by going over each of the preliminary levels. Then, begin dictating sentences from passages you read to your student as described in Chapter 2. Here's an example of a lesson you might devise.

Excerpt from "The Great Mouse Plot," found in Roald Dahl's memoir, *Boy*.

My four friends and I had come across a loose floor-board at the back of the classroom, and when we prised it up with the blade of a pocket-knife, we discovered a big hollow space underneath. This, we decided, would be our secret hiding place for sweets and other small treasures such as conkers and monkey-nuts and birds' eggs. Every afternoon, when the last lesson was over, the five of us would wait until the classroom had emptied, then we would lift up the floor-board and examine our secret hoard, perhaps adding to it or taking something away.

One day, when we lifted it up, we found a dead mouse lying among our treasures. It was an exciting discovery. Thwaites took it out by its tail and waved it in front of our faces. "What shall we do with it?" he cried.

'It stinks!" someone shouted. "Throw it out of the window quick!"

"Hold on a tick," I said. "Don't throw it away."

Thwaites hesitated. They all looked at me.

When writing about oneself, one must strive to be truthful. Truth is more important than modesty. I must tell you, therefore, that it was I and I alone who had the idea for the great and daring Mouse Plot. We all have our moments of brilliance and glory, and this was mine.

"Why don't we," I said, "Slip it into one of Mrs. Pratchett's jars of sweets? Then when she puts her dirty hand in to grab a handful, she'll grab a stinky dead mouse instead."

The other four stared at me in wonder. Then, as the sheer genius of the plot began to sink in, they all started grinning. They slapped me on the back. They cheered me and danced around the classroom. "We'll do it today!" they cried. "We'll do it on the way home! You had the idea," they said to me, "so you can be the one to put the mouse in the jar."

Twaites handed the mouse to me. I put it into my trouser pocket. Then the five of us left the school, crossed the village green, and headed for the sweet-shop. (p. 35 – 36)

Sentences for Dictation and Grammatical Analysis

                                                     D.O.   D.O.

1. [Every afternoon], we would lift [up] the floor-board and examine our secret hoard.

                               D.O.   D.O.   prep   o.p.

2. [One day], when we lifted it [up], we found a dead mouse lying (among our treasures).

                     D.O.   prep   o.p.   D.O. prep o.p.   prep   o.p.

3. Thwaites took it [out] (by its tail) and waved it (in front) (of our faces).

                     D.O.   prep o.p.   o.p.

4. We all have our moments (of brilliance and glory).

                        prep o.p. prep   o.p.

5. The other four stared (at me) (in wonder).

                    D.O.   prep.   o.p.

6. They cheered me and danced (around the classroom).

            D.O. prep   o.p.

7. We'll do it (on the way) [home]!

                   D.O.   prep o.p.

8. Thwaites handed the mouse (to me).

            D.O. prep   o.p.

9. I put it (into my trouser pocket).

             prep o.p.   D.O.   D.O.   prep   o.p.

10. [Then] the five (of us) left the school, crossed the village green, and headed (for the sweet-

    shop).

LEVEL 2: COMPOUND AND COMPLEX SENTENCES.

Compound sentences combine two independent clauses with a coordinating conjunction; complex sentences combine a main clause and a subordinate clause with a subordinating conjunction. Grammatically, the patterns for both are similar.

Compound Sentences

In a compound sentence, two independent clauses are combined with a coordinating conjunction such as *and, but, or, so, yet,* and *for.*

- This is an independent clause, <u>and</u> this is also an independent clause.

Complex Sentences

In a complex sentence, an independent clause and dependent clause are combined with a subordinating conjunction such as *because, since, while, when, whereas,* and so on.

- This is an independent clause, <u>while</u> this is a dependent clause.

- <u>Because</u> this subordinating conjunction appears at the beginning of this clause, this sentence takes a comma before the main clause.

This point brings us to a few important yet frequently broken comma rules:

Comma Rules for Compound and Complex Sentences

1. Place a comma before the coordinating conjunction in a compound sentence.

2. Place a comma before the main clause of a complex sentence that begins with a subordinating conjunction.

3. Do not use a comma before a dependent clause that follows the independent clause except to show contrast or a reversal in the direction of the sentence's logic, as here:

    Jill wears a dress to parties, <u>whereas</u> Stephanie wears pants.

4. Subordinating conjunctions that often indicate contrast include: *although, even though, though, since, while* (when it means whereas) and (you guessed it) *whereas.*

Sample Lesson for Compound and Complex Sentences

Excerpt from *Charlotte's Web* by E.B. White:

Far into the night, while the other creatures slept, Charlotte worked on her web. First she ripped out a few of the orb lines near the center. She left the radial lines alone, as they were needed for support. As she worked, her eight legs were a great help to her. So were her teeth. She loved to weave and she was an expert at it. When she was finished ripping things out, her web looked something like this: [picture in the text]

A spider can produce several kinds of thread. She uses a dry, tough thread for foundation lines, and she uses a sticky thread for snare lines—the ones that catch and hold insects. Charlotte decided to use her dry thread for writing the new message.

"If I write the word 'Terrific' with sticky thread," she thought, "every bug that comes along will get stuck in it and spoil the effect."

Charlotte climbed to a point at the top of the left hand side of the web. Swinging her spinnerets into the position, she attached her thread and then dropped down. As she dropped, her spinning tubes went into action and she let out thread. At the bottom, she attached the thread. This formed the upright part of the letter T. Charlotte was not satisfied, however. She climbed up and made another attachment, right next to the first. Then she carried the line down, so that she had a double line instead of a single line. "It will show up better if I make the whole thing with double lines."

She climbed back up, moved over about an inch to the left, touched her spinnerets to the web, and then carried a line across to the right, forming the top of the T. She repeated this, making it double. Her eight legs were very busy helping. (p. 92-93)

Sentences for Dictation and Grammatical Analysis

1. [Far] (into **the** night), <u>while</u> **the other** <u>creatures</u> <u>slept</u>, <u>Charlotte</u> <u>worked</u> (on **her** web).

2. [First] <u>she</u> <u>ripped</u> [out] **a** few (of **the orb** lines) (near **the** center).

3. **A** <u>spider</u> <u>can produce</u> **several** kinds (of thread).

                   D.O.   prep   o.p.   D.O.   prep .

4. She uses **a dry, tough** thread (for **foundation** lines), and she uses **a sticky** thread (for **snare**

     o.p.

lines).

                      prep   o.p.   prep   o.p.   prep   o.p.   prep   o.p.

5. Charlotte climbed (to **a** point) (at **the** top) (of **the left hand** side) (of **the** web).

                                   prep   o.p.   D.O.

6. As she dropped, **her spinning** tubes went (into action) and she let [out] thread.

     prep   o.p.   D.O.

7. (At **the** bottom), she attached **the** thread.

                       D.O. prep   o.p. appositive[3]

8. This formed **the upright** part (of **the** letter T).

                    D.O.   D.O. complex prep   o.p.

9. [Then] she carried **the** line [down], so that she had **a double** line (instead of **a single** line).

                             prep   o.p.   prep o.p.   D.O.

10. She climbed [back] [up], moved [over] (about **an** inch) (to **the** left), touched **her** spinnerets

     prep   o.p.   D.O.   prep   o.p.

(to **the** web), and [then] carried **a** line [across] (to **the** right).

---

[3] An appositive gives a more specific name to a noun in a sentence: in this case, 'T' re-names 'letter.'

LEVEL 3. LINKING VERBS AND COMPLEMENTS

Unlike active verbs, linking verbs describe or define subjects by linking them to nouns and adjectives. The most common linking verb is the verb 'to be' and its conjugations: am, are, is, was, were, be, being, been. Linking verbs never have direct objects; rather, they "link" subjects to either a noun or an adjective that complement the subject. Label linking verbs and complements like this:

        LV   LVC-N   LV   LVC-A

Noun: **An <u>adult</u> <u>is</u> a mature** person. Adjective: **Barn <u>owls</u> <u>are</u>** awesome!

Less common linking verbs can be remembered with the acronym GRABS:

Grow, remain, appear, remain, become, seem

Also, verbs that describe the physical senses sometimes act as linking verbs:

Appear, look, sound, smell, feel, taste

Sometimes, GRABS and sensing verbs are active verbs, and sometimes they're linking verbs. You can tell the difference by asking if the subject is literally doing the action of the verb. Another way to tell is by whether you can substitute a conjugation of 'to be,' 'become,' or 'seem' for the verb. If you can, then the verb is linking. The following sentences use a few verbs once each way.

I tasted the hot pizza. *('Tasted' is active since I literally tasted the pizza.)*

The pizza tasted delicious. *('Tasted' is linking; I could just as well say, "The pizza was delicious.")*

My mother grows daisies in her garden. *('Grows' is active.)*

She grows weary of all the weeding. *('Grows' is linking since I could substitute 'becomes.')*

The food looked edible at first glance. *(The food seemed to be edible at first glance.)*

Then the hungry camper looked closer. *(The camper literally looked; 'looked' is active.)*

TIP: Do not confuse linking verbs with active progressive verbs, which often take a form of the verb 'to be' as a helping verb for the main, active verb: For instance:

I am writing this sentence as I type. *('Am' is the helping verb, 'writing' is the action in progress)*

A phone was ringing in the background. *('Was' is the helping verb, 'ringing' was the action.)*

Sample Lesson: Linking Verbs

First, make sure your student can identify the function of every word in a simple independent clause as described in Level I. Then, allow your student access to the Conjunctions Cheat Sheet and begin dictating sentences from passages as described in Chapter 2. Here's an example of a lesson you might devise.

Excerpt from *Farmer Boy*, by Lauren Ingalls Wilder:

> **The cold was cruel. The night was black and still, and the stars were tiny sparkles in the sky. Almanzo was glad to get into the big kitchen, warm with fire and candle-light. He was very hungry.**
>
> **Soft water from the rain-barrel was warming on the stove. First Father, then Royal, then Almanzo took his turn at the wash-basin on the bench by the door. Almanzo wiped on the linen roller-towel, then standing before the little mirror on the wall he parted his wet hair and combed it smoothly down.**
>
> **The kitchen was full of hoopskirts, balancing and swirling. Eliza Jane and Alice were hurrying to dish up supper. The salty brown smell of frying ham made Almanzo's stomach gnaw inside him.**
>
> **He stopped just a minute in the pantry door. Mother was straining the milk, at the far end of the long pantry; her back was toward him. The shelves on both sides were loaded with good things to eat. Big yellow cheeses were stacked there, and large brown cakes of maple sugar, and four large cakes, and one whole shelf full of pies. One of the pies was cut, and a little piece of crust was temptingly broken off; it would never be missed.**
>
> **Almanzo hadn't even moved yet. But Eliza Jane cried out: "Almanzo, you stop that! Mother!"**
>
> **Mother didn't turn around. She said:**
>
> **"Leave that be, Almanzo. You'll spoil your supper."**
>
> **That was so senseless that it made Almanzo mad. One little bite couldn't spoil a supper. He was starving, and they wouldn't let him eat anything until they had put it on the table.** (p. 23-24)

Sentences for Dictation and Grammatical Analysis

   LV LVC-A LVC-A   LV LVC-N prep o.p.

1. **The** <u>night</u> <u>was</u> **black** <u>and</u> **still,** <u>and</u> **the** <u>stars</u> <u>were</u> **tiny** sparkles (in **the** sky).

   LV LVC-A prep   o.p.   prep o.p.   o.p.

2. <u>Almanzo</u> <u>was</u> **glad** [to get]⁴ (into **the big** kitchen), **warm** (with fire <u>and</u> candle-light).

    prep   o.p.   prep o.p.

3. **Soft** <u>water</u> (from **the** rain-barrel) <u>was warming</u> (on **the** stove).

       D.O. prep o.p. prep   o.p.   LV LVC-A prep

4. <u>Mother</u> <u>was straining</u> **the** milk, (at **the far** end) (of **the long** pantry); **her** <u>back</u> <u>was</u> (toward

 o.p.

him).⁵

    prep   o.p. LV LVC-A prep   o.p. Adjective Infinitive

5. **The** <u>shelves</u> (on **both** sides) <u>were</u> **loaded (**with **good** things) **to eat.**

     LV LVC-A   prep   o.p.

6. **Big yellow** <u>cheeses</u> <u>were</u> **stacked** [there], <u>and</u> **large brown** <u>cakes</u> (of **maple** sugar), <u>and</u> **four**

          prep o.p.

large <u>cakes,</u> <u>and</u> **one whole** <u>shelf</u> **full (**of pies).

    prep o.p. LV LVC-A   prep o.p. LV   LVC-A

7. <u>One</u> (of **the** pies) <u>was</u> cut, <u>and</u> **a little** <u>piece</u> (of crust) <u>was</u> [temptingly] **broken** [off].

   LV LVC-A   D.O. phrase   D.O. prep   o.p.

8. <u>He</u> <u>was</u> **starving,** <u>and</u> <u>they</u> <u>would</u>[n't] <u>let</u> him eat anything <u>until</u> <u>they</u> <u>had put</u> it (on **the** table).

---

⁴ Ignore 'to get' in your grammar analysis or explain that it is an infinitive acting like an adverb.
⁵ As you will soon learn, a prepositional phrase usually acts as either an adjective or an adverb. Here, a prepositional phrase serves as the linking verb complement adjective.

Linking Verbs, Part II: Transitive vs. Intransitive; Active vs. Passive Voice

By now, you will have observed that many sentences have no direct object nor do they need one when the verb is intransitive and the action of the verb does not apply to any object, as here:

The Christmas lights twinkled. *(There is no answer for, "Lights twinkled who or what?")*

Some verbs may be transitive or intransitive: "I run" is intransitive; "I run a store" is transitive. Linking verbs are intransitive because no object receives the action of the verb.

Transitive: I taste the pizza. *(The action of tasting applies to the object, 'pizza'.)*

Intransitive: The pizza is delicious. *(No object receives the action from the verb, 'is'.)*

The Passive Voice

Some linking verb sentences are written in the passive voice. In the passive voice, action is implied, but no actor performs it, although the actor sometimes appears in a prepositional phrase.

The cookies were baked yesterday. *(We don't know who baked the cookies; there's no actor.)*

The cookies were baked yesterday by Jill's grandmother. *(Jill's grandmother is the actor.)*

The passive voice tends to obscure information; however, writers sometimes choose to use it for that very reason, as in the fable on page 113. In your analysis, you will sometimes be forced to decide whether a past participle reflects the passive voice or whether the past participle is acting as a linking verb complement adjective.

The potatoes were baked, not mashed.

The potatoes were baked in an oven, not in the microwave.

The answer lies in whether you could supply a subject (try 'someone' as a generic subject) and convert the sentence into an active sentence: <u>*Someone*</u> <u>baked</u> the potatoes, not mashed. (Hmmm: the point of this sentence was probably the nature of the potatoes: 'baked' and 'mashed' are probably best designated as linking verb complement adjectives.)

Someone baked the potatoes in an oven, not in the microwave. (This conveys essentially the same point, only more actively. The original sentence was passive.) Whether a past participle following a linking verb is a complement or reflects the passive voice is a subtle distinction: don't worry about being 100% certain about these; rather, consider them opportunities to discuss subtleties of meaning.

LEVEL 4: PHRASES AND THEIR FUNCTIONS

A phrase is a group of words that together function as a single noun, adjective, or adverb. Students will learn to identify five kinds of phrases:

1. Prepositional phrases

2. Participial phrases

3. Infinitive phrases

4. Gerund phrases

5. Absolute phrases

Prepositional Phrase Functions

Of course, students have already discovered prepositional phrases. In most sentences, a prepositional phrase will function as either an adjective or an adverb. What the prepositional phrase is doing is a matter of observing what the prepositional phrase is describing.

Since students are familiar with prepositional phrases by now, this lesson will only involve suggesting that students (a) draw an arrow from the prepositional phrase to whatever it is describing and (b) observe whether the prepositional phrases functions as an adjective or adverb, based on what the phrase is modifying.

Assess Progress

This is a good point to stop and assess how many prompts your student needs to complete the process. Can your student follow the process without prompts? For instance, if you say nothing, does he or she first look for the verb and then the subject? Can he or she find prepositional phrases without help? Does your student know the difference between adjectives and adverbs?

The next lessons involve some of the concepts that confuse students most. If your student is still depending heavily on prompts from you, stop here and just practice until your student demonstrates confidence in analyzing independently.

Participial Phrases

Participial phrases are formed with either the present participle or the past participle of a verb. If you've forgotten what these forms look like, this chart will remind you:

Infinitive	Present Participle	Past Participle (* are irregular verbs)
To Do	Doing	Done*
To Make	Making	Made*
To See	Seeing	Seen*
To Fluctuate	Fluctuating	Fluctuated
To Cook	Cooking	Cooked

Although participles are sometimes used by themselves as adjectives, many times an adverb, object, or prepositional phrase completes their meaning, converting them into participial phrases.

Bobbing and weaving skillfully, the boxer evaded his opponent's jabs.

A participial phrase preceding a clause should describe the clause's subject and a comma should separate it from the sentence's main clause, as in the sentence above.

When the participial phrase comes after the noun it modifies, you'll need a comma to show where it begins and to suggest a pause to readers that intuitively tells them that the phrase modifies something that appeared earlier in the sentence, as in the sentence below:

The bakery worker kneaded the dough steadily, **blinking in the floury dust.**

Similarly, when you interrupt the subject and verb of a sentence with a participial phrase that shows simultaneous action, you'll need to set the phrase off with commas, as here:

The bakery worker, **blinking in the floury dust**, kneaded the dough steadily.

Participial phrases that show simultaneous action like these are adjectives because they describe a noun, but they are unusual in that they don't really answer any of the four questions that adjectives normally answer. Participial phrases that do answer one of the four adjective questions generally don't need to be set off with commas in the same way:

The **recently hired** baker worker knew practically nothing about making bread.

Students can treat participial phrases as a single unit and simply circle the whole thing.

Excerpt from *The Hobbit*, by J.R.R. Tolkien:

> **To the end of his days Bilbo could never remember how he found himself outside, without a hat, walking-stick or any money, or anything that he usually took when he went out; leaving his second breakfast half-finished and quite unwashed-up, pushing his keys into Gandalf's hands, and running as fast as his furry feet could carry him down the lane, past the great Mill, across The Water, and then on for a whole mile or more.**

> **Very puffed he was, when he got to Bywater just on the stroke of eleven, and found he had come without a pocket-handkerchief!**

> **"Bravo!" said Balin who was standing at the inn door looking out for him.** (p. 41 – 42)

Sentence for Dictation and Grammatical Analysis

prep   o.p.   prep   o.p.

(To **the** end) (of **his** days) <u>Bilbo</u> <u>could</u> [never] <u>remember</u>

----------D.O. (Noun Clause) ----------   prep   o.p.   o.p.   o.p.

how <u>he</u> <u>found</u> himself [outside], (without **a** hat, walking-stick <u>or</u> **any** money,

o.p.   (this is an adjective clause, but your student will be able to identify the parts of speech within it)

<u>or</u> anything <u>that</u> <u>he</u> [usually] <u>took</u> <u>when</u> <u>he</u> <u>went</u> [out]);

participial   object of participial   (This entire phrase should be circled and an arrow drawn to Bilbo, whom it describes)

leaving **his second** breakfast

(both of these participles describe 'breakfast')

half-finished <u>and</u> [quite] **unwashed-up,**

participial   object   prep   o.p.   (Again, circle entire participial phrase and draw an arrow to Bilbo)

pushing **his** keys (into **Gandalf's** hands), <u>and</u>

participial   D.O.   (Circle from 'running' through the end of the sentence as one long participial phrase.)

running <u>as fast as</u> **his furry** <u>feet</u> <u>could carry</u> him

prep   o.p.   prep   o.p.   prep   o.p.

(down **the** lane), (past **the** Great Mill), (across The Water), <u>and</u> [then] [on]

prep   o.p.

(for **a whole** mile) <u>or</u> **more.**

Infinitive Phrases

An infinitive (or infinitive phrase) begins with 'to' (for example: to do, to make) and can function as a subject, direct object, adjective, or adverb—anything, really, except a verb.

I don't have time **to bake cookies** today.

('To bake cookies' is an adjective infinitive phrase; it describes what kind of time I don't have.)

Bilbo wanted *to impress the dwarves* by tricking Smaug.

(Direct Object Infinitive Phrase: answers what Bilbo wanted)

To tame a dragon, first shoot one down from the sky. *('To tame a dragon' is an adverb infinitive phrase: it answers why you should shoot a dragon down from the sky.)*

<u>To inspire others with my awesomeness</u> is my only aim.

(This is an infinitive phrase noun; it answers the question, "What is my only aim?")

TIP: Be careful not to confuse infinitives with prepositional phrases that begin with the preposition, 'to.' 'To' is a preposition when followed by a noun.

In 1969, America sent three astronauts to the moon. *('To the moon' is a prepositional phrase.)*

To walk on the moon was Buzz Aldrin's dream. *('To walk on the moon' is an infinitive phrase.)*

Excerpt from *Aesop's Fables*

> **For many years the mice had been living in constant dread of their enemy, the cat. They decided to call a meeting to determine the best means of handling the situation. Many plans were discussed and rejected.**
>
> **At last a young mouse got up. "I propose," said he, looking very important, "that a bell be hung around the cat's neck. Then whenever the cat approaches, we always have notice of her presence, and so be able to escape."**
>
> **The young mouse sat down amidst tremendous applause. The suggestion was put to a motion and passed almost unanimously.**
>
> **But just then an old mouse, who had sat silent all the while, rose to his feet and said, "My friends, it takes a young mouse to think of a plan so ingenious and yet so simple. With a bell about the cat's neck to warn us we shall all be safe. I have but one brief question to put to the supporters of the plan: Which one of you is going to bell the cat?"**
>
> **Moral: It is one thing to propose, another to execute.** (p. 12)

Sentences for Dictation and Grammatical Analysis

prep   o.p.   prep   o.p.   prep   o.p.   appositive

(For **many** years) the <u>mice</u> <u>had been living</u> (in **constant** dread) (of **their** enemy, **the** cat).

                    Infinitive D.O. phrase   (Infinitive adverb phrase answers "Why they decided to call a meeting".)

<u>They</u> <u>decided</u> to call a meeting [to determine the best means of handling the situation].

prep o.p.   participial phrase describing 'he'   LV

(At last) **a** young <u>mouse</u> <u>got</u> [up]. "<u>I</u> <u>propose</u>," said <u>he</u>, **looking very important**, "<u>that</u> **a** <u>bell</u> <u>be</u>

LVC-A   prep   o.p.

<u>hung</u> (around **the cat's** neck).

                                              D.O.   prep   o.p.   LV

[Then] <u>whenever</u> **the** <u>cat</u> <u>approaches</u>, <u>we</u> [always] <u>shall have</u> notice (of **her** presence), <u>and</u> [so] <u>be</u>

LVC-A Infinitive adverb

able [to escape]."

                          LV LVC-A prep   o.p.

The <u>suggestion</u> <u>was put</u> (to **a** motion) <u>and</u> <u>passed</u> [almost] [unanimously].

                                       prep   o.p.   noun of direct address   D.O.

<u>But</u> [just] [then] **an old** <u>mouse</u> <u>rose</u> (to **his** feet) <u>and</u> <u>said</u>, "My friends, <u>it</u> <u>takes</u> **a young** mouse

Infinitive adverb phrase answers why it takes a young mouse.

[to think] (of a plan) [so] **ingenious** <u>and</u> [yet] [so] **simple**.

                           D.O.   Inf. Adj. prep   o.p.   prep   o.p.

<u>I</u> <u>have</u> [but] **one brief** question to put (to **the** supporters) (of **the** plan):

                    prep o.p.   Infinitive phrase; 'the cat' is the object of the infinitive phrase.

<u>Which</u> one (of you) <u>is going</u> [to bell the cat]?"

                LV   LVC-N Inf. Appositive   Inf. Appositive (Appositives re-name "thing.")

Moral: <u>It</u> <u>is</u> **one** thing *to propose,* **another** *to execute.*

Gerund Phrases

A gerund is a verbal, which means that it is formed from a verb. A gerund always ends in "–ing" and functions as a noun.

Simple Gerund Subject: *Skiing* is fun!

Sometimes, the gerund will have a complement or a completer, making it a gerund phrase:

Gerund phrase subject: *Running marathons* takes perseverance.

Either the gerund or the gerund phrase may serve as any noun in a sentence: subject, direct object, object of a preposition, appositive, etc.

Subject: *Yawning* in the middle of a lecture is a sign of boredom.

Direct Objects: Dentists recommend *brushing and flossing* regularly.

Linking verb complements: Two of my hobbies are *reading and gardening.*

Subject and object of preposition:

- *Gaining weight* is a direct consequence of *eating junk food.*

- *Picking raspberries* requires a lot of *stooping and bending.*

Tip: Do not confuse gerunds (which are always nouns) with progressive verbs, which show action in progress, or participles, which always act as adjectives.

Progressive Verb: The doctor <u>is recommending</u> Vitamin D to his patient.

Participial Phrase: **Juggling oranges**, the teacher explained gravity to his class.

Fun Fact: While all gerunds end with "–ing", not every noun with an "–ing" ending is a gerund. Gerunds conceptualize the activity of a verb, whereas some nouns ending in "ing" represent concrete objects.

Not a gerund: The *building* obstructed our view. (Building is a concrete object.)

Gerund: *Building sand castles* is fun! (Building sand castles conceptualizes activity.)

Gerund: *Writing books* takes dedication.

Not a gerund: Shakespeare's *writings* have stood the test of time.

Excerpt from *The Wind and the Willows* by Kenneth Grahame:

> **"Well, well," said the Rat. "I suppose we ought to be moving. I wonder which of us had better pack the luncheon-basket?" He did not speak as if he was frightfully eager for the treat.**

"O, please let me," said the Mole. So, of course, the Rat let him.

Packing the basket was not quite such pleasant work as unpacking the basket. It never is. But the Mole was bent on enjoying everything, and although just when he had got the basket packed and strapped up tightly he saw a plate staring up at him from the grass, and when the job had been done again the Rat pointed out a fork which anybody ought to have seen, and last of all, behold! The mustard-pot, which he had been sitting on without knowing it – still, somehow, the thing got finished at last, without much loss of temper. (p. 14)

A Very Long Sentence for Dictation and Grammatical Analysis

Gerund phrase subject   LV   LVC-N   prep   gerund phrase o.p.

Packing the basket <u>was</u> [not] [quite] [such] **pleasant** work (as *unpacking the basket*).

LV LVC-A prep   gerund phrase o.p.

<u>But</u> **the** <u>Mole</u> <u>was</u> bent (on *enjoying everything*), <u>and</u>

D.O.   (this participle and participial phrase both describe basket)

<u>although</u> [just] <u>when</u> <u>he</u> <u>had got</u> **the** basket **packed and strapped [up] [tightly]**

D.O.   (this participial phrase describes the plate)   LV LVC-A

<u>he</u> <u>saw</u> **a** plate **staring** [up] (at him) (from **the** grass), <u>and</u> <u>when</u> **the** <u>job</u> <u>had been done</u> [again]

                    prep   o.p.   Infinitive phrase   prep o.p. Interjection!

the <u>Rat</u> <u>pointed</u> (out **a** fork) <u>which</u> <u>anybody</u> <u>ought</u> [to have seen], <u>and</u> **last** (of all), behold!

            D.O. (D.O. of "saw" above, I think)   prep   gerund phrase o.p.

the mustard-pot, <u>which</u> <u>he</u> <u>had been sitting</u> [on] (without *knowing it*) –

                LV⁶   LVC-A   prep o.p.

[still], [somehow], **the** <u>thing</u> <u>got</u> **finished** (at last),

prep   o.p.   prep   o.p.

(without **much** loss) (of temper).

---

6 'Got' isn't usually a linking verb, but you can substitute 'was' in this sentence without changing the meaning, so I'm treating it like one. Sentences like this one make you think about how a word's being used.

Absolute Phrases

Absolute phrases combine a noun and a participial phrase but lack a verb; unlike participial phrases, however, they refer to no specific noun in the sentence.

The storm having destroyed the neighborhood, the people stood gaping in the street.

The emergency room having been busy all night, the doctor looked bleary eyed.

Because absolute phrases occur rarely and may be treated almost exactly as participial phrases, I'm not including any sample lessons for them. Simply be aware of them, especially as your student begins to demonstrate confidence with all of the preceding concepts, so that you can teach the concept when you happen upon one in a passage for dictation.

LEVEL 5. COMPLEX SENTENCES WITH DEPENDENT CLAUSES

The first type of dependent clause is the adverb clause, which your student will already know from the lesson on complex sentences. Adverb clauses answer one of the adverb questions about the main clause: when, where, how, how much, plus a bonus one: why. Adverb clauses begin with a subordinating conjunction.

Begin your study of dependent clauses by explaining the adverb clause and its function in a sentence. If you like, you may have students bracket off dependent adverb clauses as well as identify the parts of speech within the clause. Since your student already knows adverb clauses, he or she will probably be ready to move on to adjective clauses almost immediately.

Adjective Clauses

Like adverb clauses, adjective clauses contain a subject and verb, must be attached to an independent clause, and need some kind of connector to the main sentence. Unlike the adverb clause, this connector is sometimes implied. For instance, compare these sentences:

Connector present: The classes **that I liked best in high school** were foreign languages.

Connector implied: The classes **I liked best in high school** were foreign languages.

Adjective clauses begin with either a relative pronoun or a subordinating conjunction; in analysis work, go ahead and treat both as conjunctions, since both serve connecting functions:

Relative Pronouns: **Who, Whom, Whose, That, Which**

Subordinating Conjunctions: **Where, When, Since, While**

Ex: That is the house **where my mother grew up**. *('Where my mother grew up' describes the house.)*

Essential versus Inessential Clauses

Punctuating adjectives clauses confuses some people because the rule is that they must be set off with commas when they are inessential to the meaning of the sentence. But many people ask, "What is essential?" I like Sister Miriam Joseph's explanation here: "If a modifier describes in order to point out, it is a definitive . . . if the individual [or thing] is already designated by a proper name [or by other means], the modifier no longer needed to point out the individual, [and it] becomes . . . descriptive" (p. 60). Merely descriptive clauses are the ones that need to be set off with commas.

Example 1: Laura Ingalls Wilder's book *Farmer Boy* is about her husband, Almanzo. *(Farmer Boy points out which book is meant; it is definitive and thus essential.)*

Example 2: Laura Ingalls Wilder's books, which remain popular today, mostly describe her own childhood. *("Which remain popular today" does not designate or point out which but rather describes Laura Ingalls Wilder's books; the clause is descriptive and thus inessential to the sentence, requiring commas.)*

Excerpt from *The Wizard of Oz* by L. Frank Baum:

> The Winged Monkeys seized the Tin Woodman and carried him through the air until they were over a country thickly covered with sharp rocks. Here they dropped the poor Woodman, who fell a great distance to the rocks, where he lay so battered and dented that he could neither move nor groan.

> Others of the Monkeys caught the Scarecrow, and with their long fingers pulled all of the straw out of his clothes and head. They made his hat and boots and clothes into a small bundle and threw it into the top branches of a tall tree.

> The remaining Monkeys threw pieces of stout rope around the Lion and wound many coils about his body and head and legs, until he was unable to bite or scratch or struggle in any way. Then they lifted him up and flew away with him to the Witch's castle, where he was placed in a small yard with a high iron fence around it, so that he could not escape.

> But Dorothy they did not harm at all. She stood, with Toto in her arms, watching the sad fate of her comrades and thinking it would soon be her turn. The leader of the Winged Monkeys flew up to her, his long, hairy arms stretched out and his ugly face grinning terribly; but he saw the mark of the Good Witch's kiss upon her forehead and stopped short, motioning the others not to touch her.

> 'We dare not harm this little girl,' he said to them, 'for she is protected by the Power of Good, and that is greater than the Power of Evil. All we can do is to carry her to the castle of the Wicked Witch and leave her there."

So, carefully and gently, they lifted Dorothy in their arms and carried her swiftly through the air until they came to the castle, where they set her down upon the front doorstep. (p. 83 - 84)

Sentences for Dictation and Grammatical Analysis

                        D.O.   D.O.   prep   o.p.

The Winged Monkeys seized **the** Tin Woodman and carried him (through **the** air) until they

LV   prep   o.p.[7]   prep   o.p.

were (over **a** country) [thickly] **covered** (with **sharp** rocks).

         D.O.   D.O. prep o.p.

[Here] they dropped **the poor** Woodman, who fell **a great** distance (to **the** rocks), where he lay

[so] **battered and dented** that he could neither move nor groan.

    prep   o.p.   D.O.   prep   o.p.   D.O.

Others (of **the** Monkeys) caught **the** Scarecrow, and (with **their long** fingers) pulled all

prep o.p. prep o.p.   o.p.

(of **the** straw) [out] (of **his** clothes and head).

     D.O.   D.O.   D.O. prep   o.p.   D.O.

They made **his** hat and boots and clothes (into **a small** bundle) and threw it

prep   o.p. prep o.p.

(into **the top** branches) (of **a tall** tree).

     D.O. prep o.p. prep   o.p.   D.O.

The remaining Monkeys threw pieces (of **stout** rope) (around **the** Lion) and wound **many** coils

prep o.p. o.p. o.p. LV LVC-A Infinitive Adverb phrase

(about **his** body and head and legs), until he was unable [to bite or scratch or struggle]

prep o.p.

(in **any** way).

---

[7] This prepositional phrase serves as the LVC-A.

      D.O.   prep o.p. prep   o.p.

[Then] they lifted him [up] and flew [away] (with him) (to **the Witch's** castle), where

  LV LVC-A prep   o.p.   prep   o.p.   prep o.p.

he was placed (in **a small** yard) (with **a high iron** fence) (around it), so that he could [not]

escape.

      D.O.   prep o.p.

But Dorothy they did [not] harm (at all).

      prep   o.p.   prep o.p.   (participial phrase describing "leader")

The leader (of **the** Winged Monkeys) flew [up] (to her), **his long, hairy arms stretched out**

    (participial phrase, continued)   D.O. prep   o.p.   prep

and **his ugly face grinning terribly**; but he saw the mark (of **the Good Witch's** kiss) (upon

     o.p.   (another participial phrase describing "leader")

her forehead) and stopped [short], **motioning the others not to touch her.**

                    D.O. prep   o.p.   D.O.   prep

[So], [carefully] and [gently], they lifted Dorothy (in **their** arms) and carried her [swiftly] (through

  o.p.   prep   o.p.   D.O.   prep   o.p.

the air) until they came (to **the** castle), where they set her [down] (upon **the front** doorstep).

Noun Clauses

Noun clauses are nouns; they may serve any of the noun functions in a sentence: subject, direct object, indirect object, object of preposition, or appositive. A noun clause begins with one of the following words:

        What, when, where, how, whether, why, who, whom, that

        Whatever, whenever, wherever, however, whoever, whomever

Whoever submits the best entry will win the prize.

I don't understand **why people behave rudely**.

ABRIDGED GLOSSARY OF GRAMMAR TERMS

PARTS OF SPEECH

A. Nouns are subjects, objects, and appositives in sentences. A word is a noun if it's acting like a noun in a sentence.

B. A verb describes the action of a sentence's subject, sometimes in combination with a helping verb, which indicates the verb's tense, voice, or mood. Some sentences show no action; these sentences employ linking verbs to equate a subject with a noun or adjective.

C. Adjectives describe nouns.

D. Adverbs describe verbs, adjectives, and other adverbs.

E. Conjunctions combine words, phrases, and clauses and show the relationship between whatever they combine as either of equal or unequal importance.

F. Prepositions show relationships between nouns. Occasionally, a word that normally serves as a preposition acts as an adverb, as in "Go on!", "Get off!", and "Shut up!"

G. Pronouns replace or refer to nouns in sentences.

H. Interjections have no syntax; they are exclamations: "Ouch!" "Wow!" "Hey!"

ADDITIONAL GRAMMAR TERMS

A. Phrases comprise two or more words that serve a single grammatical function. A phrase contains neither subject nor verb.

B. Clauses comprise two or more words and always contain a subject and verb.

    1. Independent Clauses contain a subject and verb and express a complete thought; they can stand alone as a sentence.

    2. Dependent Clauses contain a subject and verb but do not express a complete thought. Most dependent clauses modify either an independent clause or a noun within an independent clause. Less often, a dependent noun clause replaces a noun in an independent clause.

C. Appositives rename a noun: "The author Frank Smith did such and such," or "The colors purple and green combine to make a hideous shade of brown."

D. Nouns of Direct Address directly name the audience, often as an introductory word or interruption, requiring a comma or commas: "Alice, you are making too much noise." "I wish, Alice, that you would kindly stop coughing."

A FEW USEFUL COMMA RULES

1. Place a comma between items in a series of three or more.

   I purchased eggs, milk, and a tur-duc-hen at the store.

2. Place a comma before the coordinating conjunction in a compound sentence.

   The alarm clock blared, and Jim fell out of the bed.

3. Place a comma before the subject of the main clause in a sentence that begins with an introductory word, phrase, or dependent clause.

   Suddenly, the pitcher threw the ball.

   In his confidence, the runner had gone halfway to second base.

   By the time the runner made it back to first, the first baseman was holding the ball.

4. Place a comma before a parenthetical or tagged-on bit at the end of a sentence.

   This is an excellent sentence, right?

   Natalie fluffed the pillow, hoping more loft would help her sleep.

5. Place commas around interruptions between the subject and verb as well as between the verb and direct object or completer.

   The dog, exhausted from his adventures, slept on the floor.

   The pickled cockroach and Brussels sprout salad smelled, strangely enough, quite good.

6. Place a comma between adjectives wherever you could say 'and.'

   - Wrong: *I ate a delicious, hot dog.* ("I ate a delicious and hot dog" doesn't make sense.)

   - Right: *I ate a delicious hot dog.*

   - Right: *I ate a delicious, spicy hot dog.* ("I ate a delicious and spicy hot dog" works.)

NOUNS

A word is a noun if it's acting like a noun in a sentence; for instance, if a word is a subject, object, or an appositive, it is acting like a noun.

Noun: *Television* entertains people.

Direct Object: Eugene has a *television* in his minivan.

Appositive: Some people consider video programming, or *television*, bad for children.

Object of preposition: These people identify several problems with *television*.

Object of gerund phrase: Instead of watching *television*, they recommend reading books and playing outside.

BUT: There's something gooey all over the **television** screen. ('Television' describes screen; making it an adjective in this sentence.)

Note that words that look and seem like verbs can be nouns:

Skiing takes a lot of coordination.

Jerry's favorite summer activity is *mountain-climbing*.

PRONOUNS

Pronouns replace nouns in sentences; there are several types.

Personal pronouns

	Nominative		Objective		Possessive	
	Singular	Plural	Singular	Plural	Singular	Plural
First Person	I	We	Me	Us	My	Our
Second Person	You	You	You	You	Your	Your
Third Person	He, She, It	They	Him, Her, It	Them	His, Her, Its	Their

Demonstrative Pronouns

This	That	These	Those

Relative Pronouns

That	Which	Whom
What	Who	Whose

VERBS

Main Verbs

A main verb normally describes the action of a sentence, although sometimes, linking verbs serve to equate a subject with another noun or describe the subject with an adjective.

Active main verb: The boy chews gum. ('Chews' shows action.)

Linking Verbs

A special kind of main verb is the linking verb, which shows no action but equates or links two objects, as in, "The woman is a doctor" or an object with an attribute, as in "The woman is nice."

Common Linking Verbs: am, are, is, was, were, be, being, been.

GRABS Linking Verbs: Grow, remain, appear, remain, become, seem

Sensing Linking Verbs: Appear, look, sound, smell, feel, taste

Note that 'to be' can also function as a helping verb; GRABS and sensing verbs are sometimes active.

Helping Verbs (also called auxiliary verbs)

Helping verbs combine with main verbs to show tense, voice, or mood.

Tenses: I will finish this project tomorrow. Sally finished hers yesterday.

Voice: The hurricane devastated the town; Hilda was devastated by the news.

Mood: I would eat some grapes if there were any.

Helping verbs are always verbs in sentences. Many people find it helpful to memorize this list:

has	do	are	be	may	shall
have	did	is	being	might	could
had	does	was	been	must	should
	am	were	can	will	would

PARTS OF SPEECH CHEAT SHEET

A. Simple Prepositions (Most Common)

about	beside	like	throughout
above	besides	near	till
across	between	of	to
after	beyond	off	toward
against	but (as in except)	on	under
along	by	onto	underneath
among	despite	out	unlike
around	down	outside	until
as	except	over	unto
at	for	past	up
before	from	plus	upon
behind	in	since	with
below	inside	than	within
beneath	into	through	without

B. Participial Prepositions

assuming	concerning	during	provided	respecting
barring	considering	notwithstanding	regarding	owing to

C. Complex Prepositions

according to	by way of	in consideration of	next to
along with	contrary to	in front of	on account of
as well as	for the sake of	in regard to	out of
because of	in accordance with	in respect to	with reference to
by means of	in addition to	in spite of	with regard to
by reason of	in case of	instead of	with respect to

Coordinating Conjunctions

More common: And, But, Or

Less common: For, Nor, Yet, and So

Subordinating Conjunctions

after	as well as	inasmuch as	until
albeit	as though	once	when
although	because	since	where
as	before	than	while
as if	even though	that	why
as far as	except	so that	without
as long as	if	though	
as much as	in order that	unless	

Relative Pronouns

More common: That, which

Less common: Who whom whose what when where

Adjectives

Adjectives describe nouns. An adjective answers one of four questions:

- Whose [thing]? Ex: **Sally's** bike is red.

- How many [things]? Ex: **Nine** cats ate the tuna.

- Which [thing]? Ex: **This** towel is mine.

- What kind of [thing] is it? Ex: **Striped** shirts flatter you.

Adverbs

Adverbs describe verbs, adjectives, and other adverbs; they answer four questions:

- When? Ex: I'll phone you *later*.

- Where? Ex: My aunt lives *nearby*.

- How? Ex: Harold sings *boldly*.

- How much? Ex: Harold sings *very* boldly.

Appendix B: Reading Program Helps

This appendix is designed to help you solicit your student's input as you organize work for the reading program. It contains the following:

- Literary Preferences Questionnaire

- Reading Lists

- Library Planning Worksheet

- Reading Log Template

- Glossary of Literary Terms

- Discussion Questions

Of the items here, the literary preferences questionnaire, planning worksheet, and reading log are for your student to complete, while the reading lists are for you and your student to peruse together. The reading lists are not necessarily my recommendations, since not all of the titles represent my personal taste, but rather are intended to provide a starting point for you and your student as you discuss what kinds of books belong in his or her personal library. You will notice that some titles appear in bold; this signifies that that particular work has endured in print long enough to be considered a classic. Where applicable, I've tried to note whether a video adaptation exists that might help familiarize your student with the classic; most classics are now available in various audio formats, many of them free. I've also tried to give you a sense of how difficult books in each genre might be by listing titles by difficulty and shading selections as follows:

(No shading) Not difficult; most students would find these books comfortable to read

Average level of difficulty for most sixth graders

Intermediate level reading; probably appropriate for most seventh graders

Difficult for sixth graders, appropriate for eighth graders

Very Difficult—these books would be more appropriate for high school students

Other Factors

A few other factors that might affect whether a book might appeal to a student are indicated by the following symbols:

           ▨   Means that a book contains illustrations or visual elements

           ☺   Means that a book is considered humorous

           🎭   Means that a book is more emotional or psychological

           🏃   Means that a book has a lot of action

           ➤➤   Means that a book is fast paced

           🚭   Means "No Smoking"

Use the questionnaire on the next page to get a sense of your student's current preferences and help you zero in on the kinds of books that are most likely to engage your reader. Try to identify three genres that will really appeal: books from these categories will represent about a third of your home library. Another third will come from the books that, while not your student's first choice, might appeal enough to help your student expand his or her tastes. Try to determine books from at least six fiction genres for your initial library, and don't forget to stock a few non-fiction selections that represent intriguing topics as well.

Also consider classics with your student, and pick out a few that sound interesting. Classic literature tends to be heavy on unfamiliar terminology and slow pacing, so short stories are probably the best bet for students who want to sample a project that won't be too exhausting. Also, while I've indicated available video adaptations, remember that these sometimes slightly distort classic literary works, so in most cases, it's best to follow up watching a video adaptation by either reading the text or listening to an unabridged version of the work.

Questionnaire Instructions:

First, answer the questions; then, number the items from one to ten according to which preference matters most.

Literary Preferences Questionnaire

1. On the lines below, list the four books you liked best over the past two years.

_____   _____

_____   _____

2. Of your all-time favorite books, would you say they mostly make you laugh or cry?

Laugh   Cry

3. When you read, do new or long words force you to slow down or lose focus on the story?

Yeah—it's annoying   Sometimes   I never notice new words

4. Do you prefer books with boys or girls as the protagonist?

I prefer books about boys   Doesn't matter to me   I prefer books about girls

5. Do you prefer stories that take place in familiar, foreign or exotic, or unrealistic settings?

Familiar World   Foreign (like Africa)   Fantasy World

6. How often would you read books with lots of pictures if it were up to you?

I don't care about pictures   Sometimes   I love comic books & manga

7. Do you prefer stories where dogs act like dogs or stories where dogs talk like people?

Realistic Animals   Anthropomorphic Animals

8. If a book's title sounded good, but the book was really long, would you still read it?

Probably not.   Probably.   Sure, why not?

9. Would you say the best books are more humorous or the best books are more inspiring?

Humorous   Inspiring

Length

Take a book's length into consideration for readers who feel daunted by hefty volumes, especially when gathering books that aren't necessarily their favorite types. For books that fit their tastes, books that are a bit longer than usual are a good opportunity to really get into a book. Also, think about trying short stories as a less intimidating way to sample new genres or difficult classics.

Difficulty

The lists below are shaded to show the level of difficulty. Students who feel flustered by unfamiliar vocabulary will probably prefer books toward the top of the lists. However, as you collect books for your library, focus less on difficulty and more on taste. Most people can read more difficult books when they're appealing than when they're not, so your student will probably be able to read more difficult books in their favorite genres than they can in less preferred ones. If a book that should be appealing strikes your student as boring, it's possible that the book is still a little too hard. That's okay; put it aside, and he or she will probably enjoy it much more in a year or two.

Protagonist Gender

This item might seem inconsequential, but a protagonist's gender can tell you a lot about a book: books with male protagonists typically contain more action and excitement while books with female protagonists tend to focus more on psychological processing. Of course, there are exceptions, but be aware that boys in general will probably be more reluctant to pick up a book with a female protagonist than girls tend to be about books with male ones.

Overall Tone

The very best books make readers either laugh or cry, but a lot of books that are written for middle schoolers are primarily one or the other. A book's tone might be serious or contemplative, humorous, sarcastic, irreverent, or sardonic. In general, expect coming-of-age, historical fiction, survival and pet stories to be more of the thought-provoking or even tear-jerker variety and adventures, thrillers, science fiction, and most fantasy to be more upbeat and entertaining.

Pace

A fast-paced story has a lot of action, dialogue, and usually, frequent snippets of humor. In a fast-paced book, a lot happens fast. Most books are average-paced; they blend action, dialogue, and description very comfortably. Books that are slow-paced normally have lots of description; the characters in them don't just talk, they expound. Most classics are more or less slow-paced. These books tend to be long but worthwhile reads for students who are ready for them.

Adventure: Off to hunt the manticore and conquer the mighty river . . .

Out from Boneville by Jeff Smith: A graphic novel series about the Bone cousins' humorous adventures. ▨ ☺

Sonic the Hedgehog series by Mike Gallagher, Dave Manak, Patrick Spaziante: A comic book series based on the popular video game. ▨ ☺

The Authoritative Calvin and Hobbes by Bill Watterson: The smart but silly comic. ▨ ☺

The Gollywhopper Games by Lori Feldman: A boy competes in a toy company's contest. �

The Adventures of Captain Underpants series by Dav Pilkey: Popular irreverently humorous boy adventures with bonus comics & flipbook. ▨ ☺ ➡

The Melvin Beederman Superhero series by Greg Trine are a less irreverent option for readers who are into pseudo-superheros. ▨ ☺ ➡

The Choose Your Own Adventure series by R.A. Montgomery. An interactive series with titles such as *The Abominable Snowman, Journey Under the Sea* and *Lost on the Amazon* in which readers make decisions that affect how the story ends. 彡 ➡

Take me to the River by Will Hobbs: Two boys raft down the Rio Grande by themselves. 彡 ➡

Flush by Carl Hiaasen: A boy helps his dad catch a local polluter in the act. Similar titles by Hiassen include *Hoot* and *Scat.* 彡

Cryptid Hunters by Roland Smith: Two siblings join their archeologist uncle's hunt for cryptids (mystical creatures believed to be extinct). 彡 ➡

A Whole Nother Story by Cuthbert Soup: The quirky and humorous adventures of a family on the run from people who want to steal their time travel machine. ☺ 彡 ➡

The Adventures of the Great Brain by John Fitzgerald: Set in Utah about a hundred years ago, a boy describes his older brother's conniving ways. ☺ 彡

The Diary of a Wimpy Kid series by Jeff Kinney: The humorous adventures of a middle school boy basically trying to make good. ▨ ☺ ➡

Call it Courage by Armstrong Sperry: An islander boy sets out on a quest to prove his courage. 🐚

Congo by Michael Crichton: A quest to find rare blue diamonds becomes a survival story. 彡 ➡

The Adventures of Tom Sawyer by Mark Twain: A boy's scheme leads his friends into danger.

I'd Tell You I Love You But Then I'd Have to Kill You by Ally Carter: A girl at a spy academy meets a boy who thinks she's normal, and it's up to her to pretend she is. ☺ ➡

Mr. Midshipman Hornblower by C.S. Forester: A young man's experiences as a seaman on a British ship during the Napoleonic Wars. A&E's video Horatio Hornblower series would be a good introduction for this and other titles in the series. 🏃

Around the World in 80 Days by Jules Verne is the story of a wealthy gentleman's race against time to win a bet that he can travel around the entire world in (you guessed it) eighty days. Video adaptations include an entertaining 2004 movie starring Jackie Chan; the 1989 mini-series starring Pierce Brosnan is a little more faithful to the novel.

Going Solo by Roald Dahl: The author's experiences, training to fly a fighter plane in WWII. 🏃

Carry On, Jeeves by P.G. Wodehouse: A collection of humorous short stories about a wealthy British bachelor whose manservant is smarter than he is. A&E has adapted the stories in a series starring Stephen Fry and Hugh Laurie. ☺

Treasure Island by Robert Louis Stevenson: The classic pirate tale complete with sabotage and treasure; a number of video adaptations are available. Other classics by Stevenson include another adventure, *Kidnapped*, and the novella *The Strange Case of Dr. Jekyll and Mr. Hyde*. 🏃

The Three Musketeers by Alexandre Dumas is about a poor boy's adventures attempting to become a Musketeer. Originally written in French, English translations vary quite a bit, but William Barrow's translation tones down the explicit references in the original. The 1993 Disney film adaptation emphasizes humor in this classic. Other classics by Dumas include *The Count of Monte Cristo* and *The Man in the Iron Mask*, both of which have also been adapted into popular movies. 🏃

Ivanhoe by Sir William Scott is a historical fiction adventure story set just after the Third Crusade's failure. With a personal quest, political tension, romantic chivalry, and a cameo appearance by Robin Hood, Ivanhoe has something for everyone! It's been adapted for film many times; the 1982 Sony version is considered well-done.

Don Quixote by Miguel de Cervantes was the one of the first novels written. It's an episodic tale that describes the comic adventures of Don Quixote and his faithful squire, Sancho Panza, as they set out to revive chivalry in Medieval Spain. Although the text is very long and difficult, but you might to enjoy watching the 1973 musical adaptation, *Man of La Mancha*.

Mystery: A story built around discovering the truth (detectives optional)

The 39 Clues books by various authors: Interactive mysteries featuring sibling protagonists. 🏃 ➳

Chaderick: Not a Vampire. Not a Zombie. Not a Superhero by Lauren DW Luchsinger Fox. A boy who lives in Hero Town dreams of being superhero—but is he up to the job? ☺

The *Bunnicula* series by James Howe: A cat and dog suspect the new pet bunny's a vampire. ☺ ➳

The Adventures of Hank the Cowdog by John Erickson: A bumbling anthropomorphic cowdog and his inept deputy solve mysteries on the ranch. ☺ ➤

The Alex Rider series by Anthony Horowitz: A fourteen-year old boy is recruited to be a spy for the British Secret Service. ⚡ ➤

The Strange Case of Origami Yoda by Tom Angleberger: A boy wears an origami Yoda on his finger and talks with it. But is it real? 🀫☺➤

From the Mixed-up Files of Mrs. Basil E. Frankweiler by E. L. Konigsburg: A girl convinces her brother to run away to the Metropolitan Museum of Art, where a new art exhibit poses a mystery.

The Westing Game by Ellen Raskin: A millionaire bequests his fortune to whomever solves his own murder.

The Nancy Drew series by Carolyn Keene: The popular mysteries starring the famous female sleuth.

Science Fair by Dave Barry and Ridley Pearson: A middle school boy must stop stupid terrorists: fast-paced and funny suspense. ☺ ⚡ ➤

Murder on the Orient Express by Agatha Christie: The famous detective Hercule Poirot investigates a murder on a train in the middle of nowhere. Agatha Christie is one of the most famous mystery writers of all time. Other great titles (although it's hard to name just a few) include *And Then There Were None, Death on the Nile*, and *The Murder of Roger Ackeroyd.*

The Mysterious Benedict Society by Trenton Lee Stewart: Four pre-teens a spy on an evil schoolmaster.

The Andromeda Strain by Michael Crichton: Scientists investigate when a satellite falls to earth, killing humans who approach it. ➤

The Importance of Being Earnest by Oscar Wilde: A man lost as an infant needs to discover his identity to marry the girl of his dreams in this witty play. ☺

The Legend of Sleepy Hollow and **Rip Van Winkle** by Washington Irving: these short stories pair mystery with elements of fantasy: in one, cranky schoolmaster Ichabod Crane is chased by a Headless Horseman; in the other, a lazy man falls asleep and wakes twenty years later.

"The Fall of the House of Usher," "The Tell-Tale Heart," and Other Tales and Poems by Edgar Allan Poe is a collection of mysteriously dark, super creepy short stories.

The Adventures of Sherlock Holmes by Arthur Conan Doyle is a collection of short stories, written from the first person perspective of the famous detective's friend and assistant, Dr. John Watson. More than 211 movie adaptations have been made that feature Sherlock Holmes; however, the BBC series starring Jeremy Brett follows Conan Doyle's plots well and is considered "definitive." Try watching an episode and seeing how it compares with the corresponding short story.

Science Fiction: a story based on scientific understanding or predictions

The My Teacher is an Alien books by Bruce Coville: A girl and boy team up to expose their substitute teacher (who happens to be an alien). ☺➤

Things Not Seen by Andrew Clements: A boy whose body has become invisible befriends a blind girl.

The *Star Wars Trilogy* by George Lucas: These movie novelizations are action-packed, easy-reads. ⚡

The Martian Chronicles by Ray Bradbury: Interwoven short stories vividly describe the colonization of Mars. Classic sci-fi.

A Wrinkle in Time quartet by Madeline L'Engle: Two siblings travel in space and time to save their father and oppose an evil cosmic force.

The Missing series by Margaret Peterson Haddix: Teens investigate a mystery that sends them "hurtling through time." ➤

Have Space-Suit, Will Travel by Robert Heinlein: A boy enters a contest to win a trip to the moon but ends up kidnapped by aliens. ⚡

I, Robot by Isaac Asimov: Classic short stories about all manner of artificial intelligence (i.e., robots). Asimov's **Foundation** series is considered among the best in science fiction.

Dune by Frank Herbert: A sci-fi epic in which a boy must save his civilization.

The *Interstellar Pig* books by William Sleator: A boy is intrigued by an intergalactic role-play game. "Twilight Zone-ish."

Doctor Who: Prisoner of the Daleks by Terrance Baxendale: A tie-in novel based on the BBC series about a world-saving time traveler. ⚡

20,000 Leagues Under the Sea by Jules Verne: Classic adventure full of exploration, conservation, and revenge. Other classic science fiction works by Jules Verne include *Journey to the Center of the Earth, From the Earth to the Moon,* and *Around the World in Eighty Days.* ⚡

The Time Machine by H.G. Wells: This classic novella is probably the first story about time travel. Other classic science fiction works by H.G. Wells include *The War of the Worlds, The Invisible Man,* and *The Island of Dr. Moreau.*

2001: A Space Odyssey by Arthur C. Clarke is among the more scientifically accurate science fiction novels. The "epic" 1968 movie of the same name is famous for its special effects and soundtrack.

Frankenstein; or the Modern Prometheus by Mary Shelley is the considered by some to be the first science fiction story. In it, a scientist's experiments result in the production a living creature that turns out to be a monster. Although the book isn't terribly long, the slow pace and unfamiliar vocabulary make it somewhat challenging. Several movies have been produced, but the 1931 movie starring Boris Karloff gets the highest ratings.

Epic Fantasy: in which a protagonist confronts evil for the good of all

The Pendragon series by D.J. MacHale: A 14-year-old boy saves multiple worlds from evil. ➤

The City of Ember by Jeanne Deprau: Two teens in a post-disaster, underground refuge realize that their city's generator is running out of power. Also, see *The City of Ember: The Graphic Novel* by Jeanne Deprau and Niklaus Asker: The same story, depicted visually. ▨ ➤

The *Percy Jackson* series by Rick Riordan: A boy discovers his father is actually the Greek god Poseidon and the fate of the world rests on his half-god shoulders. ☺ ⚐ ➤

Fablehaven series by Brandon Mull: A brother and sister visiting their grandparents discover a kingdom where mythical creatures are real—and sometimes dangerous. ⚐ ➤

The *Inkheart* series by Cornelia Funke: A girl's bookbinder father "reads" characters into life

The Ranger's Apprentice series by John Flanagan: A teenaged boy learns to be a Ranger in this engaging and action-packed series. ⚐ ➤

The Chronicles of Prydain by Lloyd Alexander: A discontented pig-keeper gets accidentally waylaid and finds himself part of a quest to save his homeland from evil forces.

The Narnia Chronicles by C.S. Lewis: Classic series about four children who travel to a magical world. Disney's recent Chronicles of Narnia movies are a good introduction to the books.

Into the Land of the Unicorns by Bruce Coville: A bit darker than the title suggests, a girl is transported into a magical land where she is accompanied by a unicorn on a dangerous mission. ⚐

Watership Down by Richard Adams: Anthropomorphic epic fantasy about warring hares. Some might appreciate the cartoon movie version; however, others find the violence disturbing. ⚐ 🎬

The *Pellinor* series by Allion Croggon: A slave girl inherits a gift that enables her to save her world.

The Dark is Rising sequence by Susan Cooper: A simple family holiday turns into an Arthurian epic when siblings discover that a map in the attic is more than it seems.

The Harry Potter series by J. K. Rowling: A boy must fight an evil wizard to save the wizarding world. The first three books are about half the length of the final four. ☺ ⚐ 🎬 ➤

The Lord of the Rings by J.R.R. Tolkien: The epic fantasy about an unassuming hobbit who sets out to destroy the One Ring that the evil Sauron seeks. Also, well worth reading is Tolkien's prequel to the trilogy, **The Hobbit**. While some people love Peter Jackson's movie adaptations, I prefer the books' richer language and character development. ☺ ⚐ 🎬

The Wonderful Wizard of Oz by Frank L. Baum: A relatively short allegorical story about a girl's experiences in the fantasy land of Oz. The 1939 movie starring Judy Garland is a classic in its own right.

Anthropomorphic Fantasy: where animals teach us how to be more human

Aesop's Fables by Aesop, written by a Greek slave about 600 B.C.E., are a collection of very short stories that teach timeless truths.

Upchuck and the Rotten Willy by Bill Wallace: Fast-paced and funny chapter books. ☺ ➽

Bambi by Felix Sarten: A beautiful coming-of-age story about a deer. 🐾

The Little Prince by Antoine Saint Exupèry: Charming tales of a prince from outer space who needs humans explained. ▣ 🐾

Mrs. Frisby and the Rats of NIHM by Robert C. O'Brien: A field mouse seeks the assistance of genetically advanced rats to save her son. 🐾

The Guardians of Ga'Hoole by Kathryn Lansky: Medium length books about rival owl kingdoms. 🏃

The Warriors series by Erin Hunter: Popular fantasy series about warring feral cat clans. 🏃

Winnie the Pooh by A.A. Milne: Short stories with humorous true-to-life characters; don't assume that these stories are for little kids—Milne's stories are witty and wonderful at any age. ☺

A Dog's Life: The Autobiography of a Stray by Ann Martin: A stray dog narrates her experiences. 🐾

Black Beauty by Anna Sewell: the first of its kind, in this novel, the first-person narrator is Black Beauty himself, and he describes his experiences as he passes from owner to owner. The 1994 film adaptation is well done. 🐾

Alice in Wonderland by Lewis Carroll is a fantasy in which a girl falls down a rabbit hole and discovers a strange world with quirky characters. Several movie adaptations exist, but since Carroll's witty wording hold the work's charm more than the plot, listening to an unabridged audio version and reading along would be preferable. ☺

The Phantom Tollbooth by Norton Justin: A boy who enters a tollbooth and meets quirky characters on a series of strangely philosophical adventures.

Babe by Dick King-Smith: A pig learns to herd sheep; for once, the movie is as good as the book.

Animal Farm *by George Orwell* is an allegorical novella depicting the evils of the Communist Revolution in Russia; however, the story itself features engaging farm animal characters who overthrow human farmers and try to run the farm themselves. 🐾

The Wind in the Willows by Kenneth Grahame: Classic, whimsical tale of Ratty, Mole, Toad, and Frog's "misadventures." Many DVD adaptations exist, though the story would make for an even better read aloud.

The Jungle Book by Rudyard Kipling is a collection of character-forming short stories set in the Indian jungle; among the most famous are "Rikki Tikki Tavi" and stories featuring Mowgli, a boy raised by wolves. The Chuck Jones 1970's cartoons capture Kipling's stories faithfully.

Fairy Tale Fantasy: Charming, moral, and sometimes romantic stories

Ella Enchanted by Gail Carson Levine: Popular, unconventional retelling of Cinderella. ➔

Rapunzel's Revenge by Shannon Hale: Rapunzel gets a humorous, slightly romantic, western twist in this graphic novel. 🖼☺

Peter and the Starcatchers by Dave Barry and Ridley Pearson: A fast-paced re-telling of Peter Pan. ☺➔

Charlie and the Chocolate Factory by Roald Dahl: A tear-jerker turns knee-slapper, rags-to-riches tale told with fantastic characters.

Half Magic by Edward Eager: Four cousins find a curious coin that grants half their wishes.

Dealing with Dragons by Patricia Wrede: A tomboyish princess prefers hanging out with dragons; a fairy tale with a twist. ⸖ ➔

The Goose Girl (Books of Bayern series) by Shannon Hale: A princess loses her rightful place and must decide whether to seek justice.

The Princess Bride by William Goldman: A book with everything: pirates, giants, swordfighters, an evil prince, a beautiful peasant girl—more action than romance, but it's got that, too. ☺ ⸖ ➔

The Princess Academy by Shannon Hale: After a prophecy, common village girls prepare to become a princess, but only one will be chosen by the prince.

Peter Pan by J.M. Barrie: Charming classic about a boy who never grows up.

Tales from the Perilous Realm by J.R.R. Tolkien: Well-written, short stories about all things fantasy.

The Blue Sword by Robin McKinley: A girl is kidnapped and then mentored and trained; lots of action plus a bit of romance. This book's sequel, The Hero and the Crown, won the Newbury. ⸖

The Princess and the Goblin by George MacDonald: A princess and common boy team up against evil goblins. Also, see MacDonald's *The Princess and Curdie* and short story collections.

How to Train Your Dragon by Cressida Cromwell: A boy named Hiccup sets out to kill dragons and ends up befriending them. ☺ ⸖ ➔

The Complete Hans Christian Andersen's Fairy Tales: Classic short story collection of timeless fairy tales, back when fairy tales were written for adults, not children.

The (Red, Blue, Violet, Yellow) Fairy Book by Andrew Lang: Collections of classic fairy tales from a variety of sources.

People are Funny About their Pets. (Spoiler alert: Half of the animals die.)

Because of Winn-Dixie by Kate DeCamillo: A romp of a girl-meets-dog, dog-charms-everyone, makes-everything-better story.

The Black Stallion by Walter Farley: A survival story about a shipwrecked boy who tames a wild horse on a deserted island as well as an adventure story once they reach the mainland. 🏃

Where the Red Fern Grows by Wilson Rawls: A boy saves up to buy and train his own coonhounds in the sparsely populated Ozarks. 🏃 🎭

National Velvet by Enid Bagnold: A girl wins, trains, and races a horse in a national derby. 🏃

Gentle Ben by Walt Morey: In a twist on the typical boy-loves-dog-fare: boy befriends bear. 🎭

Misty of Chincoteague by Marguerite Henry: Two siblings save up for a Chincoteague pony at the annual auction. 🏃

The Tarantula in My Purse by Jean Craighead George: Humorous collection of memoirs about ducks, boas, skunks—you get the picture. ☺

Lassie Come Home by Eric Knight: A beloved pet is sold due to hard times but repeatedly returns to his original owners. 🎭

Old Yeller by Fred Gipson: A boy and his dog protect his family in rural Texas during his father's absence. 🏃 🎭

Big Red by Jim Kjelgaard: Another gripping adventure about a boy and his dog. 🏃

All Creatures Great and Small by James Herriot is a collection of short stories about a veterinarian's experiences doing his rounds in rural Great Britain.

Lad: A Dog by Albert Terhune: A realistic, descriptive account of a heroic Collie. 🏃

My Life in Dog Years by Gary Paulsen: A collection of memoirs about dogs that can make readers laugh and cry. ☺

The Call of the Wild by Jack London is an adventure novella about a dog named Buck that is kidnapped and sold as a sled dog during the Yukon-Klondike Gold Rush. A number of film adaptations have been made. 🏃 🎭

Rascal by Sterling North: A boy adds a raccoon to his menagerie of pets.

Born Free by Joy Adamson. A couple in Kenya raises a lion cub and releases it back into the wild. 🎭

Never Cry Wolf by Farley Mowat: A researcher dispels misconceptions about wolves in the Artic.

Survival: People fighting elements, beasts, or other people to survive

Fantastic Mr. Fox by Roald Dahl: Mr. Fox leads wild animals in a brilliant heist. (Anthropormophic.)

The Cay by Timothy Taylor: A boy, after being blinded and shipwrecked, must overcome his prejudice and depend upon a West Indian for his survival.

Avalanche by Arthur Roth: A teenage boy gets buried alive in an avalanche.

Jurassic Park by Michael Crichton: Several people are stranded on an island with dinosaurs.

The Lord of the Flies by William Golding: Stranded on a deserted island, teenage boys try to organize themselves in this disturbing modern classic.

The Shadow Children series by Margaret Peterson Haddix: In this dystopia set in a disturbing future, outlawed third-born children fight for survival.

My Side of the Mountain by Jean Craighead George: A boy runs away to the wilderness.

Sing Down the Moon by Scott O'Dell: Historical fiction about the Navajo people's loss of freedom

A Night to Remember by Walter Lord: Gripping historical account of the night the Titanic sank.

Julie of the Wolves by Jean Craig George: A girl survives among wolves on the frozen tundra.

The Island of the Blue Dolphins by Scott O'Dell: An Indian girl lives for many years alone on an island.

Hatchet by Gary Paulsen: After a plane wreck, a boy survives in the wilderness.

A Series of Unfortunate Events by Lemony Snicket: Three resourceful orphans escape their fortune-seeking relative in a series of unfortunate and generally bizarre events.

The Mysterious Island by Jules Verne: A true account of five men's survival on an island off the coast of Chile. Some consider this to be Jules Verne's masterpiece.

Robinson Crusoe by Daniel Defoe: Published in 1719, this didactic, epistolary novel was one of the first stories not to be based on mythology or previous literature. It is the original stranded-on-an-island survival tale. A few video adaptations are available.

Tarzan of the Apes by Edgar Burroughs is one of the most well-known literary characters: marooned and orphaned off the Atlantic coast of Africa, an English boy is raised by apes. The character is, in many ways, the ideal natural man, with tanned skin, athletic prowess, superior intelligence, and an exceptionally well-formed moral character as well. The book has been adapted (and parodied) in numerous movies and TV shows.

The Swiss Family Robinson by Johann Wyss: One of the first Robinson Crusoe wannabes that also became a classic: a shipwrecked family makes a deserted island their home and accumulate an impressing array of improbable pets. This book, which is somewhat episodic, makes for a wonderful read aloud. The 1960 Disney movie, while not a very faithful adaptation of the novel, is charming in its own way.

Boys Coming-of-age: Realistic stories of boys learning through experience

Al Capone Does My Shirts by Gennifer Choldenko: Forced to care for his autistic older sister while his parents work, a boy grows up on Alcatraz Island.

Holes by Louis Sachar: Falsely accused of stealing, a boy learns perseverance at a reform camp. ☺

The Outsiders by S.E. Hinton: A teen being raised by his older brothers grapples with social tension and loss. Written by a teenager, this is considered by many to be the first YA novel.

Crispin: Cross of Lead by Avi: In the fourteenth century, an orphan sets out to discover his identity.

Danny: Champion of the World by Roald Dahl: A boy conspires with his father to poach a wealthy landowner's pheasants.

The Sign of the Beaver by Elizabeth George Speare: A boy holds down his family's claim and is befriended by Indians when his parents' return is delayed.

Game by Walter Dean Myers: A high school senior pins his hopes on a basketball scholarship.

The Summer of the Monkeys by Wilson Rawls: A boy tries to capture escaped monkeys in order to get money to buy a horse.

Preacher's Boy by Katherine Paterson: A boy rebels against the pressure he feels to be a perfect preacher's son.

Shane by Jack Schaefer: A boy admires a mysterious cowboy who helps his father defend his land against a powerful rancher.

Dandelion Wine by Ray Bradbury: Semi-autobiographical novel about growing up in the Midwest.

The Red Badge of Courage by Stephen Crane is considered one of the greatest novels about the Civil War. In it, a boy struggles with cowardice so much that he hopes he gets wounded, which he thinks will prove that he's not. Although neither long nor extremely difficult, the book's slow pacing and emphasis on psychological exploration make it a challenging read.

Freak the Mighty by Rodman Philbrick: Two boys, one large but slow, the other gifted but ill, go on heroic adventures.

Boy by Roald Dahl: Charming, episodic memoirs about growing up a hundred years ago.

The Adventures of Huckleberry Finn by Mark Twain is considered by many to be one of the greatest contributions to American literature. In it, a boy runs away with a slave on a journey down the Mississippi River. Huck is often a hilarious narrator, though the book overall is thought-provoking. The characters' dialect can make the text a little challenging at times, but Twain's storytelling voice is so compelling, it's worth the extra effort. ☺

Great Expectations by Charles Dickens: A poor orphan boy inherits a fortune but his vanity and pride impoverish him. Other novels written by Dickens include *Oliver Twist*, *A Tale of Two Cities*, and *David Copperfield*; the novella, *A Christmas Carol*, is a good introduction to Dickens.

Girls Coming-of-age: Realistic stories of girls learning through experience

Smile by Raina Tegemeier: A graphic novel about a girl who has to get braces in middle school. ▨

A Year Down Yonder by Richard Peck: Set during the depression, a girl is sent to live with her quirky grandmother in a small town.

The Summer of the Swans by Lois Lowry: When her disabled brother goes missing, a brooding teen gains perspective. ✎

The Little House on the Prairie books by Laura Ingalls Wilder: I'm pretty sure you can never be too young or too old to love Laura Ingalls Wilder's books.

I Capture the Castle by Dodie Smith: Growing up in a deteriorating castle, two poor sisters dream of a better future. ☺

Heidi by Joanna Spyri: An orphan girl charms her hermit grandfather—almost sickly sweet, but for some reason you just want to read it over and over again

Rebecca of Sunnybrook Farm by Katherine Wiggins: Sent to live with spinster aunts, a girl learns to appreciate their ways.

The Anne of Green Gables series by L.M.M. Montgomery: is the first of a series of stories about an impetuous and talkative red-headed orphan Anne Shirley. Kevin Sullivan's 1980's miniseries is a good introduction to the books.

Diary of a Young Girl by Anne Frank was never meant for publication: it is literally a diary, written by a young Jewish girl who hid in the upper rooms of her father's office building during World War II. Kenneth Branaugh's 1995 DVD documentary, "Anne Frank Remembered" would be a good introduction to Anne's story. ✎

Up a Road Slowly by Irene Hunt: When her mother dies, a girl moves in with her a strict schoolteacher aunt.

The Midwife's Apprentice by Karen Cushman: An orphan taken in by a gruff midwife gradually discovers her own worth. Also see *Catherine, Called Birdy* by the same author.

Jane Eyre by Charlotte Bronte: A stubborn orphan learns personal integrity through some very unusual circumstances. The 2005 BBC adaptation is perhaps more faithful to the text than some of the others that are available, but I like the five-hour 1983 BBC version.

Northanger Abbey by Jane Austen: Enamored of gothic novels, a foolish girl suspects foul play when visiting her new friends' castle. Also, consider *Pride and Prejudice*, which many consider Austen's funniest novel. Great video adaptations include A&E's six-hour *Pride and Prejudice*, Ang Lee's *Sense and Sensibility*, Masterpiece Theater's 2008 *Northanger Abbey*, and the 1996 *Emma* starring Gwyneth Paltrow.

Little Women by Louisa May Alcott: Four sisters support one another during the Civil War. ✎

Historical Fiction: Stories that show you history as if you were there yourself

Carry On, Mr. Bowditch by Jean Lee Letham: Fiction-like biography of an indentured servant who founded modern navigation.

Nine Days a Queen by Ann Rinaldi: Lady Jane Grey, crowned Queen of England as a teenager, reigns for just nine days.

Night by Elie Wiesel: A Jewish boy describes his experiences in Nazi concentration camps.

Uprising by Margaret Peterson Haddix: Union organizers encourage immigrant workers to protest working conditions.

Dave Barry Slept Here by Dave Barry: Hilarious parody of a textbook—not really historical fiction, but it does reinforce American history. ☺

The Invention of Hugo Cabret by Brian Selznick: This highly acclaimed rags-to-riches story is a graphic novel depicting the birth of cinematography.

Johnny Tremain by Esther Forbes: After injuring his hand, a boy becomes a Minuteman.

The Witch of Blackbird Pond by Elizabeth George Speare: A girl in colonial Connecticut befriends an outsider and is accused of witchcraft.

To Kill a Mockingbird by Harper Lee is told from the perspective of eight-year-old Scout, who observes racial tensions in her town when her father defends an unjustly accused black man.

Roll of Thunder, Hear My Cry by Mildred Taylor: An African-American girl describes her family's struggles during the Depression.

Bud, Not Buddy by Christopher Paul Curtis: An orphan seeks an identity during the Great Depression.

Amos Fortune, Free Man by Elizabeth Yates: A man, kidnapped in Africa and enslaved in America, dreams of freedom.

The Prince and the Pauper by Mark Twain: A look-alike swaps places with the crown prince of England; adventures ensue. Also, consider Twain's even funnier time traveling adventure, **A Connecticut Yankee in King Arthur's Court.**

Across Five Aprils by Irene Hunt: A farm boy grows up during the Civil War.

Uncle Tom's Cabin by Harriet Beecher Stowe was one of the most influential books prior to the Civil War. In it, a good and faithful slave is sold and later mistreated by his new master.

Gone With the Wind by Margaret Mitchell: Long but compelling classic romance set in the South, during the Civil War. The 1939 movie starring Clark Gable and Vivien Leigh is a classic.

Ben Hur by Lew Wallace tells the tale of Judah Ben Hur, a Jewish merchant whose story runs parallel to that of Jesus of Nazareth. Considered the most influential novel of the 19th century, the book is extremely long and difficult with many digressions from the story line. The 1959 MGM film starring Charlton Heston is considered a classic.

Non-fiction

It's hard to make recommendations for non-fiction choices because non-fiction is good when it's (a) well-written, and (b) about a topic of interest to the reader. Find out what your middle school students wants to know more about, and see what you can find. For visual learners, consider especially texts with visual aids or graphics; meanwhile, students who really want to learn about a topic won't be satisfied with the level of information available in books aimed at a juvenile market. As you consider what sorts of books your student might find appealing, consider the following genres within non-fiction: history, biography, autobiography/memoir, inspirational, informational, explanatory, instructional, practical tips or how-to.

Poetry

Similarly, I won't make any recommendations for poetry except to suggest that you include poetry. If possible, include a book or two of humorous poems for children such as Shel Silverstein's *Where the Sidewalk Ends* or a collection such as *Kids Pick the Funniest Poems*, edited by Bruce Lansky. In addition, look for an anthology or a collection that includes poems by noteworthy poets such as William Blake, Lord Byron, Samuel Taylor Coleridge, e. e. cummings, Emily Dickenson, T.S. Eliot, Ralph Waldo Emerson, Robert Frost, Langston Hughes, John Keats, Henry Wadsworth Longfellow, Alexander Pope, William Shakespeare, Lord Alfred Tennyson, Henry David Thoreau, Walt Whitman, and William Wordsworth.

Mythology and the Bible

These are the works of literature that appear most in literary allusions. The more familiarity readers have with these, the more they'll understand and appreciate in the high school literature to come. Consider stocking appealing books to entice your student to explore mythology. Depending on your student's preferences, you might want to stock either Bulfinch's or Edith Hamilton's *Mythology*, which are fairly difficult, text versions; Roger Lancelyn Green's *Tales of the Greek Heroes* is mostly text but somewhat less intimidating; for more visual learners, *D'Aulaire's Book of Greek Myths*, the *National Geographic Treasury of Greek Mythology;* or, for kids who like their mythology a bit more visual and tongue-in-cheek, check out the *Mythlopedia* series.

Similarly, readers who have some familiarity with the Old and New Testaments are much better prepared for high school literature than those who have none. Even if your family isn't religious, it's worthwhile to stock a readable paperback or hardcover Bible (as opposed to one of those giant "Family" Bibles or fancy leather ones with frail pages) or, alternatively, an appealing storybook such as *The Random House Book of Bible Stories.*

What about Shakespeare?

After Greek mythology and the Bible, the single most important influence on the body of literature—and thus, the most literary allusions—come from William Shakespeare. But whereas I would recommend stocking some kind of enticing books about mythology and the Bible for your home library, I would hold off on Shakespeare, for now.

Don't get me wrong: I love Shakespeare. At least, I do now. But when I was in eighth grade, I hated it. Well, maybe hate's too strong, but the foreign wording was just way too weird for me, and the stories didn't seem all that great, either.

Here's the thing about Shakespeare: Shakespeare is most amazing for his rich use of language and deep, thought-provoking themes, but expecting students to appreciate all that richness and deepness before they're ready as readers is unrealistic. In order to really appreciate Shakespeare's plays, you have to be able to simultaneously interpret foreign-sounding prose, cull themes from plots and character development, take into account a very different cultural context, and appreciate imaginative and sometimes figurative uses of language, all of which is complicated by the fact that modern readers don't understand about a fifth of the vocabulary Shakespeare used. These are all advanced abilities that most middle school students haven't yet developed. But with practice reading increasingly difficult and diverse texts and deriving more and more sophisticated meaning from them, by high school, they'll find it much easier to take in new vocabulary and interpret meaning from Shakespeare's complicated plots, characters, themes, and language.

Finally, Shakespeare's plays are almost all a little racy, and some of the characters in Shakespeare's plays can be rather crude in their sense of humor. Some people think that it's a good idea to at least introduce Shakespeare with a resource like Charles and Mary Lamb's *Tales from Shakespeare,* which turns the plays into prose. I guess there's nothing wrong with that, except that the beauty and enduring value in Shakespeare's plays come more from his use of language than from the storylines. In a way, I feel like reading Shakespeare in order to know the names of the characters and have the gist of the stories kind of misses the point.

All things considered, I think Shakespeare is best postponed until students are ready to spend some time with the text itself and can at least attempt to interpret its meaning independently. Also, since reading Shakespeare is almost like learning another language, it's not a bad idea to view and read several plays in succession so that the strange language becomes more familiar.

Library Planning Worksheet: Student Survey

1. Circle your top three, most appealing genres, given your current tastes in reading.

Comic Books	Fairy Tale Fantasy	Coming-of-age Stories
Manga	Science Fiction	Anthropomorphic Fantasy
Graphic Novels	Survival	Informational Non-fiction
Mythology	Adventure	History & Biography
Mystery/Thrillers	Realistic Pet Stories	Instructional or How-To
Epic Fantasy	Historical Fiction	Inspirational Non-fiction

2. Now, cross off the three or four genres that you think sound the least appealing.

3. Beyond genre, which of the following items are most important to a book's appeal?

Pace	Topic	Difficulty
Tone	Length	Gender of Protagonist

4. Of the items on this list, which would prevent you from even attempting a book? For instance, if you came across a book that looked really interesting but was really long, would you even pick it up? If not, list length as something that you consider a factor in whether a book holds appeal for you.

Things to Avoid in Books : _____

In the table below, list the classic literary works that sound most interesting, and with your teacher, decide which of the options for gaining familiarity seem most appropriate.

Intriguing Classic	Just read	Listen and read along	Watch first and then read	Watch, then listen & read along	Just watch

Reading Log

Student_____Semester_____

Date	Author	Title	Genre	Classic?	Rating

HOW TO DESIGNATE RATINGS FOR BOOKS

5 = You love it. You intend to read it again, maybe often. You like the book so much that you recommend it to all of your friends.

4 = You really liked it. You intend to read it again someday. If a friend asked you if you would recommend it, you would say, "Yeah, it's pretty good."

3= You like it okay. You don't think you'll want to read it again, but it was good enough that you never thought about giving up on it. If a friend asked you if you would recommend it, you would say, "Maybe. It depends on what you like."

2 = You don't like it. Not only would you never read it again, you weren't sure you wanted to finish the first time. If a friend asked if you would recommend the book, you would say, "No."

1 = You hate it. You maybe couldn't even finish it. It was so bad that it actually offended you. You go out of your way to warn your friends not to read it.

LITERARY GENRES

I. Poetry
II. Nonfiction
A.   Opinionated essays (sometimes called op-eds) reveal someone's opinions about a subject
B.   Autobiography, biography, and memoir tell you about a real person's life. Autobiographies are fairly all-encompassing accounts of the life of the author; memoirs usually focus on a particular time period or aspect of a person's life. Biographies tell an individual's life story but are written by another person.
C.   History describes historical events as they occurred; it includes many facts.
D.   Informational books transmit knowledge and explain concepts.
E.   Instructional or How-to books explain how to do something.
III. Drama (plays)
IV. Fiction
A.   Mystery involves discovering the truth about something, usually a crime.
B.   Suspense/thriller involves people trying to survive dangerous situations.
C.   Horror usually involves people pitted against supernatural threats.
D.   Action/Adventure involves people experiencing unusual and exciting situations that may be dangerous, but usually danger is limited to specific episodes (as opposed to thrillers, where the danger remains intense right up to the end).
E.   Science Fiction involves imaginative applications of science and technology.
F.   Fantasy involves realistic characters in imaginary settings or imaginary characters in realistic settings.
G.   Romance involves two individuals either finding love or losing it.
H.   Coming-of-Age involves the wisdom a person gains through maturing.
I.   Historical Fiction sets a story and characters in realistic historical periods.
J.   Literary Fiction usually features vivid description and well-developed characters but weak plots and ambiguous themes.
K.   Sociological books make a point about an issue affecting society in general.
L.   Psychological books focus on the way characters think and feel.
M.   Short Stories compress narrative elements into few words; many contemporary short stories are more literary and lack clear resolutions and themes.

Glossary of Literary Terms

Plot: what happens in a story to resolve a conflict. In a sense, the plot is the story itself. A plot begins with the exposition, continues with rising tension, has its defining moment in the climax, and wraps up any loose ends in the resolution.

Exposition: the opening scenario in which the author introduces the main characters and gives them a setting so that readers can visualize the story.

Setting: the time and place of a story.

Conflict: the main problem the protagonist has to solve or overcome in the story. A conflict is an essential ingredient to any good story; without a conflict, all you have is a series of events.

Rising Tension: the complications that get in the way of the main character solving the conflict.

Climax: the defining moment of a story when the conflict is resolved, one way or the other.

Outcome: how things turn out in the end.

Resolution: the part of the story where the author wraps up any loose ends and bring things in the story world back to normal. Some people refer to this part of the story as 'Denouement.'

Episodic plot: the story unfolds through separate episodes; you could almost rearrange the various episodes without affecting the overall story too much.

Formulaic plot: a plot that unfolds according to a pattern that is typical to a genre. For instance, a detective story will almost always follow the same pattern.

Unified plot: a work of fiction where everything revolves around a central problem that must be resolved in the climax.

How the Author Tells the Story

Description: when the author provides details about the setting or a situation to add depth to the story rather than tell what the characters do next to solve the conflict.

Scenes: individual segments of the plot that use a combination of dialogue and description to tell what happens next in the story.

Dialogue: what the characters say to one another in the story.

Monologue: an extended speech by a single character.

Pace: how fast the story seems to move. A story that has a briskly moving dialogue and minimal description feels like it moves very fast, while a story with page upon page of descriptions broken up by characters expounding in long monologues feels very slow.

Tone: the way the author feels about his story. You can usually tell whether the author has a sense of humor or if the author feels like his story is very serious.

Theme: either what the author was grappling with or what the protagonist learns in the outcome.

The Story's Perspective

Characters: the people who act and speak in fiction.

Protagonist: the character who has a problem or who has the most at stake in a story.

Antagonist: the character who opposes the protagonist most or who is vying for the same goal or object, causing conflict.

Character Development: the way a character learns and changes in a story. Not every character in a story necessarily develops: sometimes a bad guy is always a bad guy and never reforms.

POV: or Point of View, is the perspective from which the story is told. A POV can be 1st person, 2nd person, or 3rd person, or Omniscient.

1st Person POV: is when the narrator refers to himself or herself as "I." In a story with a 1st person POV, the narrator may or may not be the protagonist.

2nd Person POV: is when the narrator addresses the reader directly as "you." 2nd person POV stories are very rare.

3rd Person POV: is when the narrator refers to characters as 'he' or 'she'. Usually in a story with a 3rd person POV, the narrator will tell readers what only the protagonist is thinking. Knowing what just one character thinks helps readers identify with that character.

Omniscient POV: is technically also a 3rd person POV, but in this case, the narrator knows what everyone is thinking, and sometimes even breaks into the story to make a comment on the characters' actions.

Narrator: the character or the unnamed voice that tells the story.

Likeability: the criteria by which readers judge characters, especially the protagonist of a story. If you don't like the main character in the story you're reading, chances are you, you won't like the story. It's hard to enjoy identifying with a character you really don't like. That's why authors usually try to strike a balance between having a protagonist that's too perfect (which gets annoying after a while) and one that's too imperfect (which just makes us judge that person as bad).

Plausibility: Whether you just a work of fiction good or bad has everything to do with how plausible or believable you felt the story was. If you don't believe the main character would have acted the way he or she did in the story or that the chain of events in the story were realistic enough, you probably won't think the story was very good.

The Author's Style and Literary Devices

Style: the way an author tells a story. For instance, some authors rely more on the plot to tell their story, while others use a lot of descriptive imagery, symbolism, allusion, or figurative language.

Symbol: an object that stands for an abstract concept. For instance, the One Ring in *The Lord of the Rings*, the Jedi's Light Saber in *Star Wars*, and the Elder Wand in *Harry Potter* all symbolize power. Some authors purposely embed lots of symbols in their stories, while others don't bother with symbols at all.

Flashback: allows authors to tell readers something that happened before the story began that explains why a character would act or feel a certain way in the story. Flashbacks can help a plot-line seem more plausible ("It was weird how the main character went berserk like that, but knowing that a frog attacked him like that when he was a small child, I guess it makes sense") or a character more human ("Wow; I feel like I understand Bill so much better now that I know about that frog.").

Foreshadowing: when the author hints at what is going to happen later in the story.

Figurative language: means using words in a way otherwise than in a literal sense. Four common kinds of figurative language include metaphors, similes, and clichés (idioms) and allusions.

Metaphor: when an author likens two dissimilar things, as in "That man is a rock." The man is not literally a rock, but by calling him one, the author suggests the man is like a rock, probably because he is hard and strong.

Simile: a type of metaphor in which two dissimilar things are compared using a comparing preposition such as 'like,' 'as,' or 'than.' For instance, "Sue ran like the wind," compares Sue to wind, suggesting speed.

Cliché: when a simile is overused, as in the last example. When people have heard a simile before, it comes off as cheap. Most writers avoid using clichés. (Also known as 'idioms'.)

Literary allusion: lends a richness to the story by making readers think of another story. For instance, a story might suggest that someone was a Jezebel. If readers catch the allusion to the Old Testament, they will not only know that means that the person is not a very nice lady, but also recall how persistently nasty the biblical Jezebel was and understand even better what the author is trying to say.

DISCUSSING BOOKS

Among real readers of literature, conversation begins with two questions:

"What are you reading?" & "Do you like it?"

When a sophisticated reader answers the second question, he or she will volunteer the answer to the next question, which is:

"Why?"

Here is a list of possibilities that students can choose from to answer this question with the terms that educated, literate people use:

- The *protagonist* is likeable (funny, humble, brave, clever, witty, kind, realistic)

- The *plot* is exciting, original, or unpredictable (the story is unlike any I've read before)

- There's a strong *theme* (the main character learns something powerful in the end)

- The *resolution* was satisfying (the characters all got the outcomes they deserved)

- The author used language well (lots *description* and *figurative language*)

- The *pace* was fast or the story was well-paced (the story didn't seem boring in parts)

- The *tone* was light-hearted, funny, or appropriate to the story

- The *premise* was unique (the book is based on a really interesting idea)

Of course, sometimes a reader won't like a book as well. In that case, your question will be:

"Why not?"

(1) The story isn't *plausible*: either the characters don't seem like real people, don't act like normal people would given the situation, the setting isn't detailed enough for the reader to visualize the events, or the situation would never occur.

(2) They don't find the main character or narrator *likeable*: either the *protagonist* or *narrator* is too boring, self-obsessed, goody-two-shoes, boy (or girl) crazy, immature, disrespectful, or mean; the *tone* of the book might be too didactic (obviously meant to teach a lesson), brooding, silly, sarcastic, or irreverent; or the *pace* of the story is too slow, boring, and devoid of action (which usually goes along with brooding characters).

Appendix C:

Writing Program Helps

This appendix contains a number of helps for the writing program:

- Resources for Student Writers

- Projects for Students to Consider

- Suggestions for Publication

- Writing Log Template

With the exception of this opening section and the list of resources, I address this section directly to students. You can look over it together with your student to get ideas for projects—or even just hand it to a students feeling stuck for ideas. Too often, people assume that upper elementary and middle school students should be writing stories. I don't know why. Storywriting is not an essential skill. Not everyone is a storyteller, and not everyone needs to be. But everyone occasionally needs to communicate messages, ideas, opinions, and information. Most people have to advertise something at some point or participate in social conventions like holiday greetings or conveying thanks. It's important for you to think in terms of a wide range of projects and to point your student toward the ones that make the most sense for him o her to attempt. You can also use the project descriptions to guide your feedback when your student brings a project to you for a response. For instance, if a student brings you a thank you letter that has no details about the gift, you can point to the description here when suggesting revisions.

The categories here might deviate somewhat from what you may have seen elsewhere. For instance, my first writing project category is called "Collected Thoughts." This category is unusual in that projects like list-writing and collecting quotes don't call for a lot of original content or grammatical correctness on the part of students. So why do I include such projects? Well, first of all, because real people collect quotations and make lists. More importantly, however, students who aren't in the habit of writing or who feel no particular inclination to write can get started moving their hands and compiling something they find personally meaningful. There's probably no better category to point a student who's stuck for ideas to than this one; in fact, you could even have a student generate a list of potential topics to write about.

Another unusual category is writing with graphics. Not only are some students terrific artists, many realistic writing projects require graphics. Think of greeting cards, brochures, picture books, and PowerPoint presentations: all of these projects call for meaningful writing and illustrations. Students who are more visually oriented than linguistically gifted might get much more excited about writing than they would were you to require solely text projects. Students who are more visually gifted might even get excited about designing a comic strip or composing a graphic novel.

A few categories clarify the distinction between writing that serves for purposes of reflection, expressing opinions, and informing others of facts. This, for me, is an important distinction. A lot of students have a hard time maintaining a reasonable, intelligent tone while writing because they blend their reflections and opinions with facts—usually shortchanging the latter. When you look over your student's writing, be clear about what kind of project your student has attempted, and use the descriptions to gauge how well your student has achieved the effect he or she wants. For instance, if your student writes a report, it should contain no opinions at all. If persuasion, the writing should support an opinion with facts. But in a reflection, anything goes, including nothing but personal opinions. Knowing the difference between these three will do your student a world of good later in life.

For inspiration and models for your student, bear in mind that most writers learn their craft by initially imitating the authors they admire. The books in your student's library constitute your best sources for pointing your student toward writing projects. Whatever your student reads, encourage him or her to imitate. If your student has a lively sense of humor, encourage him or her to parody anything they see in real life or read in print that strikes him or her as ridiculous.

Finally, don't overlook the value in playing word games and letting your student log them in lieu of other more tangible or lasting projects from time to time. Not only are word games a welcome break from the pressure to always produce, but word games can help students develop the skills they need as writers. A few games I find valuable for training students good writing habits include the acrostics game described below, Scattergories, and Balderdash.

The Acrostics Game

One of my favorite games is based on an obscure game I found at a thrift store. The board game and the directions that came with it soon fell by the wayside—they were too cumbersome to bother with—but the heart of the game, which involved turning regular words into acrostic sentences, became one of our favorite games.

Here's how you play. You take a word, any word (although its best to start with short, three or four-letter words), and you write the word in all caps vertically on a page. Then, you use the letters as the first letters in words that you turn into a complete, grammatically correct—but not necessarily sensible—sentence.

For instance, take the word 'FOX.' I might make it into the sentence:

Frank

Ostracizes

Xylophones.

"DENA" might become "Dejectedly, Evelyn nudges alligators." My last name can become: "Luckless, unfortunate children huddle sadly in northern Georgia, eating rocks."

The trick to this game is knowing that the best sentences begin with a great verb. The more vibrant, descriptive, and unusual the verb, the more interesting the sentence will be. Compare Evelyn above with "Daphne eats nine apples." Both sentences work, but 'nudges' is more interesting, and obviously nudging alligators can hardly be smart for anyone, especially Evelyn.

I love pulling this game out with students because it underscores the importance of writing with verbs. You can tell kids to write with specific verbs a hundred times, but until they get a sense of their power—i.e., until they see how a vibrant sentences lights up their audiences whereas the dull-verb sentences leaves them flat—it's really hard to convince them to discipline their brains to search for the right verb.

I've used acrostics as a game in a number of ways. The simplest way is to simply agree on the same word for everyone and set a timer. At the end of a minute or two, everyone compares sentences. Since the sentences must be grammatically correct but can be nonsensical, sharing the sentences in a group is usually reward enough; no score is kept or necessary. If you've got students who enjoy competition, you can add scores to the game by having players vote on the most successful sentence.

Scattergories

A second game I like to pull out is the board game, Scattergories. In it, players have a limited amount of time to come up with words that begin with a certain letter to fit certain descriptions, like "A kind of sandwich" or "Things you put in a suitcase." When you play Scattergories, your brain has to work to find specific words that serve a specific purpose, so it helps students develop their capacity to do a mental search for just the right way of saying something.

Balderdash

Balderdash can be played with a board game or with just a dictionary, but it works best with groups of at least five or six people. The game works like this: one person reads a word that most people are unlikely to know. Then, everybody else in the group makes up a definition for the word and passes it to the person who read the word to be defined. When everyone has submitted a definition, that person reads all of the definitions, including the word's real definition somewhere in the mix. The remaining players vote on the one they think is correct. Players get points for every vote their made-up definition gets as well as for guessing the correct definition. Players take turns reading the words and definitions out to the others.

A variation for fewer people involves one person leaving the room while the remaining players write as many definitions as they can think up, either on little slips of paper or on a whiteboard. One player makes sure the correct definition gets added to the mix. Then, when the person comes back in the room, he or she reads the definitions and tries to pick out the right one. If the person guesses correctly, he or she gets to be the guesser again; otherwise, the player whose definition won out gets to be the next person to guess. Once again, I like this game because it forces everyone to generate ideas and use words well. Also, players who get the most points tend to be the ones who figure out how to mimic the tone of a legitimate definition; then again, everyone has the most fun when players opt to forego the points and develop funny definitions instead.

Resources for Every Writer

Every writer should have a good dictionary and a copy of *Roget's Thesaurus*. Also, Internet access is a wonderful all-purpose resource where you can access specialized dictionaries (for instance, rhyming dictionaries), encyclopedias, advice for writing projects, and lots of writing samples.

The Elements of Style by William Strunk & E.B. White is a succinct and inexpensive guide to writing well, with advice for grammar and usage.

On Writing Well by William Zinsser offers advice for students who intend to write memoirs or sports reports, conduct interviews, or attempt humor.

Image Grammar by Harry Noden and *Self-Editing for Fiction Writers* by Renni Browne & Dave King are two great resources for students who want to improve their skill as fiction writers.

Understanding Comics and *Making Comics: Storytelling Secrets of Comics, Manga, and Graphic Novels* by Scott McCloud are excellent resources for students who intend to write stories with pictures.

Pigs, Pizza, and Poetry: How to Write a Poem by Jack Prelusky and *Poetry Matters: Writing a Poem from the Inside Out* by Ralph Fletcher are two resources for students interested in writing poetry.

Eats, Shoots, & Leaves by Lynne Truss explains punctuation humorously.

Woe is I Jr. by Patricia O'Conner explains grammar with lost of humorous examples and illustrations.

TYPES OF WRITING PROJECTS

Book of Quotations	Annotated Timeline	Anecdote
Top Ten Lists	Advice Column	Fable
Wish Lists	How-To Article	Parable
To-Do or "Bucket" List	Cookbook	Fairy Tale
Journal Entry	Textbook	Fan Fiction
Reflection Essay	Glossary	Short Story
Rhyming Poems	Essay	Chapter Book
Imagist Poems	Sports Report	Skit or Script
Free Verse	Current Event Report	Greeting Card
Parodies	Feature Article	Poster
Thank You Notes	Profile	Pamphlet
Sympathy Notes	Interview	Brochure
Congratulation Notes	Book or Movie Reviews	Advertising Flyer
Letter of Inquiry	Blog	Calendar
Letter of Complaint	Op-Ed	Coloring Book
Letter to a Friend	Letter to the Editor	Picture Book
Fan Letter	Persuasive Speech	Comic Strip
Newsletter	Commercial Script	Manga
Notes and Memos	Memoir	Graphic Novel

COLLECTED THOUGHTS

This is the category I'd look to if I were ever looking for a project and feeling a bit stuck. People have been collecting their own thoughts for centuries—not only is it fun to look back at what you were thinking years after the fact, but it can actually be fun to come up with lists of whatever interesting ideas you have now.

Book of Favorite Quotations

In Jane Austen's *Pride and Prejudice*, Lizzie's little sister Mary had a quotation for every situation—most of them annoying. Apparently, people used to collect their favorite quotations in books, kind of like journals. Why not start your own book of favorite quotations? Designate a notebook or get a special journal and consider assigning sections for different kinds of quotes. For instance, you might designate a section for Quotes from Movies, Humorous Quotations, Great Lines from Books, Things You or Your Friends Said That Made Everyone Laugh—whatever!

The great thing about compiling a book of quotations is that the pressure for coming up with stuff is off (for once!) but you get all the benefit of writing down some great material and keeping it in a collection that is uniquely your own.

Top Ten Lists

This could be anything from your top ten favorite movies to your top ten favorite foods to the top ten best action movies of all time (in your "humble" opinion) to the top ten most important Presidents of the United States (complete with the reasons why you think so) to your top ten pet peeves. A top ten list can be pure opinion, pure academia, pure fact, or pure fun.

Wish Lists

I feel like I don't need to explain this one. Basically, you make a list of dreams you have (i.e., "To Climb Mount Everest", "To be a Plumber"), heartfelt hopes you share with others (i.e., "World Peace", "Global Cooling"), or stuff you want (i.e., "Marbles", "A Lot More Marbles").

Things To-Do or Bucket List

A Bucket List is a list of things you want to do before you die. You could do this assuming that you will live another 70 years or you could write a list of things you want to do before you turn 18. One of the most poignant bucket lists I've seen was written by a 16-year-old girl who has terminal cancer—on her list were items like go to prom, train dolphins, and start a charity. What would be on your bucket list if you had only one year left to live?

Journal Entry

A journal entry is meant for your eyes only: it's your thoughts about life, whatever you're thinking about at the time. A journal entry is not quite the same as a diary: whereas a diary might describe the mundane (Laura Ingalls Wilder kept track of the daily temperature in one of her diaries; my friend who was a doctor kept notes on his own health in his), in a journal, an entry would not only state that it had been 101 and humid, but describe how the mugginess affected your day or maybe help you remember another muggy day that was important to you in some way.

Reflection Essay

A reflection essay is where you sort out your feelings. When you write a reflection, you reflect on specific experiences you've had that were important to you personally. In contrast, you wouldn't usually write about major societal issues like peer pressure or kids doing drugs (unless you've had personal experiences with them that you want to think through). For instance, you might fill a whole page on topics like "My First Blue Ribbon at the County Fair (Finally!)", "Babysitting: Not What I Thought It Would Be" or "Regrets after Fighting with My Brother."

POEMS

Poems can seem lame if you only write them because you have to, like for a school assignment. But when you write a poem because you want to play with words, poems can be super fun to write. Or, maybe you've been through a huge disappointment or a really sad experience. In times like that, writing a poem can help you find words to express your feelings.

The best way to learn about poems is reading them. Really good poets take things like nuances in meaning and accents on syllables to design poems that are really precise and perfect. Novices like me tend to focus on the more obvious stuff, like rhyming patterns and the number of syllables. The suggestions here will get you thinking about composing poems, but if you find you really like poetry, ask your parents to help you find collections of poetry and maybe a book or two about how to write poetry well.

Rhyming Poems

When most people think about poems, the words "Roses are red, Violets are blue" often come to mind: they think about quatrain poems, or stanzas of four lines that rhyme. What most people don't realize is that there are different patterns of rhyme to choose from. For instance, "Roses are Red" and all its variations usually follow the pattern ABCB: the second and fourth lines rhyme.

One popular kind of poem is a ballad, which tells a story in a number of stanzas that rhyme according to the same ABCB pattern. Although many ballads are more sophisticated, some of the most popular children's rhymes are actually ballads. For instance, consider the children's rhyme, "Mary's Lamb" (more often known as "Mary Had a Little Lamb") by Sarah Josepha Hale: it tells a story using stanzas that rhyme. Here are the first two stanzas:

> Mary had a little lamb,
> Its fleece was white as snow;
> And everywhere that Mary went,
> The lamb was sure to go.
>
> He followed her to school one day,
> Which was against the rule;
> It made the children laugh and play
> To see a lamb at school.

To read more sophisticated ballads, you can go to www.bartleby.com. Click on the verse tab and search for the term 'Ballad.' You'll find hundreds.

A heroic quatrain follows the pattern, ABAB, in which the first and third lines rhyme as well as the second and fourth. A poem that follows this pattern is Lewis Carroll's famous, nonsensical "Jabberwocky." Here are the first two stanzas:

'Twas brillig, and the slithy toves
Did gyre and gimble in the wabe;
All mimsy were the borogoves
And the mome raths outgrabe.

"Beware the Jabberwock, my son!
The jaws that bite, the claws that catch!
Beware the Jubjub bird, and shun
The frumious Bandersnatch!"

A triple quatrain rhymes according to the pattern, AABA. An example of this pattern is seen in Robert Frost's "Stopping by Woods on a Snowy Evening." Here's the first stanza:

Whose woods these are I think I know,
His house is in the village, though;
He will not see me stopping here
To watch his woods fill up with snow.

A limerick is a usually amusing poem with lines that rhyme according to a pattern: AAbbA. Here's a short untitled limerick by an anonymous poet:

A diner while dining at Crewe,
Found a rather large mouse in his stew.
Said the waiter, "Don't shout and wave it about
Or the rest will be wanting one too."
(as cited in Joseph, p. 260)

Imagist Poems

Imagist poems capture an image and usually a feeling associated with the image with very few words. Rather than rhyming schemes, imagist poems are formulated with counted syllables. One example of an imagist type of poem is Haiku, which is comprised of seventeen syllables, usually broken up into lines of five, seven, and five. Here's an example of a Haiku by written by a poet named Basho, who lived from 1644-1694 and was considered the first Haiku poet ever:

An old silent pond...
A frog jumps into the pond,
splash! Silence again.

Here's one I made up myself:

Near my kitchen sink,
Dried cereal sticks on sides
Of abandoned bowls.

Another type of imagist poem is cinquain, which involves twenty-two syllables arranged in five lines. Here's a cinquain written by Adelaide Crapsey, entitled "Snow":

Look up . . .
From bleakening hills
Blows down the light, first breath
Of wintry wind . . . look up, and scent
The snow!

Parodies

A parody takes a popular literary work and makes fun of it by mainly imitating it but changing it in some way. While you could parody almost any literary work, I think it's most fun to parody song lyrics. All you have to do is switch out the rhyme schemes. Here's a couple of stanzas of one I came up with one day, just goofing around. Sing it to the tune of the folk song, "On Top of Old Smoky:"

On top of 'No smoking,'
'No dogs are allowed.'
One Way and No Parking
In church, don't talk loud.

No running with scissors,
Sit straight and don't slouch,
'No shoes, shirt, no service,'
No shoes on the couch.

For some pretty amazing song parodies, look up Weird Al Yankovic, who parodies popular music. My favorite will always be his "Eat It" which parodied Michael Jackson's "Beat It" video, both of which you can watch on YouTube.

Of course, you can parody anything: songs, poems, novels, TV shows, commercials, even people. My daughter had the idea to write a fan-fiction story that parodied reality TV using characters from J.R.R. Tolkien's *Lord of the Rings*. (See an excerpt below.)

Free Verse

Free verse poems don't have to rhyme or follow any particular rhythm or rules about syllables. And yet, free verse poems aren't just a mess of words; they kind of march to their own beat and create an impression. Free verse can be somber, serious, impressive, or totally whimsical. You'll come across some free verse in almost any modern collection of poems.

CORRESPONDENCE

Special Occasion Notes

These are notes you write to say thanks when someone's done you a favor or given you something, notes of sympathy to console someone whose spouse or close relative has died, or to congratulate someone who's accomplished something extraordinary, like graduating from high school or college. A special occasion note has just three essential ingredients:

- a general statement of (choose one): thanks, sympathy, congratulation

- a sentence or two (more if you like) that gives more details—why you appreciate the favor or why the gift means a lot to you, why you appreciated the person who died or how that person affected you, or why an accomplishment impresses you

- finally, a reiteration of your purpose. Here's a sample thank you note.

Dear Flopsy,

Thank you for the beautiful sweater. I can tell that you put a lot of yourself into it—it's so soft! I will think of you every time I wear it. Thanks again,

Your friend,

Susie

P.S. I hope your hair grows back real soon.

Letter of Inquiry

Write a letter of inquiry when you want someone important to consider doing something for you, like hiring you for a job, or publishing an article you wrote, or hosting an event you want to sponsor. When writing a letter of inquiry, make sure you

- state your purpose for writing

- explain in a sentence or two (more if you like) why the recipient appeals to you as the best way to achieve your purpose and why your proposal might appeal to them

- tell the recipient how to contact you and close the letter graciously

Here's a sample letter of inquiry:

Dear Mr. Important Dude,

I am writing to you to apply for the position of King in your company. I am particularly interested in your opening because ruler positions are hard to come by in these hard economic times. You will find me, I think, to be a perfect tyrant, unreasonable in my demands and universally difficult to work with. If you have any questions, you may contact at 555-9029. Thank you for your consideration.

Sincerely,

Royal Hyness

Letter of Complaint

Like other letters, this letter calls for a professional tone and four basic ingredients:

- a statement of your purpose for writing

- specific, detailed examples that prove your contention

- what you want the recipient to do (and how to contact you)

- a gracious closing sentiment

Here's a sample letter of complaint:

Dear Greasy Hole Restaurant,

I am writing to inform you of my family's unsatisfactory experience at your establishment. My daughter and I both ordered the Reuben sandwich, but when our orders came, mine had mostly meat and hers had mostly sauerkraut. My oldest daughter's salad was wilted, and my son's hamburger was so tough that he could not eat it, not even when he extracted the meat patty from the bun and gnawed on it. Furthermore, none of us had more than twelve French fries. We counted. Unfortunately, our server did not reappear except to drop off the bill. Considering the price of food in restaurants these days, I feel that we deserve a refund for this inadequate and disappointing dining experience. I would be happy with either a check refund or even a gift certificate for another meal, preferably at a different restaurant. If you have any questions, I can be reached at (385) 437-8592.

Thank you for your attention to this matter.

Sincerely,

Fred Upp

Letter to a Friend or Relative

Writing a letter to a long distance relative or to a friend who's moved out of town can really make that person's day. Don't worry, a letter doesn't have to be long, just tell your recipient what you've been doing or write up a brief narrative about something interesting that happened to you. Grandparents especially love letters that remind them of your shared history, or stories that you remember of times you spent together when you were younger. Friends, in general, prefer stories that make them laugh.

Fan Letter

Write a fan letter to show your appreciation to someone who has made your life better, but may not know it. Don't limit yourself to famous people. Although you can certainly consider famous authors, actors, and singers as potential recipients, such people get a lot of fan mail and they might not always have the time to respond to yours. Think about writing a fan letter to a less well-known author or to someone in your community who really makes a difference. Make sure you:

- state your purpose for writing

- explain in a sentence or two (more if you like) why you felt compelled to write to the recipient and what about their work or influence you have most appreciated

- close the letter graciously

Here's a sample fan letter:

Dear Nifty Rider,

My name is Gina Lubbux, and I am writing to you because I really enjoyed every one of the 150 books in your Good-Natured Kids Do Good Deeds series. I love the way the characters always do nice things for less fortunate people and the way the people they help are always so grateful. I especially like Julie because she's so pretty and smart and always gets along with her mildly quarrelsome younger brother. Your books have been a real inspiration to me, and I hope you keep writing more stories about well-behaved children.

Your fan,

Gina

Personal or Family Newsletter

Every December, people send end-of-the-year newsletters to keep in touch and let people know about the highlights of their years. The standard format for newsletters seems to include a brief summary of each family member's main activities, major accomplishments, and travel destinations. Some of them, I'm sorry to say, are rather boring. To make your newsletter more interesting, add a few anecdotes (see the anecdote section below). Also, try adding some kind of twist to your newsletter to make it interesting. Here's an excerpt from one of my newsletters.

Last year, a friend aptly noted that everyone tends to list the year's highlights in these Christmas newsletters. It's true: highlights of fun vacations, happy families, and updates in home décor do get old, so we thought we'd spread a little holiday cheer by identifying the Luchsinger Lowlights of the year:

Number 10: When Tom left a hose to siphon out the water from the hot tub, Andrew decided to relocate the other end of the hose to our carpeted bedroom floor. Some folks think very highly of their waterbeds, but just in case you were wondering, water-bedrooms are not as cool. Plus, after a few days, they start to stink.

Number 9: We took the Andrew and Lauren bowling and the only spare I got was when Andrew helped me. Needless to say, I was the big loser. (No one in the bowling alley would look me in the eye – I was that bad.)

Number 8: Meanwhile, Kristen was at summer camp, where she got stung by a bee and her hand swelled up to the size of a small basketball. Apart from her deformed member, Kristen reports a good time was had by all.

Obviously, there's more, but I think that gives you the idea. Close your newsletter with a positive note that says how much you appreciate your friends or with a wish for their well-being.

INFORMATIVE WRITING

Whatever you write to inform someone of something, the trick is to rely on objective facts as much as possible. Your opinions about matters dilute the information you want to get across and weaken any point you want to make. Even in the note and memo below, the writer doesn't dilute her point with an opinion but tells her readers authoritatively what's going to happen. In short, when you write informative pieces, stick to the facts!

Advice Column

Everybody loves giving advice (whether or not the enjoy receiving it is a different story.) Writing an advice column can be fun, because you can give real, good advice—or you can turn your advice column into a parody and make your advice funny. Or, especially if you've got a hobby you know a lot about, you can use your advice column to answer the questions everybody asks you, like "How do you always pick out such cute outfits?" or "How do you always get such good grades?"

To see what a real advice column looks like, check out a major newspaper's advice column or go on-line and search for popular advice columns. One of the most famous advice columns is called Dear Abby. To write your own advice column, either invite people you know to submit real or made-up dilemmas for you to respond to via e-mail or, if you don't want to do that, write the letters yourself, possibly even writing them as if you were people you know and describing the problems they would be smart to ask you advice about! Then, answer the letters, making sure to take that friendly know-it-all tone of someone who has all the answers.

Notes and Memorandum

Kids write notes, grown-ups write memos. Both of these are a semi-formal way of communicating something of importance (or, in the case of memos, usually something that matters to absolutely no one but the writer). The main differences between the two kinds of writing are most obvious in the memo's specific formatting and tone, which is semi-formal (some might say, "obnoxious"). Compare the memo and the note below to see the difference.

Memo

To: Luchsinger Family Members

From: Dena Luchsinger

Date: April 2, 2011

It has come to my attention that miscellaneous items have accrued on the dining table to such a degree that the management has deemed their continued presence to be unacceptable. Please remove any personal effects forthwith; any unclaimed items will be confiscated and dealt with accordingly.

Note (Scribbled on a Whiteboard)

I don't know whose stuff is all over the kitchen table, but if you don't put your junk away by dinnertime, I'm throwing it out!!!

Mom

The next time you have a message to convey, try writing a memo. Make sure you work in a few sesquipedalian, or super-long, words to make your memo sound really official.

How-To Articles

In a How-To Article, you teach someone how to do something you do especially well. A How-To Article is normally about a page or two in length. It will have an introduction in which you try to convince your readers that they really want to do whatever you're going to teach them how to do, a main body where you tell them how to do it, and a conclusion that says something encouraging, like "You can do it!" but in more interesting words.

The main part of the how-to article is, of course, the part where you explain how to do something. Happily, this is also the easiest part of the article to write. Just figure out the order of the steps involved in whatever you're teaching, and list them in the right order. Readers will find your instructions easier to follow if you include helpful words like 'First', 'Second', 'Third', 'Next', and 'Finally'.

If any of the steps in your process involve mini-steps, try listing them with bullets. People like bullets. They make instructions look cool.

Use lots of commands. Let's face it, most people don't like taking orders from anyone, so there's not a lot of opportunity in life to boss people around. But good news! In a how-to article, you get to do it all the time. And it works, because when you're telling people how to do something, you come off as being helpful, not bossy. Try it! It's fun!

Finally, close your how-to article with a word of encouragement that your readers can be successful if they follow your instructions.

Cookbook

A cookbook is a great project if you like to cook (or eat), and it can make a great gift, too.

Some cookbooks have a theme, like a whole cookbook full of recipes for different kinds of gumbo. Unless you're a gumbo expert, I wouldn't recommend being quite that specific, but you might have a number of cookie, desserts, or main course recipes you could group together.

A cookbook can doesn't have to be massive. Unless you're very ambitious and want to do more, consider compiling a cook-booklet of about a dozen recipes. For each recipe, include the name of the dish, a blurb that describes it or explains why someone would want to prepare it, and of course, the recipe and instructions for making it.

Your descriptive blurb should highlight a good reason to try your recipe, such as one of these:

- It's inexpensive to prepare.

- It doesn't take too long to make.

- Most people have actually heard of the ingredients in it.

- It's easy to make.

- It tastes good.

For the recipe part, list ingredients, quantities, and preparation of each—i.e., "½ cup green pepper, chopped," before explaining how to prepare the dish. You can do this with either a paragraph of text or a numbered list with each step explained in order. Conclude each entry with serving instructions ("Serve with chips") or a pleasant salutation such as "Bon Appetit!" or "Enjoy!"

Textbook

Okay, I know this doesn't sound like fun, but it could be. A friend of mine actually came up with this idea when her son told her he was sick of doing his vocabulary workbooks. So my friend suggested that instead of doing vocabulary workbooks, he make his own. She had him go find a pile of books that were about his level of reading, and she told him to find words in them that he thought kids his age should know the meaning of. When he finished, he was pretty pleased with his project, but he asked his mom if he actually had to do the exercises. His mom asked if he knew the meaning of the words in his book, and he answered that he had to; he wrote the book. So his mom said, "Then, nope."

Moral: If you hate doing exercises in workbooks, ask your teacher if you can write your own!

Glossary

A glossary is a short, themed dictionary, in which you write brief definitions for terms that apply to a specific topic. You could make a glossary of cooking terms to put at the end of your cookbook—or, you could write a glossary of football terms or technology terms to help your clueless relatives keep up with the things you're involved with. If you know and enjoy a topic, writing a glossary is surprisingly satisfying. To write one, first make a list of all the terms that a novice would need to know to understand your topic; then, decide whether you're going to organize them alphabetically or by some other logical order. Finally, add your definitions. Definitions can be complete sentences or not—your choice—but whatever you decide, try to be consistent.

Format your glossary to suit your purpose—for instance, if you're giving it to Grandma, try turning your glossary into a booklet—print it out, and you're done! For a few examples of glossaries, you can check out the ones in this book on pages 121 and 148.

News, Sports, or Current Events Report

In a report, you always want to answer the readers' questions: Who, What, When, Where, Why? Start a report by answering who, what, when, and where in a single sentence:

Last week, Harry Fludbuster broke the record for trampoline jumping in his backyard in Chicago.

The next sentence should answer WHY.

Fludbuster was inspired by an episode of "The Brady Bunch" in which Bobby and Cindy tried but failed to break the World Record for teeter-tottering.

The main part of your report should provide the reader with interesting details about the event, ideally including quotations from the people involved.

You can write a report like this about major sporting events, like the Superbowl, or minor ones, like your little league team's recent showdown with its rival. A fun take on a current events report is to write up what others might see as insignificant. Picture the headline (and imagine the details you'd include) in an article like: "Joey Fargus Actually Cleans Bedroom!"

For examples of real reports, check out your favorite local newspaper or newsmagazine.

Feature Article

In a feature article, reporters try to find out answers to questions like, "What would it be like to be a black person living in the South?" (*Black like Me* by John Howard Griffin), "What's it like to try to get by on minimum wage jobs?" (*Nickel and Dimed* by Barbara Ehrenreich) "What goes on behind the scenes of the fast food industry?" (*Fast Food Nation* by Eric Schlosser).

A feature article is basically a really long, in-depth report: it answers all the questions of a regular report (Who, What, Where, When, Why?), but from a behind-the-scenes perspective. A feature article is often written from the reporter's perspective, in the first person.

Whereas most reports get straight to the point (as in the Fludbuster example above), a feature article usually begins with an intriguing anecdote to hook the reader, followed by a blend of detailed information and quotes from people who you interviewed about the topic. Also, whereas a typical news report is about one to two pages in length, a feature article is usually between two and eight pages.

Profile or Interview

Just as a feature article is a special kind of news report, a profile is a special kind of feature article that focuses on a specific person. An interview is a profile in which a conversation goes back and forth between the reporter (you) and the person you're interviewing.

Profile the people in your community that do good in a small way—or interview the ones who do it in a big way. What really matters is the good they do, and the fact that someone noticed.

I'll give you just a couple of tips for doing a profile: first, request an interview with the person you're interested in profiling, and if the person agrees, prepare a list of maybe ten questions to ask. Don't worry if you don't get to all of your questions in the actual interview; people being interviewed tend to say unpredictable things, so don't be surprised if the interview goes a different direction than you originally planned. The questions you prepare are just to help you make sure you have an idea of the types of things you want to know, especially if the person is the type to wait for you to lead the discussion. If the person you're profiling says something you know you're going to want to include in your profile, it's okay to say, "Can you repeat that?" Finally, it's a good idea to record the interview with a digital device, but you should also take notes, just in case your device malfunctions.

Tribute

A tribute honors the memory of someone you love who has died. In a tribute, list a few of the qualities of whomever you're writing the tribute about as well as a few anecdotal memories that capture how you feel about the individual. Writing a tribute is something people do because they feel like they have to, never because someone else thought it would be a good idea for them to do. In a sense, a tribute is one of the most personal forms of writing. Our relationships with others and our sense of loss when they die are among the most profound experiences we have. If you are ever in a position to write one, you might want to consider making a copy for someone else who loved the same person. He or she will treasure your tribute and be comforted by your gift.

OPINIONATED WRITING

In a democracy, everybody is entitled to an opinion—but not all opinions are alike. Some opinions come across as crazy-people rants, while others hold a lot of weight. What's the difference? People whose ideas influence others support their opinions with factual evidence. When you write anything that reveals your opinions about a matter—and, in a nutshell, your opinion is whether you like or dislike something—give reasons for your point of view. Your opinion will strike your readers as reasonable and smart—and so will you.

Reviews

In a review, a writer offers a brief description of something and follows this with an evaluation. Although you can review books, movies, products, cars, restaurants, hotels, vacation destinations, hairdressers, or instructors, I'm going to focus mainly on book reviews. Here's an example:

> In *Billy's Quest*, a twelve-year-old boy named Billy sets off to recover his sister's stolen Barbie doll. The quest takes Billy all the way to Thailand, and Billy gets into a lot of scrapes along the way. The plot was totally viable, and Billy and his sidekick Poodle were really likeable, heroic characters. I especially liked the part where Poodle gave Billy mouth-to-mouth resuscitation after Billy almost choked on the last morsel of food he stole from Poodle. I highly recommend *Billy's Quest* to anyone who likes adventure stories.

Now, let's look at what goes into a good review. A review should begin with a summarizing statement that gives the reader an idea what the review is essentially about. If you look at my review, you'll notice that I tell my reader about the main character and the basic plot of the book. Next, add just a few details about the story so that readers have a good feel for what you're talking about, especially when you give your evaluation about what is particularly good (or not-so-good) about it. Finally, end with either a recommendation as in the review above, or a rhetorical question and a challenge ("Will Billy ever find Suzy's Barbie? Read *Billy's Quest* and find out!")

One thing you should never do in a book or movie review is tell your reader how the story ends. You can, however, tell your reader if a product doesn't work.

Blogs

A blog is a website where you regularly post your ideas and opinions on the Internet. You'll have to check with your parents before you do this one, and since anyone can read anything you post online, it's probably good to have your parents preview anything you think you might want to post. Some teenagers have set up blogs with themes, where they write about a hobby, advise others about something they're particularly knowledgeable about, or describe their day-to-day experiences as a way to keep in touch with family and friends.

Almost any blog could be entitled, "What I Think About _____" or "What I Think I Know About _____." However, like every piece of opinionated writing, the more you support your ideas with good reasons, the more people will consider your blog thoughtful and want to read more. Apart from reflecting your perspective, a blog has no particular rules about length or format—simply write what you think, and make sure you proofread your writing before you post it online. Remember, anything you post online can be read by anyone, so represent yourself well. It's not hard to set up a blog: just search the Internet for "free blog." A few popular and currently free blog sites include Blogger (also known as blogspot), Squidoo, and Wordpress.

Letters to the Editor and Op-Eds

A letter to the editor is, as you might guess, a letter you write to the editor of a newspaper or magazine in response to an article that was published. A letter to the editor normally praises a piece and agrees with it, or identifies problems with an article or position taken by an article's author. In contrast, an op-ed isn't necessarily a response to any particular article, it just sets forth a writer's opinion about something important like politics or societal values. Normally, a letter to the editor is short—maybe two or three paragraphs in length, while an op-ed might go on for several pages.

Persuasive Letter, Essay, or Speech

As with all opinionated writing, if you want to persuade someone of something, you need to give them good reasons to do so. But before you can persuade your audience of your position, you have to convince them that there's a problem that needs addressing. When you write to persuade, it's helpful to think in terms of a few things you need to do:

1. Provide statistics or describe a situation that highlights the problem.

2. Either list reasons why a solution must be found or propose a solution and explain why it's the best one. Depending on how complex the problem is, you might be able to do this in a list or you might need to write a paragraph for each one.

3. Close by reiterating the urgency of the issue, and it can never hurt to

4. Appeal to the audience by affirming your belief that they'll do the right thing.

Commercial Script

I put commercials in the opinions category because commercials are designed to persuade people to buy a product, not state facts as informative writing does. Obviously, you're going to have limited opportunities to produce a real commercial (unless you have an actual product you're trying to sell), but that doesn't mean you can't play around with writing a commercial for fun. Because commercials so often exaggerate their claims, they're great fun to parody. Here's one I wrote as filler for Kristen's "Double Take" fan fiction, (an excerpt of which appears below):

> "You got orcs. I got orcs. Orcs are a fact of life. But why live with orcs when you can get Orc-B-Gone! Simply spray it at 'em and you'll never be bothered by those pesky beasts again! Smells like happiness! Orcs really don't like it very much!"

> Cut to a Warrior of Gondor using the spray against charging Orcs. Warrior smiles dazzlingly while spraying; orcs hack warrior with scythes and axes. Warrior continues to spray. Orcs frown, make crazy motions, and leave. The happy warrior bleeds.

> Cut to ugly dude. "Order your can today — but wait — there's more! Call today and we'll throw in this lovely Orc-Swatter!"

> An attractive house-hobbit in a kitchen is surprised by an Orc that steals a freshly baked biscuit. The she-hobbit swats. Orc takes cookie anyway. She swats again. Orc scowls but leaves.

> "Orc-B-Gone and Orc-Swatter combo will meet all of your Orc removal needs for a mere $19.99 — you won't get this in stores! Call now!"

> Scenes of smiling hobbit fingering swatter and confidently bandaged warrior flash in sequence as announcer says rapidly:

> "Orc-B-Gone is not for pregnant women or women that may become pregnant. Or children. Or anyone over 11. Orc-B-Gone may cause goosebumps, numbness, and shivering if used in walk-in refrigeration units. Orc-B-Gone is not for internal use. If accidental contact with eyes occurs, it is going to hurt like you will not believe, but nothing else will probably happen. We accept no liability for any use of Orc-B-Gone that does not comply with the package directions, or that does. If you swat yourself with the Orc-Swatter, you have only yourself to blame. Shipping and Handling fees are additional and unconscionable.

> "Don't live with Orcs – Orc, Be Gone! Call Now."

NARRATIVE WRITING

Narrative means story-telling, but don't assume that all narratives are just made-up stories; a lot of narrative involves telling stories that actually happened. In general, the only reason to ever write a story is because it occurs to you and you feel like you want to tell it. It's really hard to write a good story on demand, although if you practice writing them, developing storylines gets easier. Writing narrative is more a craft and an art than a science, so if you aspire to be a writer of fiction, plan on lots of practice.

Memoir

A memoir is a story that you tell from your own stock of memories that has a powerful emotional effect on your reader. That emotional effect part is important. If you've ever listened to small children tell you about what they'd done one day or, worse, listened to anyone describe a dream, you know that people telling pointless stories is horribly boring. But a story that makes you laugh along or go, "Awwwwwww!" at the cuteness or even, "That's horrible!" at the tragedy—those are the stories that are really good to listen to. A story has to affect people to be any good.

Memoir, as a genre, is all about emotion. In fact, unless a photograph reminds them of something, most adults only remember things from their childhoods that have powerful emotions attached to them. That's why memoir is not just a matter of describing experiences, but about narrating them to specifically elicit the same emotions in your reader.

How do you elicit an emotion in a reader? Usually, the best way is with sensory details: a smell or a feeling or a specific image that makes your readers feel like they're right there in your memory, experiencing what you experienced. You might have heard the advice, "Show, don't tell." What that means is that it is better to use little details to convey an emotion than to name it. When readers understand what you were feeling from the details you write, they feel for the writer much more than if you had spelled out, "I felt angry," or "I felt sad."

Here is a short memoir piece from my childhood.

Whether it was the crash or the smell that woke me, I didn't know, but Shari was still asleep. I wanted to be asleep too, but I couldn't. I got out of bed and crossed the hallway to the stairs, which I descended backwards, on my knees. When I finally got to the bottom of the stairs, my parents weren't in their comfortable chairs before the television set. I could hear voices coming from outside now, so I passed through the empty kitchen and into the entryway where Daddy kept his workclothes and his rubber boots from the barn so he wouldn't soil the carpet in the kitchen and I padded across the linoleum to the screen door where I stopped and looked outside.

Orange flames danced in and out of the garage across the driveway, even as black poured out of holes in the building that had never been there before. The noises and smells were stronger here, but they bothered me less than the presence of many strange grownups milling about the front yard, talking and watching the fire. I pressed my nose against the cool mosquito netting and examined them, but none of their forms, dark against the glowing garage, matched my mother's slender figure. I reached for the door handle and jiggled it.

Suddenly, the door gave, and I looked up. A large, vaguely familiar woman I'd seen before at church stood above me, looking down. "Oh, the poor wee girl," she said, picking me up even though I desperately wished she wouldn't. "It's okay, wee one. There's nothing to be a-scared of." I squirmed and she held me tighter. Her sour smell mixed with the foul odor from the black smoke pouring out of the garage.

More than ever, I wanted my mother.

A memoir can be no more than that: a snapshot of a memory flushed out with details. In fact, all I really remember of this event is the shocking sight of the burning garage and the desperate feeling I had when the neighbor lady picked me up. I also keenly remember the woman's smell. My dad later told me that he'd set the garage on fire himself. He wanted to build a bigger garage and figured he'd just get rid of the old one. I was two at the time.

Anecdote

An anecdote is like a memoir in many ways: the starting point for an anecdote is a memory, a snapshot of a single instant of your life. You summarize the context and add details to help your reader visualize not only what happened but also to empathize something of what you felt at the time. Finally, you conclude with whatever made this memory worth telling. But an anecdote is different from a memoir in a very significant way. Read this anecdote, and see if you can figure out what it is.

The Bunny

When I was seven years old, I won the local bank's annual coloring contest. It was a momentous occasion in my life. Every spring, the bank in town held a coloring contest, and my mother always picked up the coloring pages so that my sister and I could enter. In retrospect, I am not sure whether my parents actually conducted business with that bank; it seems to me they banked elsewhere. But the bank itself was located next to the pharmacy, and apparently our family required a great deal of medication, because I remember we walked past the bank's storefront quite often. And, not to be redundant, but the year I was seven, I won.

It was a Big Deal. I remember wearing my long dress and my mother pulling my bangs back in a barrette, which was a good look on me. We drove into town where a man in a suit awarded me a piece of paper that said 'Certificate' on the top and a stuffed purple bunny. Then, he told me to stand next to a gigantic fluorescent pink bunny that I later realized must have been a human dressed in a rabbit suit. At the time, I thought only that the bunny bore little resemblance to the rabbits we kept in a hutch on our farm and wondered what such a creature ate. But as I did not voice these questions, and as someone from the Local Newspaper was there to snap a picture, I was eventually moved closer to the creature where a picture was indeed snapped. I looked very solemn in the picture but otherwise nothing terrible happened.

Winning the contest was a turning point in my young life. Prior to the contest, I was my sister's equal, a nobody. I was just one of many kids who dared to dream that they could select the right shade of yellow with which to color a ducky without going outside the line. Oh, they wished! Of course, I did not realize the full impact of my victory until well after the award ceremony. One must have time to process the significance of events that change us so permanently. But later, in the quiet privacy of my bedroom, as I shoved over Teddy and Raggedy Andy and Henry Dog and Kanga and Roo, I realized just how much my life had changed.

I had a purple bunny.

So could you tell what makes an anecdote different from a memoir? In a memoir, you lead your reader to your conclusion so that, at the end of the memoir, your reader feels what you've been trying to get at. In an anecdote, you lead your reader right up to the opposite of your conclusion, so that the final line has almost a punch-line feel to it. In my anecdote, I led you to believe that somehow I had discovered my own self-worth or that I was not a nobody or something heady like that. But my conclusion could hardly have been more shallow. Hey, give me a break: I was seven.

Fable

A fable is a story with a moral; it teaches a general truth through a series of events, often with anthropomorphized (non-human) characters. Here's one from Aesop:

The Fox and the Grapes

Mister fox was just about famished, and thirsty too, when he stole into a vineyard where the sun-ripened grapes were hanging up on a trellis in a tempting show, but too high for him to reach. He took a run and a jump, snapping at the nearest bunch, but missed. Again and again, he jumped, only to miss the luscious prize. At last, worn out

with his efforts, he retreated, muttering, "Well, I never really wanted those grapes anyway. I am sure they are sour, and perhaps wormy in the bargain."

Moral: Any fool can despise what he cannot get. (Aesop's Fables, p. 13)

Parable

Like a fable, a parable makes a point; the difference is that a parable applies to a specific situation; it is an extended analogy for the situation. In this famous parable from the Old Testament, King David (who had a rather large collection of wives and concubines) stole another man's wife and then had the woman's husband sent off to war so the husband would not know what he had done. But the prophet Nathan came and told him this parable:

There were two men in one city, the one rich and the other poor. The rich man had a great many flocks and herds. But the poor man had nothing except one little ewe lamb which he bought and nourished; and it grew up together with him and his children. It would eat of his bread and drink of his cup and lie in his bosom, and was like a daughter to him. Now a traveler came to the rich man, and he was unwilling to take from his own flock of his own herd, to prepare for the wayfarer who had come to him; rather he took the poor man's ewe lamb and prepared it for the man who had come to him. (1 Kings 12: 1b – 4, NASB)

Hearing the story, King David grew incensed and ordered the rich man be punished, upon which Nathan answered, "You are the man!" (I King 12:7, NASB).

As you can see, a parable requires a situation to react to and a specific point about it that you want to make. Next, you need to come up with a similar situation so that you can make that point without referring to the original situation, but that convinces your audience of the point you are trying to make. For instance, if you shared a room with your sibling and your sibling kept leaving stuff on your side of the room, you might make up a parable that makes a point about the injustice of encroaching on someone else's territory. Like the parable above, your analogy shouldn't be too obvious, so that your intended audience can truly appreciate the point without getting defensive.

Whereas Nathan's parable was very clearly directed at King David, most parables apply to a more general group of people. (Most of Jesus' parables were directed at specific groups or people in general; a modern parable that makes a more general point is John Steinbeck's novella, *The Pearl*.)

Fairy Tale

A fairy tale is a story that takes place outside normal space and chronology ("Once upon a time") and involves both real and fantastic characters—like a princesses (which are rare, but real) and witches (which, as they're depicted in fairy tales, are not). In many fairy tales, someone saves someone else—i.e., Prince Charming kisses Sleeping Beauty (or was it Snow White?) to end her slumber.

One way to write a fairy tale is to take a famous fairy tale and change the characters, the setting, the perspective, or even the ending. A few examples of re-told fairy tales include John Scieszka's *The True Story of the Three Little Pigs* (a picture book) and the Disney movie *Tangled*.

To write a fairy tale from scratch, you need a combination of realistic and unrealistic characters and usually some element of magic. Then, think about who's saving whom and from what. Does a prince save a princess from a witch's spell or an evil step-mother's oppression? Could a dragon save Prince Charming from the beautiful princess? Could the step-mother turn out to be awesome and save the princess from her addiction to Angry Birds? And just what is the King doing during all of these crises, anyway? The trick to writing a fairy tale that will interest other people is to find the combination that no one's done—and that makes a subtle statement that you actually believe.

Fan Fiction

Like a retold fairy tale, a fan fiction is based on fiction that someone else has already written. You can continue someone else's story after it ends (a lot of people have tried to write the next part of *Pride and Prejudice*) or develop the story from someone else's perspective, like Tom Stoppard did in the play, *Rosencrantz and Guildenstern are Dead*. A fan fiction can be a serious continuation of the story-line (a la *Pride and Prejudice*) or more of a spoof (a la Stoppard). By the way, the works of Jane Austen and Shakespeare are all in the public domain, which means that you can write about their stories and characters without infringing on anyone's copyright. If you choose a more recently written story for your fan-fiction, it's important to add a disclaimer to your story, acknowledging that you don't own the rights to the characters.

Here is an excerpt from a fan-fiction that my daughter and I collaborated on. Based on J.R.R. Tolkien's *The Lord of the Rings*, it parodies survival-type reality TV shows. The premise here was all Kristen's, and I still think it's a pretty good one. Needless to say, neither she nor I own the rights to any of Tolkien's characters.

> **"And we're back!" Loslote said. She had joined the contestants in what was apparently some kind of cave. "We're in the entrance to the Final Challenge. But before we begin, Galadriel will present to each of you a gift."**
>
> **"Goody!" Pippin said. "Like Christmas. Does Middle Earth have Christmas?"**
>
> **"No."**
>
> **"Then it's like the time Galadriel gave us gifts."**
>
> **"Closer."**
>
> **Galadriel walked forward gracefully. "To you, Eowyn, I give a strand of my hair."**
>
> **"What for?" Eowyn held Galadriel's strand up with two fingers.**

"To Legolas, this can of aerosol Orc-B-Gone."

"Will this harm the environment?"

"Not if you don't use it. Arwen, dear, Grandma made you cookies!"

"Oreos?"

"Alright, I had a busy week. Pippin, a vial of Eärendil's light."

Pippin looked at the tub of Blistex. "Busy week again?"

"It's basically the same as mine, anyway. We're both blonde," Eowyn pointed out.

"And to Glorfindel, a magic rope."

"This is an extension cord."

"Now what do you say to Galadriel?" Loslote prompted.

"Is there even electricity in here?"

"That's my polite contestants. All right, choose one of the five entrances and go."

As soon as Loslote dismissed him, Glorfindel hurried into the closest tunnel. Hearing noises, he rounded a corner. What he saw next would forever remain in his memory as the most beautiful sight in the world.

"Is that a 96-inch plasma TV? Oh... Doritos... Mountain Dew..." Glorfindel sank into the easy chair and grabbed a handful of chips. He smiled — it was the Superbowl: the Eagles against the Trolls. Glorfindel had never seen football before, but somehow, he felt in his soul that he was meant for this, for this moment, to sit and watch and be one with the runners and the wind and the ball and the handsome man who threw the ball as if he were a dancer. Then Glorfindel frowned. He had pushed the button on the arm of the chair, but nothing happened. He was pretty sure the button meant the chair had a massage feature. He twisted around, grimacing in the discomfort of the movement. "Oh, yrch secretions! It's unplugged." He twisted back and allowed the gracefulness of the handsome one to appease him momentarily before he realized that comfort was within his reach. "My magic rope!" he said, and, blessing the wisdom of Galadriel, went to go plug the chair in.

As you can see, fan-fiction can be fun to write: since the characters are ready-made, half of the work is done for you, allowing you to play with storylines and dialogue.

You can access more examples of fan-fictions on-line on sites such as www.fanfiction.net.

Skits

As with fan-fiction, when you write a skit or a sketch, the emphasis is on a bare bones sequence of events and a dialogue that reveals the better part of the action. Of all writing projects, skits are the most fun to collaborate on with friends. Here are a few tips for a successful skit:

1. Start with an idea: a message you want to get across, a theme you want to develop, or a story you want to tell, re-tell, or parody.

2. Consider how many participants you have and what they're willing to do. There's no point writing a musical if no one's willing to sing!

3. Write with your audience in mind. If you're planning to perform your skit for little kids, make sure your humor is at their level and your lessons fairly obvious. For adults, make sure your story-line is well developed and makes a point. For peers, both the lesson and the point are probably less important than the laughs, so amp up the silliness and have fun!

4. Keep it short, as in two to five minutes. It's always better with a skit to leave your audience wanting more. Once you write your skit, practice it several times to get the timing down.

5. Have fun!

Writing Fiction

You probably know that a work of fiction is a story with a beginning, a middle, and an end:

> **Harry was hungry. He went to the kitchen, made a sandwich, and ate it. Then Harry wasn't hungry any more.**

And yet, this is not a story. It's a sequence of events, not that anyone cares. Good for Harry, right?

A good story needs a plot. A plot is not just a sequence of events. First of all, a plot implies suspense, and in order for there to be suspense, you need a main character with a clear objective. Harry's got to want something and he's got to want it bad. What might Harry want that badly?

- To survive
- To have friends

- To be respected
- To get a pony

Obviously, most characters would want to survive somewhat more intensely than they'd want that pony, but believe it or not, both objects have been done—and worked.

So far, we've got Harry sitting in his bedroom, looking out into the wide, wide world, dreaming of a pony. BORING. To liven this up, we'll need one more ingredient: an obstacle. Something's got to keep Harry from getting his beloved pony.

The more interesting your main character, and the more insurmountable the obstacle is between your character and the one thing he really, really, really wants, the more you'll build suspense and keep your reader interested in your story.

So ingredient number one in good fiction is suspense: you take a character that readers care about and you make what that character really wants unobtainable. Here's an exercise to get you thinking about how to write good fiction.

Let's start with a character and an objective: a girl (we'll call her Alice) wants to get a job. (Boring objective, Alice.) So what might make Alice an interesting character for this objective? Is Alice eighty and bored by nursing home life? Is Alice an illegal alien who has to figure out how to earn money to feed her eighteen kids? Does Alice dream of being a librarian but speak so loudly people have to clap their hands over their ears? Is Alice a monkey?

Next, consider what obstacles might make getting a job seem an impossible objective for Alice. Does Alice have a criminal history? Does Alice have to bring all eighteen of her babies along with her to work because she can't afford childcare? Does Alice belong to a religion that doesn't allow her to use vacuum cleaners or phones? Does Alice shed?

Finally, think about what kind of unusual strategies Alice will use to get a job. Does Alice show up on the doorsteps of the heads of corporations with all her babies squalling all at once? Does she fake her credentials? (Actually, that's probably not all that unusual. Strike that.) Does she start up a daycare in the park so rich mothers can just drop off their kids and go get pedicures? Does she just start working somewhere and hope some bigwig will give her some food?

Whatever you do, make your story plausible. If I don't buy Alice's story, I'm not going to like yours. If I don't care what happens to Alice, I'm going to stop reading. Don't write a story about the adventures about a tap-dancing cricket in outer space and think anyone's going to want to read it. Creativity alone doesn't make for good fiction. Plausible plots with lots of suspense and characters that make readers care what happens to them are what make people keep reading stories.

Ingredient number two in good fiction is an interesting but likeable main character. If your main character falls flat or seems annoying, people won't care whether or not he gets a pony. They'll say, "You bore me, Harry. Suck it up and get a life." Then, they'll put your story down and go play jacks. (Oh, yeah. Jacks. That's how bored they'll be!)

How do you make a character interesting? You make them complex:

- The sweet and innocent girl . . . who bullies her little brother when mom's not looking.

- The top soccer player . . . who knows that one person he wants to impress doesn't care.

- The obnoxious kid who drives everyone nuts . . . who plays Slapjack with his retarded next-door neighbor for an hour every Friday afternoon.

How do you make your character sympathetic? You give your main character some kind of flaw.

- Harry, who wants a pony, is awkward and impulsive, and because he says things without thinking them through, he doesn't have any friends.

- Alice, who wants a job, is hard-working but slow. Her bosses keep getting angry with her because her arthritis slows her down.

- Jack is good-looking, athletic, smart, and charming. But he's terrified that someone will find out that he lives with his family in a minivan.

Plots unravel in a series of scenes. Scenes can be short or long, but they take place in a setting, they have a beginning and an end, and usually, have a climax of some kind. Scenes are driven by the character's objective and made interesting by the obstacle, which continues to plague the main character, scene after scene, until he or she does finally something major to overcome the obstacle once and for all. This something major is known as a climax. The climax is like the knockout punch in a fight: it determines the outcome of the scene, and, eventually, the outcome of the main character's quest to achieve the objective.

A scene can be as short as a single paragraph or as long as twenty pages, but a scene has all of the components of a larger work of fiction:

☑ CHARACTER(S)　　　　☑ AN OBSTACLE

☑ AN OBJECTIVE　　　　☑ AN OUTCOME

A scene moves your plot one step closer to the climax of the plot by showing what the characters say and do rather than by summing up how things are progressing. This, for instance, is a summary, not a scene:

> **Susan wanted to learn how to save lives. She went to school where she had several good teachers who taught her useful skills like stitching skin and open-heart surgery. Eventually, Susan was such a good doctor, she could cure anybody.**

It's hard to imagine how that story could be interesting, but in reality, any story is going to be boring when you tell it like that. But when you tell a story with scenes that break your plot up into the little episodes that show Susan learning medicine against all odds, Susan becomes a person readers can care about, and her dream becomes interesting, especially if you make a point of adding more and more obstacles that make your character less and less likely to achieve her objective:

> **Susan looked into the open heart cavity and shook her head. "I don't think I can do this."**

> **"You have to," Betsy said. "The real doctor is dead. Only you can save Brett's life."**

> **"But we've only covered appendixes—it's all so different in real life. So . . . icky."**

"Do you want him to die?"

"You don't understand," Susan said, but she took the proffered scalpel. Concentrating on the pulsing parts, she quickly devised a strategy:

Eeny-meeny, miney-mo.

Okay, so that's maybe a little over the top, but you can probably see how scenes make almost any story more interesting to readers.

Short Story

My best advice for young writers is to write short fiction stories before attempting longer projects. When you read a lot of fiction, you tend to want to imitate what you read, and if you read books that are three hundred pages long, it's easy to think that three hundred pages is a good goal. Unfortunately, when you start out thinking three hundred pages, you tend to write meandering stories with brooding characters and overblown descriptions. The result is that you lose your reader.

Good fiction writers put nothing in their stories that don't contribute to their plots or help their readers understand their main characters better. The best way to discipline yourself to write good fiction is to make yourself write short stories first—stories of no more than twenty or thirty pages. Know how your story is going to resolve and get to the climax fast. Add only details that move the story forward, keep the suspense up, pull readers in or fake them out. Only when you've mastered writing a complete story that compels your readers from beginning to end should you increase your page count.

Chapter Books, Middle Grade, and YA Fiction

A natural progression is to go from writing short stories of twenty or thirty pages to stringing several stories with the same characters and setting together into a chapter book with an episodic plot. This is actually how a lot of writers used to work, because a lot of authors wrote stories for serial publications in magazines that were later combined in books.

Three factors distinguish chapter books and middle grade fiction: vocabulary, length, and plot unity. Chapter books tend to be shorter—between 60 and 100 pages—and more episodic with less variety in vocabulary, while middle grade fiction is normally more than 144 pages and generally develops a specific problem that unifies the story. YA fiction is usually a bit longer than that—like 300 pages or so—and always features a teenager as the protagonist. Incidentally, while grownups may play a role in chapter books and middle grade fiction, kids are almost always the protagonists.

If you want to try to write middle grade or YA fiction, remember all of the advice above and work suspense into your plot and make your protagonist likeable in some way. Then, before you start writing, chart your plot progression by mapping out at least a sketchy plan for your exposition, rising tension, climax, and resolution. That'll prevent you from writing meandering prose—and remember, write only scenes that advance your plot or develop your characters.

WRITING WITH GRAPHICS

Writing with graphics means enhancing written text with pictorial aids such as photographs, drawings, charts, or—you guessed it—graphs. If you like to draw or use images to jazz up your documents on the computer, take a look at some of the projects here.

Greeting Card

One project with obvious possibilities for publication is a greeting card, which you could design especially for a friend's or a family member's birthday or save yourself $3 next Mother's Day. You could also design a generic greeting or special occasion card.

To get an idea for your card, look at the greeting cards in the store. Most cards have an illustration as the most prominent feature on the front panel and a heading such as "For a Special Four Year Old" or "With Gratitude." Cards tend to fall into one of three categories:

- The front panel sets up a joke and the inside gives the punch-line

- The front panel basic purpose heading ("For Your Birthday") and a poem inside that matches the mood of the picture on the front, either cheerful or sentimental

- The front panel sentimental heading ("In Moments Like These") and a free verse expression of the writer's feeling for the recipient

You might want to design your artwork freehand and scan it into your computer program, so that you can print the card rather than draw the front panel freehand and try not to make a mistake. Make sure to print your card on heavy stock paper, so that it feels as substantial as store-bought cards.

Advertising Flyer

You could design a flyer for an event or for either product you're planning to sell or for a real or imaginary product you'd like to sell. The trick to designing an effective flyer is to grab people's attention with color, graphics, and big, thick, easy-to-read fonts that say exactly what people need to know (what, when, where) and no more.

Pamphlet or Brochure

Both pamphlets and brochures normally consist of text on both sides of a piece of paper, folded twice. The main difference between the two formats is that pamphlets educate people, while brochures usually advertise products or services. Because the kinds of organizations that educate tend to have less money for fancy paper and color ink, pamphlets also tend to be printed on plain or colored paper and consist of mostly text, while brochures will feature vibrant pictures and tend to be printed on expensive, glossy paper.

Pamphlets are a good way to raise awareness about something that's important to you. For example, if you noticed that a lot of people were throwing garbage on the ground in your neighborhood, you could make and distribute a pamphlet reminding people to hang on to their trash. (Although it would be ironic if your pamphlets all ended up in the gutters.)

Brochures are a great way to let people know about services, products, opportunities, or events. You could design a travel brochure, just for fun (I'm thinking parody again—I'll never forget the hotel in Costa Rica that had a gigantic iguana in bathroom); or, write a brochure to help an organization like the local animal shelter get the word out and find homes for pets.

Although the easiest way to design either a pamphlet or a brochure is with special software such as Microsoft Publisher or Photoshop, you can absolutely make one with normal word processing software. Just set the orientation of your paper to landscape and format the document to have three columns. Then, remember that the third panel of the first page will actually be the cover of your document, while the first panel is the back.

Annotated Timeline

A timeline is a line with each tick mark on the line representing dates that go from left to right chronologically. A timeline shows the order of specific events in a particular era, usually highlighting some specific type of event. For instance, a timeline might chronicle global or regional political, social, or geological events. An annotated timeline not only shows when such events occurred, but also provides some distinguishing information. If you designed a timeline to show wars in American history, for example, your annotations might consist of a paragraph explaining each war, giving details such as with whom the war was fought and why. You might even detail a few of the major battles or turning points in the war, and of course tell the outcome.

Obviously, you could do an annotated timeline like this for your history course, but you could also create a more personal timeline as well. Why not annotate a timeline of your family vacation, telling where you were when, adding a few anecdotes for each stage of the journey? Or what about doing an annotated timeline of your life, using photographs to illustrate how amazing you were at each age? ("Here I am at 7, winning my purple bunny . . .") Or what about a timeline that breaks down, minute by minute, the time the car broke down in rush hour traffic? The possibilities are endless.

Calendar

The trick to designing a calendar is to choose a theme: airplanes, kitties, mountain views, outhouses (which is the one I have hanging up in my kitchen right now). There are two major kinds of calendars: the twelve-month calendar, and the daily rip-off-one-a-day kind. The twelve-month calendar usually features an illustration opposite a grid with the days of the month identified.

To create a themed calendar, choose a theme and then make a list of twelve sub-topics. For instance, for a kitties calendar, you might make a list of twelve different kinds of cats, or twelve different cat poses, or twelve different activities cats do. For each of the twelve items on your list, either draw or take pictures, and then either write a caption, a descriptive paragraph or an explanation for the illustration. Print your calendar on cardstock, add a hole on the appropriate edge, and take it to an office supply store to have it bound with a coil: and, voila: a one-of-a-kind wall calendar.

Picture Book

If you think that picture books are kid stuff, you're right in that somewhat obviously, picture books are meant for kids, but if you think that writing a good one is so easy a kid could do it, you're wrong. A good picture book combines great illustrations with great and fun to hear and read text; to write one, you have to craft words carefully, paying attention to the rhythm of the words and sentences on the page, and include just the right amount of repetition. For an example of a great read-aloud picture book, read aloud the opening lines to Russell Hoban's *Bread and Jam for Frances*:

> It was breakfast time,
> and everyone was at the table.
> Father was eating his egg.
> Mother was eating her egg.
> Gloria was sitting in a high chair and eating her egg too.
> Frances was eating bread and jam. (p. 5)

Can you hear the rhythm? Did you hear the way the first lines bounced right along, and then the last line just fell flat, and you could actually feel the problem and the sense of humor of the story, all wrapped up in the rhythm of the words? And do you see the repetition? When words roll off your tongue like that, they're fun to read aloud to children. That's the mark of a well-written picture book.

Even picture books that don't seem obviously rhythmic will have a certain rhythm to them. If you take a close look at the books in Marc Brown's popular *Arthur* series, you'll notice that most pages have a certain pattern: a sentence of context for the page, then two or three lines of dialogue.

Marc Brown breaks the pattern up occasionally, but by and large, the pattern creates a rhythm that's pleasing to the ear and easy to read.

Many popular picture books are interactive, with flaps for children to open as in the *Where's Spot* books by Eric Hill, questions for children to answer, such as "What did the bunny see?" (next to a picture that shows whatever the bunny is seeing), or text that breaks between pages, inviting children to offer the next word in the story, as in Deborah Guarino's *Is Your Mama a Llama?*:

> "Is your mama a llama?" I asked my friend Jane.
> "No, she is not," Jane politely explained.
> She grazes on grass, and she likes to say, 'Moo!'
> I don't think that is what a llama would do."
> "Oh," I said. "I understand, now.
> I think that your mama must be a . . . ."

(The book has a picture on the next page for those of you who can't work out the answer from the fact that Jane's a calf.) Here are a few more tips for picture books:

- Keep your word count below 1,000 words. More than that and the story is too long.

- Your story should have about the same amount of text on most pages. Whatever you do, make sure your story doesn't drone on and on some pages and have only a single sentence on others.

- Make sure your words tell the story, so that you could picture the story without the pictures you add. In fact, it's best to write the story first, and add the pictures later.

Easy Reader

An easy reader is like a picture book in that most pages are illustrated, but different in that the text is meant to be easy enough for beginning readers to read for themselves. A few features of an easy reader are:

- Very limited vocabulary

- Lots of repetition

- Simple but pleasing story lines

How do you know which words you can use in your easy reader? A good rule of thumb is that any three letter word is fair game, as well as any four and five-letter words that don't include unusual spellings (like dumb, which has a silent 'b'). Longer but really common words like the prepositions 'under' and 'above' as well as common conjunctions like 'because' are also okay. Try to avoid words that are longer than that, although if you want to include one or two words like "Dinosaur" or "Hippopotamus" in your story, go ahead—readers can usually work out a few of these as long as you provide them with visual cues, but don't go crazy with them or they'll get frustrated. Finally, avoid contractions like 'don't' and 'can't', which most beginning readers don't know.

If you have a beginning reader in your family, try crafting a story from his or her spelling workbook or vocabulary words. Probably the best advice, though, for writing an easy reader is to see what others have done. Check out a few easy readers by authors such as Dr. Seuss, P.D. Eastman, and my all-time favorite, Arnold Lobel.

Comic Strips, Manga, or Graphic Novels

Comic strips are jokes or stories told though captioned pictures in sequential panels. You've probably seen short comics like *Garfield* by Jim Davis or *Peanuts* by Charles Schultz in a newspaper—if not, you can look them up online. Some comic strips take only a single panel to tell the whole story; my favorite of these growing up was always *The Far Side* by Gary Larson. Comic books take comics to a whole other level, telling stories with plots just like novels through comic strips.

Manga is a term for Japanese comics. It can refer to comic books that were published in Japan, but more often in the United States it refers to a particular style of comic.

Graphic novels are basically comic books that are bound more or less as if they were chapter books or novels, although some graphic novels don't use comic panels in quite the same way.

If you'd like to work on developing a comic strip or graphic novel, I would recommend one of Scott McCloud's books *Understanding Comic Strips* and *Making Comics*, or do an Internet search for tips to get you started. One site that seemed to have a lot of helpful advice that I found was called rabbitsagainstmagic.com. One piece of advice that I came across somewhere, though, was not to be so ambitious with your goals for writing a comic book that you never finish a project. Since that's my advice for any fiction writing project, I would agree: start small. Finish a strip with three or four panels and see what your friends have to say about it. As with any other craft, trust that your comic strips will only get better with time. And, above all, have fun with it!

Publication Options

In this course, publication simply means finding an audience for your work, however big or small. Here are a number of suggestions for publication, starting small:

Single Recipient

- Send someone you know a letter, a card you made yourself, or a story you wrote.

- Make a gift of a poem you've illustrated and framed.

- Give someone a calendar you designed or a collection of captioned photos.

- Write a letter to someone you don't know: write a fan letter or a letter of inquiry. If you want to write a letter of complaint, it's a good idea to check with an adult before actually sending it out; remember, a real person will get and read your letter, so it's important not to be too scathing or critical and to always maintain a polite tone that seeks resolution.

Limited Audience

- Write a personal or family newsletter and send it out to all of your friends.

- Offer to design brochures or posters for a community you participate in.

- Compile recipes, short stories, poems, or a book of favorite quotations and have them bound at an office store. Then, distribute them to people who will appreciate them.

- Design a coloring or activity book and give copies to the colorers in your life.

- Write and perform a skit for the people in your family or school or church community.

- Contact special education teachers at a local school to see if they could use your help designing pictorial aids for special needs students in their classrooms.

Seek a Broader Audience

- Enter an essay, poem, or short story in a local writing contest.

- Submit an op-ed, interview, or a profile you've written about someone or something of interest to members of your community to the editor of your local newspaper.

- Query a publisher or an agent about a book you've written that's gotten positive feedback. Find addresses and submission guidelines for most publishers and many literary agents on the Internet, and remember to list the query letter on your writing log.

Go Public

- Post reviews on Amazon, Barnes & Nobles, Goodreads, or ReadaRoute.com.

- Visit sites like StoryJumper.com and Studentpublishing.com to learn about publishing opportunities for student designed picture books.

- Submit your writing to websites that publish poems, stories, articles, and reviews by teen writers such as Teen Ink, Cyberteens, Figment, and Frodo's Notebook.

- Submit fan fiction stories to a website for fans of a popular book series or to a website for fan fictions in general like www.fanfiction.net.

- For a project you're very pleased with, consider POD publishing opportunities. One organization that facilitates publications for young writers is KidPub.com. For a fee, KidPub will format, publish, and distribute your collection of short stories or poems, chapter book, or novel. Once published, the book appears on Amazon.com and other online stores for sale. It falls to you to market your own book, but you can list press releases and all your query letters soliciting reviews on your writing log.

- Build your own website or blog. Believe it or not, this is not that hard to do and many websites facilitate designing websites and blogs for free. Just do a search for "free website" to find options.

Writing Log

Week	Project	Hours Spent	Polished?	Published?

About the Author

Dena Luchsinger is a homeschooling mom who tutors secondary and college writing students. Formerly a licensed minister, in 2001 she founded Proyecto Down, a non-profit, holistic ministry serving families affected by Down syndrome in Monterrey, Mexico. Since completing a Master of Arts degree with a dual emphasis in writing and practical theology, she has tutored high school and college writing students, taught supplementary advanced and remedial English classes, and facilitated workshops for high school students and their parents within her local homeschool community. The parent of three children, one with the dual diagnoses of Down syndrome and autism, and another "twice exceptional," or gifted and talented yet learning disabled, she is passionate about students of all ability levels achieving their potential. In addition to the two manuals for homeschooling high school students, *The Reader's Odyssey: An Individualized Literature Program for Homeschooling Middle and High School Students* and *Grading with a Purple Crayon: A Developmental Approach to High School Composition for Homeschooling Families* (Crecer Publications), she is the author of two children's books: *Sometimes Smart is Good/A Veces es Bueno Ser Inteligente* (Eerdman's) and *Playing by the Rules: A Story about Autism* (Woodbine House).